SCIENCE FICTION
OF THE 20TH CENTURY

This book is dedicated to the memory of Lester Anderson, Aubrey MacDermott, and Franz Grumme—loving husbands and fathers, faithful friends, and lifelong science-fiction fans and collectors. I hope they know how much I miss them.

Copyright ©1999 Frank M. Robinson

For a free catalog write to:
COLLECTORS PRESS, INC.
P.O. Box 230986
Portland, OR 97281
Toll-free: 1 800 423 1848
or visit our website at:
www.collectorspress.com

Book design DRIVE COMMUNICATIONS, NEW YORK
Copy editing ANN GRANNING BENNETT

Distributed to the U.S. Book Trade by
Universe Publishing
A division of Rizzoli International Publications, Inc.
through St. Martin's Press
175 Fifth Avenue
New York, New York 10010

Distributed in Canada by McClelland & Stewart

Printed in Hong Kong

First American Edition

9 8 7 6 5 4 3 2 1

Library of Congress Cataloging–in–Publication Data

Robinson, Frank M.
    Science fiction of the 20th century:
    an illustrated history /
    Frank M. Robinson. —1st American ed.
        p. cm.
    Includes bibliographical references (p.   ).
    ISBN 1-888054-29-8 (alk. paper). —
    ISBN 1-888054-30-1 (pbk. : alk. paper)
    1. Science fiction—History and criticism.
    2. Fiction—20th century—History and
criticism. I. Title. II. Title: Science fiction of the
20th century.
PN3433.8.R58 1999
809.3'8762'0904—dc21   99-27614
                                                    CIP

SCIENCE FICTION
OF THE 20TH CENTURY

AN ILLUSTRATED HISTORY | BY FRANK M. ROBINSON

WITH TECHNICAL ASSISTANCE BY

JOHN GUNNISON

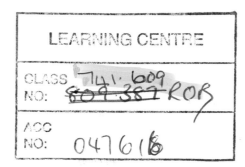

PORTLAND, OREGON

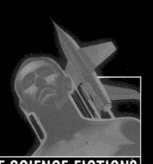

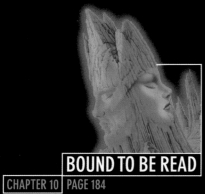

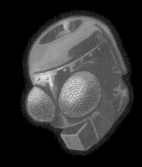

CONTENTS

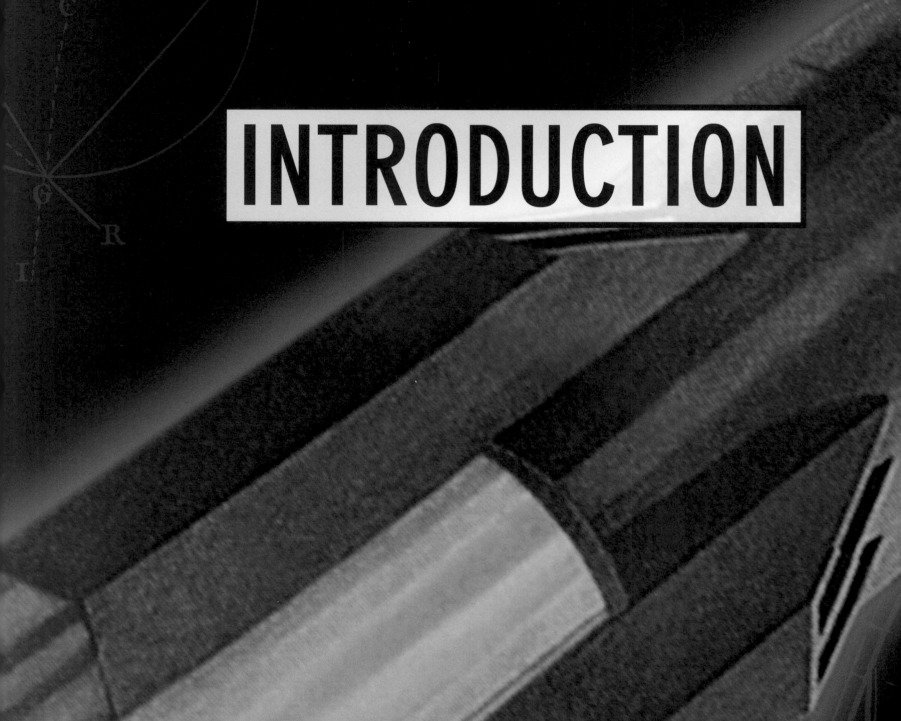

INTRODUCTION

When I was a kid, I bought my first science-fiction magazine at the age of thirteen. All older science-fiction fans remember when they bought their first magazine, and we were all about the same age—twelve, thirteen, maybe fourteen. In the 1930s and 1940s we were all pretty much alike as well. We wore knickers, sat down to a chicken dinner every Sunday, and spent Saturday afternoons at the movie theater where we saw two features, three or four cartoons, and got a free candy bar—all for a dime. Nobody had a television set, though every family had a radio. Our parents tuned in to *Lux Radio Theater* and *Fibber McGee and Molly* but most of us kids listened to *Lights Out!* and *Inner Sanctum* and *Jack Armstrong, the All-American Boy.* We made model airplanes out of balsa wood and tissue paper and rubber bands, telephones out of string and two tin cans, and occasionally we tinkered with crystal sets.

Most of us were skinny, wore glasses, were not very adept socially, and were usually sent out to left field—way out—when the Phys Ed class divided us up into baseball teams.

As writer Joanna Russ put it many years later, young science-fiction fans were "…nervous, shy, pleasant boys, sensitive, intelligent, and very awkward with people. They also talk too much." It was an accurate description. (And yes, almost all of us were boys—though with the passage of time girls became welcome.)

When we discovered science fiction, we were consumed by it. We haunted the library for books by Verne and Wells and read and re-read the cheap Grosset & Dunlap editions of Edgar Rice Burroughs that we were given for our birthdays or at Christmas. But the real epiphany came when we discovered the magazines with their fascinating covers of aliens, rocket ships, and distant planets. We read them under the tree in the backyard on sunny days, curled up on the couch on rainy afternoons, and under the covers at night.

Our neighborhood friends looked at us with contempt (an excellent reason to search for science-fiction pen pals who might live halfway across the continent—or maybe half a dozen blocks away), our parents fretted that we read too much and played too little, and our teachers were indignant that we were obviously addicted to "that trash" when we should be reading the classics.

We loved science fiction, and we wanted other people to love it as much as we did. We were dazzled by the wild ideas and the lurid artwork, we thought it was great literature (in some instances we were right), and we proselytized for it shamelessly. Almost all of us published amateur magazines—"fanzines"

SUPER SCIENCE STORIES
MAY 1942
VIRGIL FINLAY

Artist Finlay wasn't known for his ability to portray convincing machinery or scientific gadgets—but on this cover, he excelled at it.

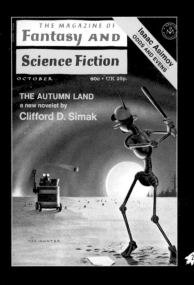

**THE MAGAZINE OF FANTASY
AND SCIENCE FICTION**
OCTOBER 1971
MEL HUNTER

Artist Hunter did a series of sly,
satirical covers featuring robots
in "normal" everyday pursuits.

🚀

LOCUS
FEBRUARY 1999
PHOTOGRAPH BY
CHARLES N. BROWN

Locus is the *Publishers Weekly* of the
science-fiction field. It includes the
latest news from the publishing and
multi-media fronts, what author has
sold what to whom, and reviews of
the novels and short fiction currently
available. Year-end summary is a
must for authors and publishers.

🚀 **4**

STAR WARS
LUCASFILM, 1977
(*ONE-SHEET POSTER*)

Star Wars was pure space opera in living color, thunderous sound and
thrilling special effects. Nothing like it had ever been seen before, though
it's been imitated many times since. With Harrison Ford (the film made
him a star), Mark Hamill, Peter Cushing, Alec Guinness, and James Earl
Jones as the voice of villain Darth Vader. (Director George Lucas)

KING KONG
RKO RADIO PICTURES, 1933
(ONE-SHEET POSTER)

The first and the best of the giant ape movies.
Willis O'Brien was the special-effects magician
who populated Skull Island with the stop-action
Kong and assorted dinosaurs. Remade in 1976.
(Producers-directors Merian C. Cooper
and Ernest B. Schoedsack)

Courtesy of Ronald V. Borst / Hollywood Movie Posters

PLANET STORIES
SPRING 1942
LEYDENFROST

Science-fiction magazines were known for
their "bug-eyed monster"—nicknamed
BEM—covers. This one for *Planet Stories*
was the best by far.

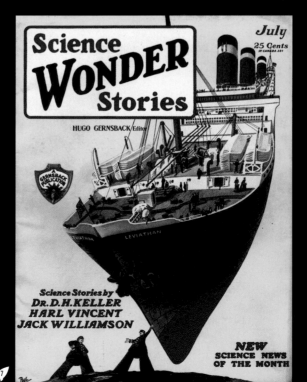

SCIENCE WONDER STORIES
JULY 1929
FRANK R. PAUL

The eye-catching cover was to
illustrate the low gravity on an
asteroid—so low one man
could lift a huge ocean liner.
But the asteroid would have to
be very small—say, 116 feet,
far smaller than the ship itself.

—devoted to it, some of us grew up to write our own science-fiction stories and others became editors or publishers of it. We went to conventions and watched them grow from a few hundred participants to the thousands, from a single convention during a year to an average of one per week.

When actor William Shatner—the beloved "Captain Kirk" of the original "Star Trek" series—stared into the camera on *Saturday Night Live* and told us to "get a life," we had to smile even in the face of betrayal. We already had a life. And to a large extent, it was one to which Captain Kirk, Luke Skywalker, the Grey Lensman, Michael Valentine Smith, and John Carter of Mars—all heroes of the science-fiction universe—had contributed an enormous amount.

Today we live in a world where a space shuttle is launched into orbit every three or four months (one of the shuttles is appropriately named the "Enterprise"). We've been to the moon where we played a round of golf and returned with a few rocks as souvenirs. We're building a space station, atomic power plants dot the globe, and almost every family has a home computer that would make the original Univac I with its tiny memory of twelve kilobytes seem like a moron. (Univac was so huge you could walk inside its garage-sized memory and gape in amazement at its thousands and thousands of vacuum tubes.)

Nobody scoffs at rocket ships today, nobody laughs when you mention the possibility of life "out there," few doubt that someday we'll go to Mars, the only question being "When?" And there is virtually nobody who hasn't read a science-fiction book or gone to a science-fiction movie or watched an

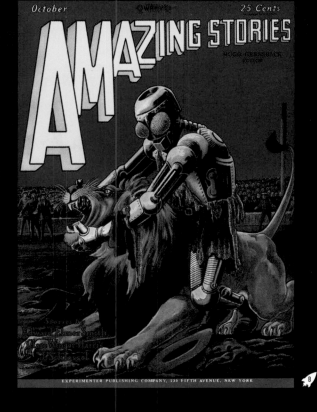

AMAZING STORIES
OCTOBER 1928
FRANK R. PAUL

One of the most unusual and dramatic of artist Frank R. Paul's covers. The lead story was by Clare Winger Harris, the first woman writer to be featured in a science-fiction magazine.

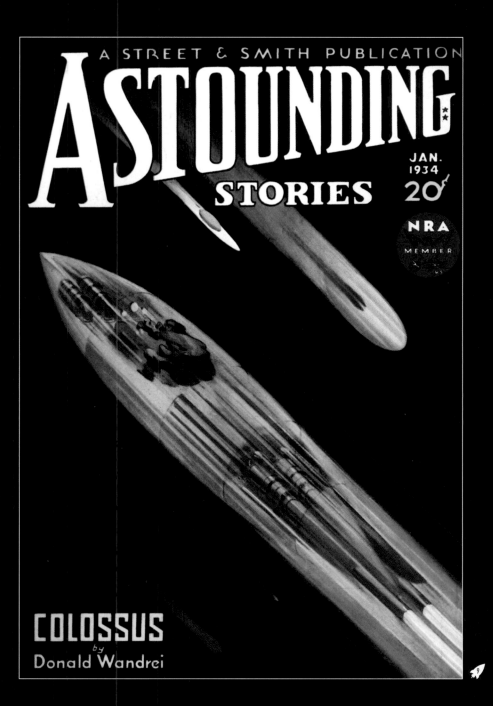

ASTOUNDING STORIES
JANUARY 1934
HOWARD V. BROWN

The first "real" science-fiction cover for *Astounding* and one of the most dramatic ever published.

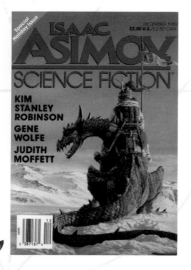

ISAAC ASIMOV'S SCIENCE FICTION
DECEMBER 1989
KEITH PARKINSON

A unique and evocative cover by artist Parkinson (poster-size reproductions were later available at conventions). *Asimov's* was an open market for new writers as well as stalwarts such as Kim Stanley Robinson and Gene Wolfe.

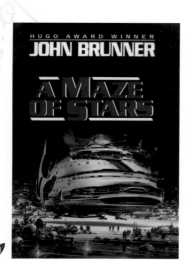

A MAZE OF STARS
JOHN BRUNNER
1991
JOHN BERKEY

This novel by John Brunner, author of the Hugo Award winning *Stand on Zanzibar*, boasted a stunning jacket by John Berkey.

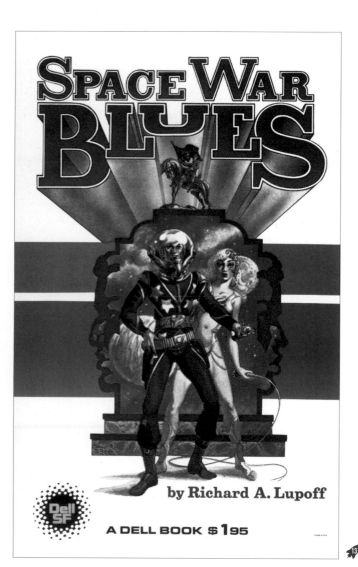

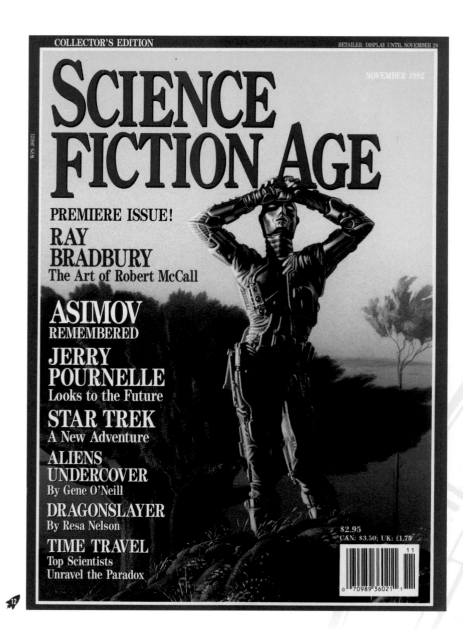

SCIENCE FICTION AGE
NOVEMBER 1992
MICHAEL WHELAN

The first issue of a slick-paper large-size magazine that rapidly grew to challenge the established titles. The magazine was ad-rich with four-color illustrations throughout. An emphasis on media helped boost circulation.

SPACE WAR BLUES
RICHARD A. LUPOFF
1978
GEORGE BARR
(PROMOTIONAL POSTER)

Originally scheduled for 1968, author Lupoff's paperback novel finally saw print in 1978. By that time it needed a promotional poster…

SCIENCE FICTION MONTHLY
JULY 1974
BRUCE PENNINGTON

A British tabloid-size magazine with the emphasis on art rather than fiction. The extra-large pages made the artwork very attractive, but short fiction and articles soon appeared.

FANTASTIC ADVENTURES
JANUARY 1941
HAROLD W. MCCAULEY

Harold McCauley painted some of the most popular covers for *Fantastic Adventures*. With his "Mac" girls he showed the flair of a pin-up artist.

MARCH | 50 CENTS

analog
SCIENCE FACT ⚛ SCIENCE FICTION

NATURAL RESOURCE | THE GAS MINE IN THE SKY

L. RON HUBBARD'S TO THE STARS

DATE UNKNOWN
UNKNOWN
(PROMOTIONAL FLYER)

A true collector's item: a promotional flyer for a magazine that never appeared. Perhaps it was an opportunity missed —if the fiction had been as sensational as the cover, the magazine would have been a sell-out. Hubbard's name certainly wouldn't have hurt it, either.

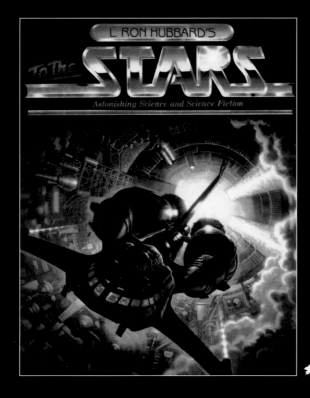

ANALOG SCIENCE FACT – SCIENCE FICTION
MARCH 1963
NAT WHITE

The first issue of the new *Analog*—a magazine with the page size of *Scientific American* printed on book paper with sixteen pages of slick stock fore and aft. The days of the old pulp *Astounding* were now behind it.

episode of *Star Trek* or *The X-Files* or *Babylon 5* on television—Captain Kirk, Captain Picard, Bones, Spock, Data, and Worf are among the most recognizable characters on the tube.

At one time, the universe of science fiction was restricted pretty much to the magazines. Aside from Burroughs and the classics by Verne and Wells, there were little else available. It was an event when a small Wisconsin specialty publisher called "Arkham House" brought out a collection of stories by H. P. Lovecraft. (Admitted that was a collection of horror stories, though some of them verged on science fiction, and it cost the enormous sum of five dollars—three if you had sent your money in early.) There were occasional anthologies that would reprint a science-fiction story or two, but there were no anthologies of all science-fiction stories, no paperback science-fiction novels at all.

Times have changed. In 1998 there were more than 1,900 books of science fiction and its related genres (fantasy, horror) published by a grand total of 233 different publishers—everybody from TOR and Random House to Buccaneer Books. More than 1,100 of these were original volumes and among them were thirty-four reference books and forty-three of history and criticism.

Science-fiction films have been around forever; they date as far back as the magazines. During the days of the Depression, *Frankenstein* and *The Invisible Man* did as much to save Universal as Mae West did to save Paramount. But it would be a few decades before science fiction shook the "B-movie" ghetto of the 1950s to dominate the ranks of the top-grossing films of the 1980s and the 1990s, to a day when a single science-fiction film could make more than a hundred million dollars in profit worldwide.

Older fans can sit back and thumb their noses at the legions of English teachers who considered science fiction trash and a waste of time. It's now taught in many high schools (where they're glad the students read anything at all) and in colleges where the writing of it is a natural adjunct to the reading of it.

There is a small part of me that resents its popularity, that wishes it was still considered at least a little trashy, and that reading it still rated as a minor act of rebellion against my parents and the scholastic powers that be. And then I remember, regretfully, that I'm no longer thirteen and the "sense of wonder" has become somewhat elusive…

Science fiction has come a long way and there have been a number of books of both text and images that have chronicled its history. The best I can do in a single volume is to offer snapshots of its past, present a visual history of the magazines and books and movies, and point out that in contrast to most literary genres, this one grew from the inside out.

Along with the visual history, I hope I can also offer a glimpse of that small band of youthful enthusiasts that grew into a subculture, largely taking over the writing, editing, and publishing of science fiction, providing endless stories and "icons" for film and TV, and forcing the field to grow up as they grew up.

They changed science fiction—they enlarged it, expanded its horizons, and made it significant without losing its ability to entertain.

And while it may seem preposterous to say so, in many respects they changed the world as well. We now realize, regretfully, that Utopias are wishful thinking, that for better or worse science and technology are rushing blindly into the Unknown and carrying us along with them, and that—whether we like it or not—the Day After Tomorrow will still arrive right on time.

Frank M. Robinson

 THE DARK BEYOND THE STARS
FRANK M. ROBINSON
1991
JOHN HARRIS

A late entry in the generation-ship sweepstakes, *The Dark Beyond the Stars* was selected as a *New York Times* "Notable Book of the Year." (A "generation ship" story was about a voyage to the stars that could take hundreds of generations for the crew.)

ASTOUNDING SCIENCE FICTION
OCTOBER 1953
KELLY FREAS

Artist Kelly Freas with a stunning cover, later used on a record jacket for the rock group "Queen."

There are many claimants as to who invented science fiction, probably starting with the ancient Greeks. But the first one of substance is Francis Godwin, an Anglican bishop, who in his posthumously published *The Man in the Moone* (1638) got his flying machine to the moon by hitching it to some accommodating wild geese who happened to winter there. A few years later, Cyrano de Bergerac (an actual person, not just a character in a play by Edmond Rostand) was a little more scientific in his *A Voyage to the Moon* (soon followed by *A Voyage to the Sun*). The propulsive power for his moon trip was furnished by rockets tied to the "space ship." Cyrano also had the ingenious idea, not entirely original with him, that the Earth and other planets revolved around the sun, the center of the solar system. This was just sixteen years after

CHAPTER 1

THE FUTURE IS HERE...
IT'S 1901!

❶

THE BOYS OF NEW YORK
NOVEMBER 20, 1886
UNKNOWN

The Boys of New York was a "story paper" in which the tales about Frank Reade, Jr., and his inventions were very popular. Luis Senarens, Jr.—the "American Jules Verne" —was nineteen when "The Electric Man" was published and had sold stories since he was fourteen.

❷

**FRANK READE
WEEKLY MAGAZINE**
MARCH 6, 1903
UNKNOWN

Frank Reade, Jr.'s, airship, complete with propeller and lifting cones, beat out the Wright Brothers by almost a year—and was far more advanced.

Galileo had recanted the same heretical views so Cyrano's books were carefully edited before they were published.

Mary Wollstonecraft Shelley started writing *Frankenstein* when she was eighteen, and it saw print (in 1818) when she was twenty. It was published anonymously, and most critics attributed it to Percy Bysshe Shelley, who had written the introduction. (Mary had run off with Shelley when she was seventeen and, after his first wife committed suicide, married him.)

Shelley and his good friends Lord Byron and Dr. John William Polidori, Shelley's physician, were fond of reading ghost stories to each other and soon started a competition to see who could write the most horrifying story. Shelley and Byron tired of the contest, and Polidori, after much effort, produced a short story, "The Vampyre: a Tale."

Mary, the youngest of the group, produced *Frankenstein.*

Edgar Allan Poe is famous for *The Narrative of Arthur Gordon Pym*, "A Descent into the Maelstrom," and "Mellonta Tauta," a story of the year 2848. Several decades later, in 1863, Jules Verne published *A Journey to the Center of the Earth*, reversed course with *A Trip from the Earth to the Moon*, and then compromised with *20,000 Leagues Under the Sea.*

Cyrano de Bergerac was French as was Verne, Mary Shelley English, and Poe American. Both Verne, along with H.G. Wells who arrived on the scene two decades later, are popularly credited with having founded science fiction, and each of the others have their adherents. But there was another American who came between Verne and Wells about whom few people know but who has just as good a claim as any of the others.

Luis P. Senarens was a prolific writer for the "story papers" of the late 1800s, specifically designed for the eleven and twelve-year-olds mentioned earlier. Senarens knew his audience well—he was twelve years old himself when he started selling stories to children's magazines and all of fourteen when he began writing novels for the story paper, *The Boys of New York*, published by Frank Tousey. (Story papers were the size of standard newspapers but devoted to fiction rather than news.)

Senarens came to write science fiction in a somewhat roundabout way. One of the early "invention" novels, printed shortly after the Civil War, was *The Steam Man of the Prairies* by Edward F. Ellis, about a gigantic metal man operated by steam (steam engines were all the rage back then). Ellis soon tired of his robot, but publisher Frank Tousey prevailed on dime novelist Harry Enton to write a cheap knockoff, *Frank Reade and His Steam Man of the Plains*.

The stories appeared irregularly in *The Boys of New York*, the last one under the house name of "Noname." Enton, offended, left, and Tousey, casting about for another writer to fill "Noname's" shoes, came up with young Senarens, who had written for him before and showed a familiarity with genuine science. At the time, Tousey had never met his fourteen-year-old wunderkind.

Senarens took over the series, recreated his hero as Frank Reade, Jr., gave him a former slave as a sidekick, and quickly electrified the steam man as well as

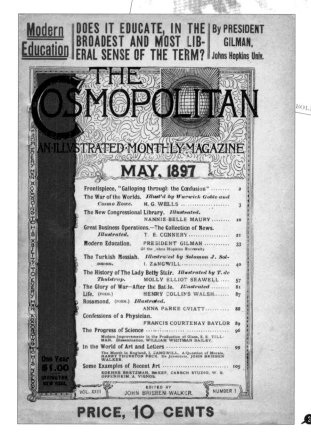

THE COSMOPOLITAN
MAY 1897
WARWICK GOBLE

The most famous novel by H.G. Wells was *The Time Machine*, but *The War of the Worlds* ran a close second. The radio broadcast by Orson Welles in 1940 caused a sensation; it was filmed by George Pal in 1953. (This issue of *Cosmopolitan* features the second installment.)

THE ALL-STORY
OCTOBER 1908
GARRY GRANT DART

A futuristic—for the period—airplane complete with pusher propeller and a gas bag above.

the steam horse. Frank soon devised a wonderful series of inventions, including a submarine (several years before Simon Lake announced the real thing in 1897), a helicopter, an airplane, an armored car—the better with which to fight Indians on the prairie—and even a manned satellite.

(Senarens may not have known of "The Brick Moon" by Edward Everett Hale, published in *The Atlantic Monthly* in 1869. Hale, best known for his story *The Man Without a Country*, proposed a "communications" satellite made of brick—for its heat resistance—about 200 feet in diameter and designed to orbit the Earth 4,000 miles up. Telescopes of the period could make out objects five feet in size at this distance, so the crew of the brick moon communicated with the Earth by cutting out large letters from cloth and placing them on the surface.)

Senarens, who became known as the American Jules Verne, corresponded occasionally with the real Verne, and they even stole from one another, apparently without any sense of guilt or complaint. One of Senarens' stories was about a trip to the center of the Earth, and Verne wrote the "anonymous" author to congratulate him. In turn, Verne swiped the idea of the steam man and incorporated it into a steam

elephant in his novel, *The Steam House*. In *Robur the Conqueror*, Verne lifted his helicopter, the Albatross, from *Frank Reade, Jr., and His Airplane* and *Frank Reade, Jr., in the Clouds*.

Senarens was predictably popular, and, as soon as the serials were finished in *Boys of New York*, they appeared complete in the *Wide Awake Library* and a little later in a weekly titled the *Frank Reade Library*. And beginning in 1902 they ran in the *Frank Reade Weekly Magazine* with fantastic covers in full color—in every sense, a one-man science-fiction magazine.

But all good things must come to an end, and the story papers and boys' papers disappeared shortly after the turn of the century. Frank Reade, Jr., was succeeded by the Tom Swift books of "Victor Appleton," which sold in the millions of copies, and similar books by "Roy Rockwood."

THE CAVALIER
JANUARY 4, 1913
CLINTON PETTEE

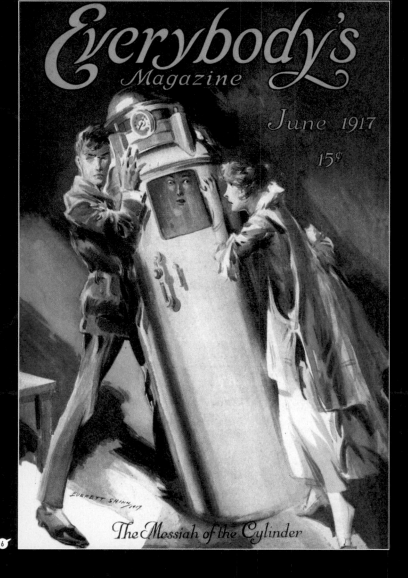

The Messiah of the Cylinder

EVERYBODY'S MAGAZINE
JUNE 1917
EVERETT SHINN

The Messiah of the Cylinder takes place a hundred years in the future in "…a world gripped by a perverted and tyrannous socialism without either religion or freedom." Interior illustrations were by Joseph Clement Coll, the best black-and-white line artist of the day.

The generation of youngsters who had devoured Frank Reade, Jr., were now older and ready for bigger and better stories. And bigger and better stories were waiting for them.

H. Rider Haggard published *King Solomon's Mines*, a "lost-race" story, in 1885 (Haggard wrote it on a bet he could outdo Stevenson's *Treasure Island*) and followed it with *She*, a novel of immortality.

But H.G. Wells overshadowed almost everything that had gone before with his *The Time Machine* published in 1895. A unique concept, it was a classic of science fiction. It also became a classic of literature. *The Invisible Man* came two years later and then *The War of the Worlds* (serialized by *Cosmopolitan* in 1898).

All of these novels (as well as most of Wells' short stories) were totally unique in concept. Wells wrote the *first* time travel story, the *first* story dealing with invisibility, and the *first* story to deal with an alien

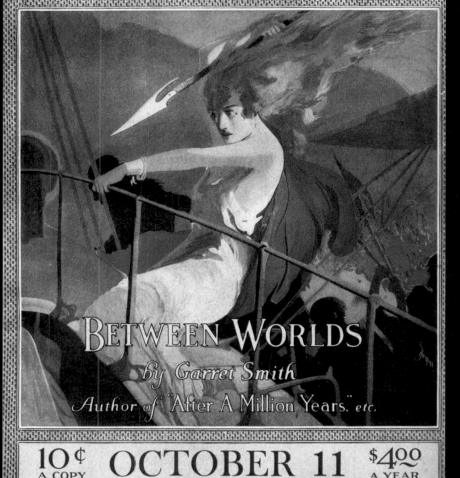

BETWEEN WORLDS
by Garret Smith
Author of "After A Million Years," etc.

10¢ A COPY   OCTOBER 11 $4.00 A YEAR

ARGOSY
OCTOBER 11, 1919
UNKNOWN

Garret Smith wrote a number of early science-fiction novels for *Argosy*. *Between Worlds* takes place on both Venus and Earth and is an early space opera.

invasion. Time-machine stories and stories about invisibility are all well and good, but stories of invasions of the Earth by aliens have become an enormous sub-genre of science fiction, spawning innumerable novels on the subject and dozens of films.

(It should be noted that a famous American writer who wrote science fiction—though his other novels overshadowed his efforts—was Jack London. His own story dealing with invisibility, "The Shadow and the Flash," appeared in the early 1900s as well as a prehistoric novel, *Before Adam.*)

Wells lived long enough to see *The War of the Worlds* adapted as a radio show by Orson Welles and his *Mercury Theater of the Air.* He didn't much care for it, though things were civil enough when Wells met Welles during a lecture tour in San Antonio in 1940. Wells was also unhappy with the film of his novel *Things to Come* for which he wrote the script. He undoubtedly would have agreed with a later writer, John le Carre, who once wrote: "Having your book turned into a movie is like seeing your oxen turned into bouillion cubes."

Orson Welles was no stranger to science fiction even before the Mercury Theater broadcast. He once confided in a letter to Nils Hardin, editor of *Xenophile*—a fan magazine of the old pulps—that he had sold stories to the pulp magazines and earned his living for the better part of a year by doing so. "There was a detective series with a rich, young aristocratic sleuth living with his three elderly aunts in Baltimore. Also a good deal of science fiction of the Lobster-Men type…"

H.G. Wells was immensely popular after the turn of the century, but for the youngsters there was nothing to take the place of Frank Reade, Jr., with his crazy inventions and his slapdash action. No

magazine ever did, though Frank A. Munsey with his pulp-paper *Argosy* and *All-Story* came close.

Munsey, a farmer's son, started *The Golden Argosy* in 1882. It was intended as a boys' paper but never quite caught fire. Munsey later began *Munsey's Weekly*, which struggled until he slashed the price from twenty-five cents to ten cents, after which circulation soared. He did the same with *The Argosy* in 1896. The magazine, which had become a slim imitator of *Munsey's*, was suddenly shorn of its slick paper, its washed-out halftones, and its dull essays and articles. It didn't even have a contents page. Nothing was left but fiction, a few poems as filler, and a plain yellow cover announcing what a bargain it was for only a dime.

(*Argosy*, like most magazines of the period, was the size of today's *National Geographic*. It had untrimmed edges and was called a "pulp" paper magazine because of the rough newsprint it was printed on.)

Like *Munsey's*, the magazine took off. In 1905, Munsey added *All-Story* and a few years after that, *Cavalier*. All three magazines published science

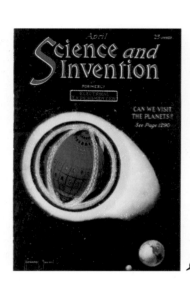

SCIENCE AND INVENTION
APRIL 1921
HOWARD V. BROWN

"Can We Visit the Planets?" was an intriguing article with an early science-fiction cover by Howard V. Brown. Inside were science-fiction stories "The Love Machine" and "In 1999," both illustrated by Frank R. Paul.

SCIENCE AND INVENTION
AUGUST 1923
UNKNOWN

A collector's item—the "Scientific Fiction Number" of *Science and Invention*. Stories included "The Man From the Atom" by G. Peyton Wertenbaker, "Dr. Hackensaw's Secrets" by Clement Fezandie, and an installment of "Around the Universe" by Ray Cummings.

fiction on a more or less regular basis, with *All-Story* publishing more rather than less. Readers soon were hanging on installments of George Allan England's *Darkness and Dawn* (a post-holocaust story), Garret Smith's *On the Brink of 2000*, and *After a Million Years*, which included a dystopian Earth, aliens, and the extinction of most of humanity. Soon to become a regular in the Munsey magazines was Ray Cummings, whose first story "The Girl in the Golden Atom" in *All-Story* proved immensely popular.

Munsey hit the jackpot with *Under the Moons of Mars* (published in book form as *A Princess of Mars*) by "Norman Bean"—a play upon "normal being"—serialized in early 1912 issues of *All-Story*. With the publication of *Tarzan of the Apes*, complete in the October issue, "Norman Bean" was revealed to be Edgar Rice Burroughs. Those two novels immediately made Burroughs the preeminent writer of science fiction in the United States. He's still vastly popular, and signed first editions of his books go at auction for thousands of dollars.

The last major player in the early days of science fiction was an immigrant from Luxembourg named Hugo Gernsback. Hugo landed in New York with two hundred dollars in his pocket and plans for selling a battery he had invented. When that failed, Gernsback formed a company to import radio parts. To sell them, he published a catalog which became the magazine, *Modern Electrics*, later retitled *Electrical Experimenter*, which in turn became *Science and Invention* a few years later.

Always fond of science fiction, Gernsback wrote a novel (*Ralph 124C41+*—read it aloud) for *Modern Electrics* when he had to fill space. In it Gernsback

predicted fluorescent lighting, plastics, the radio direction finder, tape recorders, juke boxes, vending machines, and even radar.

At first Gernsback printed simple "invention" stories, one or two to an issue, then branched out to include stories by Ray Cummings, George Allan England, and others, most of them illustrated by Frank R. Paul, a former editorial cartoonist for the *Jersey Journal*. Paul, never noted for his ability to draw people, definitely had a way with strange machinery and aliens from other worlds, the prime ingredients for the "sense of wonder" so prized by early readers.

The stories drew a lot of reader interest, and the August 1923 issue of *Science and Invention* was a special "Scientific Fiction Number" containing six stories. The cover illustrated "The Man From the Atom," by G. Peyton Wertenbaker—a precocious sixteen-year-old in the Luis P. Senarens tradition. The issue sold well and Gernsback considered publishing an all-scientific-fiction magazine. Plans didn't jell but the guests were met, the feast was set, and Hugo had better luck several years later.

Amazing Stories for April 1926 was the very first issue of the very first all-science-fiction magazine.

13
WELLS MEETS WELLES

H.G. Wells (left) met Orson Welles (right) when both were in San Antonio for a lecture by Wells in October 1940. H.G. didn't much care for Orson's radio version of his novel *The War of the Worlds*.

ISN'T IT AMAZING?

CHAPTER 2

The first issue of *Amazing Stories* wasn't much to look at—some fur-coated characters ice-skating on what is presumably a moon of Saturn (which doesn't explain the two sailing ships stuck on ice floes in the background). The sky, typical for a Gernsback publication, is not the black of space but yellow, the better to catch the passing buyer's eye. And catch it the magazine did. Gernsback reportedly printed 100,000 and sold almost all of them. *Amazing Stories* was a large-size magazine (the page size of today's *Time*) and half an inch thick—ninety-six pages printed on stock just this side of blotting paper—with an evocative "comet-tail" title design.

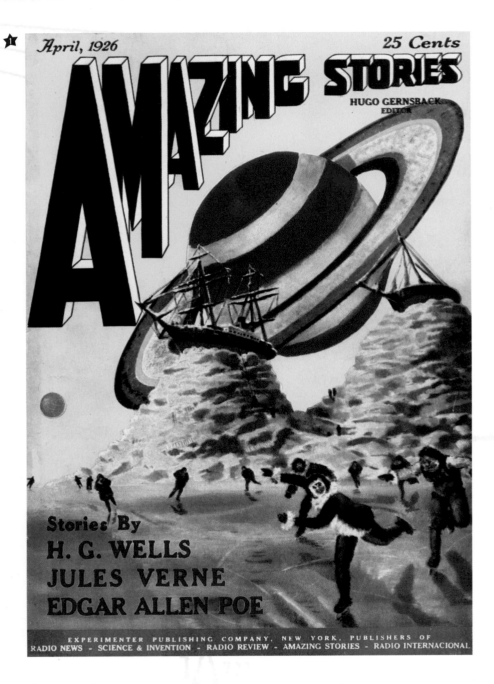

AMAZING STORIES
APRIL 1926
FRANK R. PAUL

The first issue of the first all-science-fiction magazine. Gernsback's headliners were H.G. Wells, Jules Verne and Edgar Allan Poe (misspelled on cover) — not a bad lineup for a first issue.

It cost a quarter, a high price for a magazine back then, especially for an audience primarily of teenagers and young adults, but looked like it was worth it.

The contents were almost all reprints, and remained that way for a number of issues. Wells, Verne, and Poe led the ranks of the reprint authors, with later writers added from some of the Munsey magazines and even Gernsback's own *Science and Invention*.

The initial success of *Amazing Stories* led Gernsback to toy with twice-a-month publication, but he settled for an *Amazing Stories Annual*, published in fall 1927. At 128 pages, it was only thirty-two pages larger than the monthly but cost twice as much. It featured the first appearance anywhere of *The Master Mind of Mars* by Edgar Rice Burroughs. The *Annual* was a rousing success, even at fifty cents, and Gernsback immediately converted it to a quarterly.

A year later *Amazing Stories* had added a letter column ("Discussions"), which frequently printed the full addresses of the writers, a handy guide for young readers looking for science-fiction pen pals. Many of the writers agitated for clubs to be formed in various cities.

New blood eventually started to seep into the magazine despite the low pay to authors. Among the Gernsback discoveries was Edward Elmer Smith, Ph.D.—better known as "Doc" Smith to his fans— with *The Skylark of Space*, the first of his mind-boggling space operas. Smith had started writing it in 1915, finished it in 1920, and then waited eight years for a magazine to show up that would print it.

In the same issue as the first installment of Doc's serial was "Armageddon—2419" by Philip Francis Nowlan, which introduced Anthony "Buck" Rogers

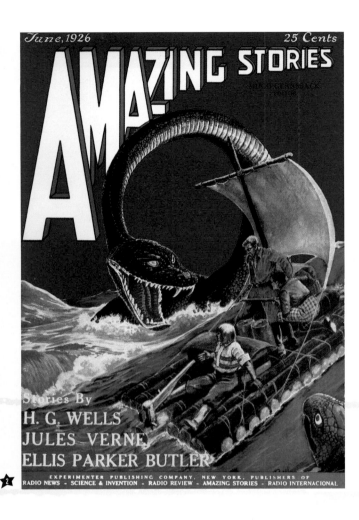

AMAZING STORIES ANNUAL
1927
FRANK R. PAUL

The *Annual* was so successful that publisher Gernsback quickly
turned it into a quarterly. *The Master Mind of Mars* was printed in
full—a bargain for fifty cents. The issue is rare, a collector's item.

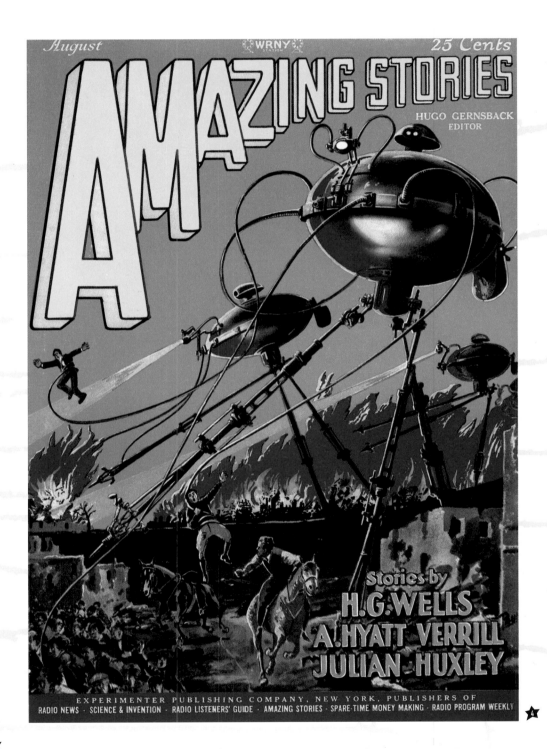

AMAZING STORIES
JUNE 1926
FRANK R. PAUL

Artist Paul was the cover illustrator for almost
every science-fiction magazine that Hugo
Gernsback published. Paul had a true sense
of wonder—and an affection for red skies.

AMAZING STORIES
AUGUST 1927
FRANK R. PAUL

The ccver was one of the more striking
representations of H.G. Wells' *The War
of the Worlds.*

AMAZING STORIES
AUGUST 1928
FRANK R. PAUL

Inside was Part I of *The Skylark of Space*, the first serial by Edward Elmer Smith, soon acclaimed the top space-opera author. Also included: "Armageddon—2419" by Philip Francis Nowlan, starring Anthony "Buck" Rogers.

AMAZING STORIES
MARCH 1929
FRANK R. PAUL

Featured was "The Airlords of Han," the second of the stories by Philip Francis Nowlan featuring "Buck" Rogers, soon to be immortalized in the comic strips and Saturday afternoon movie serials.

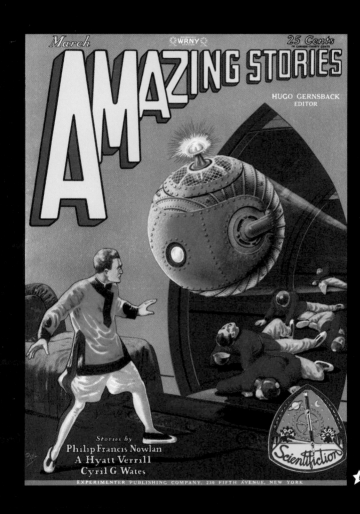

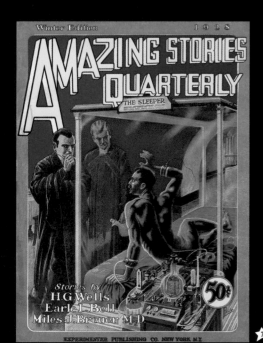

AMAZING STORIES QUARTERLY
WINTER 1928
FRANK R. PAUL

The first issue of the *Quarterly* featured a reprint of *The Sleeper Wakes* by H.G. Wells. New writers would soon be published.

SKYLARK THREE

By

Edward E. Smith, Ph.D.

Other Scientifiction Stories by:
Capt. S. P. Meek, U. S. A.
Peter van Dresser
Edmond Hamilton

AMAZING STORIES
AUGUST 1930
H. W. WESSOLOWSKI

Gernsback lost control of his publishing empire in 1929, but *Amazing* continued under the editorship of T. O'Conor Sloane, seventy-nine years old at the time of this issue.

to an enthusiastic public. Nowlan followed it with a sequel, then made Buck the hero of a comic strip— "Buck Rogers in the 25th Century."

Gernsback also discovered Dr. David H. Keller ("The Revolt of the Pedestrians") and published early stories by Edmond Hamilton and Clare Winger Harris, the first woman to write for the specialized science-fiction pulps. But his greatest discovery, though not immediately apparent, was Jack Williamson.

Williamson's "The Metal Man" ran in the December 1928 issue, though it wasn't his first appearance in the magazine. He'd had a letter in "Discussions" the year before as: "John S. Williamson" of Elida, New Mexico. In it he complains that his friends won't read the magazine because they think it's "cheap" and reading it "unhealthy."

It was the typical lament of an early science-fiction fan.

Williamson's career in science fiction was a microcosm of many science-fiction writers who came after him. He was born in 1908 in Texas and, when his father filed on a homestead in New Mexico, traveled with his family by covered wagon to his new home.

Once he discovered *Amazing Stories*, Williamson fell passionately in love with science fiction. It opened a window on a world of science and the imagination that he never suspected existed. From that moment on, the only thing he wanted to be in life was a science-fiction writer. His apprenticeship was amazingly short—from his letter in "Discussions" to a featured story in the front of the magazine took little more than a year. Though never really prolific, he wrote continuously after that. Finding a market

AMAZING STORIES QUARTERLY
FALL 1930
LEO MOREY

John W. Campbell, Jr.—later to become editor of *Astounding* —was twenty years old when the *Quarterly* published his story, "The Black Star Passes." It was pure space opera, featuring his continuing heroes Arcot, Wade, and Morey.

that paid two cents a word (*Astounding Stories*) instead of Gernsback's quarter of a cent upon lawsuit, he managed to support himself—a rarity among science-fiction writers then and still something of a rarity today.

Williamson took a break from writing to serve as a weather forecaster in the army during World War II, resuming writing after the war (including authoring a science-fiction comic strip for several years). He was never considered an old-timer—he had the happy ability to reinvent himself as an author every ten years or so, to keep up with the times. He was president of the Science Fiction Writers of America for two years, taught for a number of years, agitated to have science fiction included in the curriculum of high schools and colleges, and finally returned to writing after he retired. Williamson never became rich as an author. But money isn't everything, and in 1975 he was awarded the second Nebula Grand Master for his career in science fiction (the first went to Robert Heinlein).

(A "Nebula" is an Achievement Award given by the members of the Science Fiction & Fantasy Writers of America. A "Grand Master" is for a lifetime of work. A "Hugo," named after Hugo Gernsback, is an annual award by the membership of the World Science Fiction Convention.)

At the end of the century, Jack Williamson, age ninety-one, was still writing science fiction. The secret of his longevity was simple. At a convention some years ago, a young writer questioned Williamson about the good old days. Williamson pondered a moment, then asked the young writer what word-processing program he used.

Moral: If you want to write about the future, you can't afford to live in the past.

Gernsback lost control of his small publishing empire in early 1929 in a bankruptcy case. Whether it was the result of a plot or whether he was simply not paying his bills remains a question, but his name disappeared from the masthead of *Amazing* for May 1929, and Paul's cover for June was his last. It was the end of an era.

Gernsback's successor was T. O'Conor Sloane, Ph.D., seventy-eight years old, described by author Stanton Coblentz, as "Santa Claus in a three-piece suit." Sloane had been a boy of fourteen when the Civil War ended, and, if it had lasted a few more years, he might have fought in it (though drummer boys of fourteen were not that uncommon).

He wrote tedious editorials which got longer as he got older. Much worse, Sloane didn't believe in the possibility of space travel and frequently said so. (He didn't believe a man could climb Mt. Everest, either, but that's another story.) His editorship was erratic. He accepted a story by Clifford

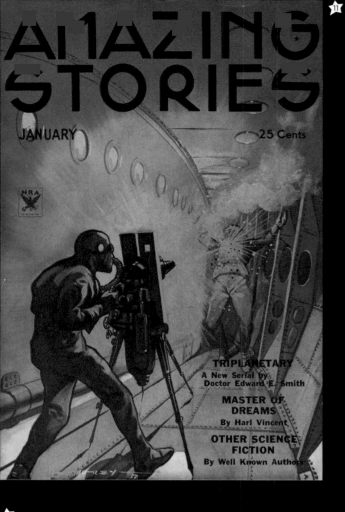

AMAZING STORIES
JUNE 1933
A. SIGMOND

One of the last large-size issues of *Amazing* (a series of Art Deco covers hadn't helped). Editor Sloane, whose editorial was on "Soap Bubbles and Candles," didn't believe in space travel—and said so.

AMAZING STORIES
JANUARY 1934
LEO MOREY

The first installment of *Triplanetary*—the last serial that "Doc" Smith would write for *Amazing*. Smith soon would become a regular for *Astounding*. The magazine was now a standard pulp, sans its famous comet tail title design.

AMAZING STORIES
MAY 1934
LEO MOREY

The only science-fiction magazine to pay tribute on its front cover to Jules Verne. The painting is of the Verne memorial at Nantes, France.

AMAZING STORIES
OCTOBER 1935
LEO MOREY

The magazine was now fading, reverting
to its old title design and a somewhat
forlorn attempt at an astronomical cover.

Simak in 1931, then returned it, unpublished, four
years later. He even lost a manuscript, *Invaders from
the Infinite*, the first story written by a teenage John
W. Campbell, Jr. (later found, it was published in
Amazing Stories Quarterly).

Sloane also had his good points. He was fond of
Edmond Hamilton and David H. Keller, M.D., and
published many stories by both. Campbell became a
regular contributor with his Arcot, Wade, and Morey
stories that established him as a competitor to Doc
Smith. As for Smith, Sloane published his *Skylark
Three*, *Spacehounds of IPC*, and *Triplanetary*.
Unnoticed by most readers, he also printed a poem,
"Elegy to a Dead Planet: Luna" in the October 1937
issue by "Elton Andrews."

Behind the whiskers and the false moustache
of the pen name was young science-fiction fan
Frederik Pohl; the poem was his first published work.
Pohl was fifteen when he wrote it, sixteen when it
was accepted, seventeen when it was published,
and eighteen when he was paid for it. Less than
two years after its publication, at age nineteen,

Pohl would be the editor of *Astonishing Stories*
and *Super Science Stories* and well on his way to
becoming one of the most significant editors and
writers in the field.

Whatever Sloane's merits, they weren't enough.
With the loss of Paul as cover artist, the magazine
also lost its visual sense of wonder. Hans Wessolowski
("Wesso") briefly replaced Paul, then defected to the
new *Astounding Stories of Super Science*. Paul was
still around—but on the covers of the new
Gernsback magazines which were replicas of his old
ones. Replacing "Wesso" was Leo Morey, who was
woefully inadequate when it came to either machinery
or astronomical scenes.

And it was, of course, the middle of the Great
Depression. The fifty-cent *Quarterly* died and the
circulation of *Amazing Stories* hit bottom at around
18,000 copies in 1938. The April issue was Sloane's last.

Amazing Stories was bought by a Chicago publisher,
Ziff-Davis, that wanted *Radio News* (*Amazing*'s big
and more profitable brother) to supplement their
existing titles of *Popular Aviation* and *Popular
Photography*. *Amazing* came along as part of the
package. (William B. Ziff had been an advertising

AMAZING STORIES
AUGUST 1938
HENRY F. KROEGER, JR.
(COVER PHOTOGRAPH)

A new publisher, a new
editor—Raymond A.
Palmer—and a modern-
ized version of the old
title. The male model
on the front cover was
twenty-one-year-old
author Robert Bloch
(or so the editor claimed),
famous later for his
novel *Psycho*.

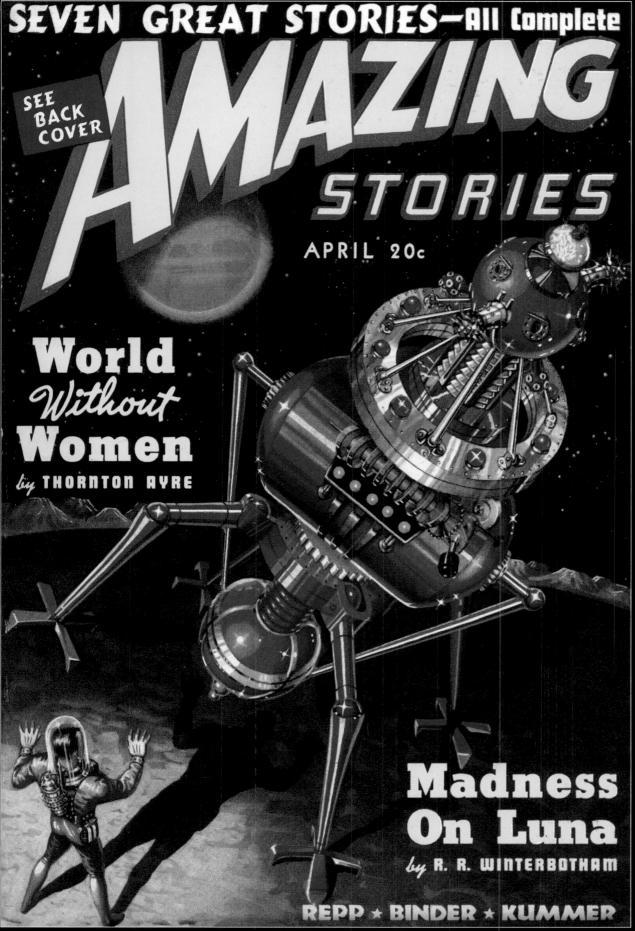

SEVEN GREAT STORIES—All Complete

AMAZING STORIES

SEE BACK COVER

APRIL 20c

World *Without* Women

by THORNTON AYRE

Madness On Luna

by R. R. WINTERBOTHAM

REPP ★ BINDER ★ KUMMER

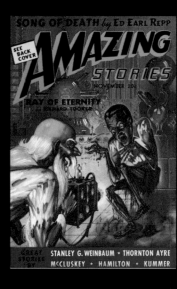

SONG OF DEATH *by* ED EARL REPP

AMAZING STORIES

RAY OF ETERNITY *by* Richard Tooker

SEE BACK COVER

GREAT STORIES BY   STANLEY G. WEINBAUM • THORNTON AYRE
McCLUSKEY • HAMILTON • KUMMER

17
AMAZING STORIES
NOVEMBER 1938
ROBERT FUQUA

Garish covers and a color scheme for the title that made it seem almost three-dimensional. Editor Palmer left no doubt that he was aiming for the younger reader.

16

18
AMAZING STORIES
APRIL 1939
ROBERT FUQUA

A robot to end all robots . . .

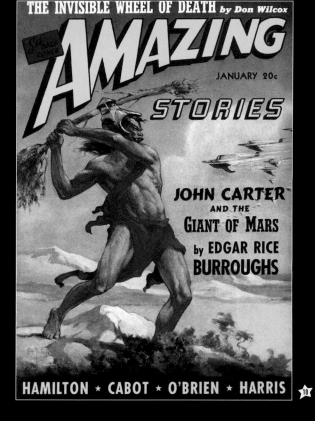

AMAZING STORIES
JANUARY 1941
J. ALLEN ST. JOHN

This issue of *Amazing* saw the first pairing of artist St. John and Edgar Rice Burroughs since St. John had painted a "Tarzan" cover for the old *Blue Book* in 1928.

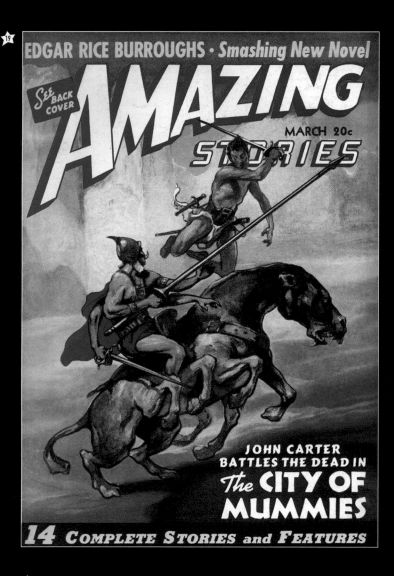

AMAZING STORIES
MARCH 1941
J. ALLEN ST. JOHN

The best painting yet of a six-legged Martian "thoat" for this story in the "John Carter of Mars" series by Burroughs.

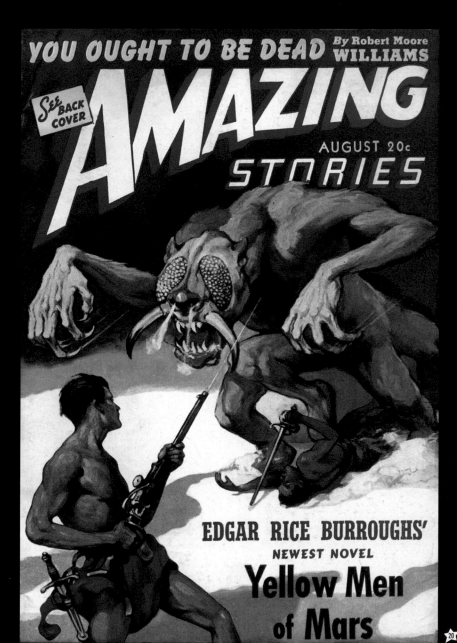

AMAZING STORIES
AUGUST 1941
J. ALLEN ST. JOHN

Amazing Stories and its companion magazine *Fantastic Adventures* featured the most eye-catching covers of the period—and the reason why were cover artists such as J. Allen St. John, Harold W. McCauley, and Robert Fuqua.

representative in Chicago and among his clients, at one time, had been the old *Weird Tales*. He later teamed up with Bernard G. Davis, fresh out of college, and founded the Ziff-Davis Publishing Company.)

Sloane died in 1940 at the ripe old age of eighty-nine. He was the oldest man to ever edit a science-fiction magazine—probably the oldest to edit any newsstand magazine. But it was not only the gulf of years that separated him from his youthful readership. He should have been the ringmaster for a future filled with hope and promise. Instead, he had acted as its caretaker.

Raymond A. Palmer was twenty-seven years old, had a history of childhood diseases (including TB), and was badly hunchbacked. Davis hired him to be the new editor of *Amazing Stories* on the recommendation of Ralph Milne Farley, an old-time pulp writer with whom Palmer had frequently collaborated.

Palmer didn't make the payroll immediately but was paid a commission depending on how many copies each issue sold. His first issue doubled in circulation, and he was put on straight salary when he began to make as much money as Bernie Davis himself.

Ziff-Davis had hired him because they knew nothing about science fiction and Farley had convinced them that Palmer, the quintessential science-fiction fan, knew everything.

Farley was right.

Palmer returned most of the stories in the Sloane inventory, doubled the word rates, saw the price of the magazine drop to twenty cents, sent out a bulletin to authors he knew asking for stories, and relied upon his old friends in the Milwaukee Fictioneers to give him a jump start.

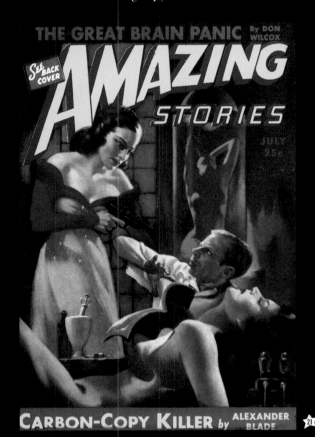

AMAZING STORIES
JULY 1943
H.W. MCCAULEY

McCauley painted a remarkable likeness of editor Raymond A. Palmer as the man in the middle—an editorial in-group joke.

AMAZING STORIES
MARCH 1945
ROBERT GIBSON JONES

Science-fiction fans were alienated by the Lemuria stories of Richard S. Shaver published as "racial memories." Shaver claimed he truly believed what he wrote. Apparently so did editor Palmer.

He threw together the first issue in two weeks, using a photograph for the front cover. The experiment was dropped after two issues, and Palmer recruited artists from the Ziff-Davis art department, primarily "Robert Fuqua" (Joe Tillotson), Julian S. Krupa, and Harold McCauley. All three, graduates of a technically oriented art department, knew how to make futuristic machinery look real. And McCauley would reveal a definite talent for airbrushed women.

They were the first major additions to the science-fiction art scene since Paul, Wesso, Howard V. Brown, and Leo Morey.

Palmer also instituted a chatty editorial column called "The Observatory," expanded the readers' page (he answered every letter published), and even had a pen-pals column, "Correspondence Corner." More than any other editor since Arthur Sullivant Hoffman of the old *Adventure*, Palmer infused the magazine with his own personality.

The transformation of the magazine was complete almost overnight. The paper was a better grade, the covers were glossy and eye-catching, the magazine cost less—what not to like?

For one thing, the fiction. Palmer saw his readers as young adolescents who wanted their stories exciting and not too heavy on the science—the same audience that would have thrilled to the adventures of Frank Reade, Jr. His advice to one writer wanting to sell him stories was simple—cross out all the passages the author thought were "fine writing." And when the action started to slow, "throw another body through the skylight."

Palmer knew what good writing was. He published Ray Bradbury, the first story by Isaac Asimov, stories by Stanley G. Weinbaum, Edmond Hamilton, William F. Temple, and Robert Bloch. And he was responsible for bringing back Edgar Rice Burroughs

with J. Allen St. John, a Chicago artist who had painted most of Burroughs' book jackets, to do the covers for issues containing a Burroughs story.

But the backbone of his magazines were simple action-adventure stories. Palmer published hackwork without apology, but at the same time was hurt by the response of the fans who considered *Amazing Stories* a juvenile magazine and a disgrace to the field. It hurt doubly because there was no more generous editor than Palmer when it came to donating artwork to help support conventions—covers and interiors by St. John (at one small convention, a St. John original cover went for twenty-five dollars), Krupa, Fuqua, and McCauley. And he always had time for fans who dropped in at the office.

He started companion magazines, some of which didn't last long. *Air Adventures* and *South Sea Stories* saw less than half a dozen issues each. *Fantastic Adventures* was more successful. Introduced in 1939 as a large-format size magazine, it didn't sell well and was retooled as a pulp. Circulation lagged until the October 1940 issue when Palmer introduced St. John's first cover—a native on a dinosaur being attacked by a red-winged pterodactyl. Sales soared and in 1941 *Fantastic Adventures* became a monthly.

Palmer's next success in magazines was with *Mammoth Detective* (May 1942), "mammoth" because it was 320 pages thick. Howard Browne joined the staff in 1943 as assistant editor, though he largely ran the magazine—Palmer didn't much care for detective fiction.

Palmer built up a small stable of local writers—William P. McGivern (who went on to become a popular mystery writer), David Wright O'Brien, William L. Hamling, Leroy Yerxa, and others—and put them on a monthly "draw." They would deliver so much wordage, he would guarantee them so

AMAZING STORIES
APRIL–MAY 1953
BARYE PHILLIPS

Howard Browne was now editor and turned *Amazing* into an upscale digest with an all-star lineup of Heinlein, Bradbury, and Sturgeon. Browne hated science fiction but recognized quality when he read it.

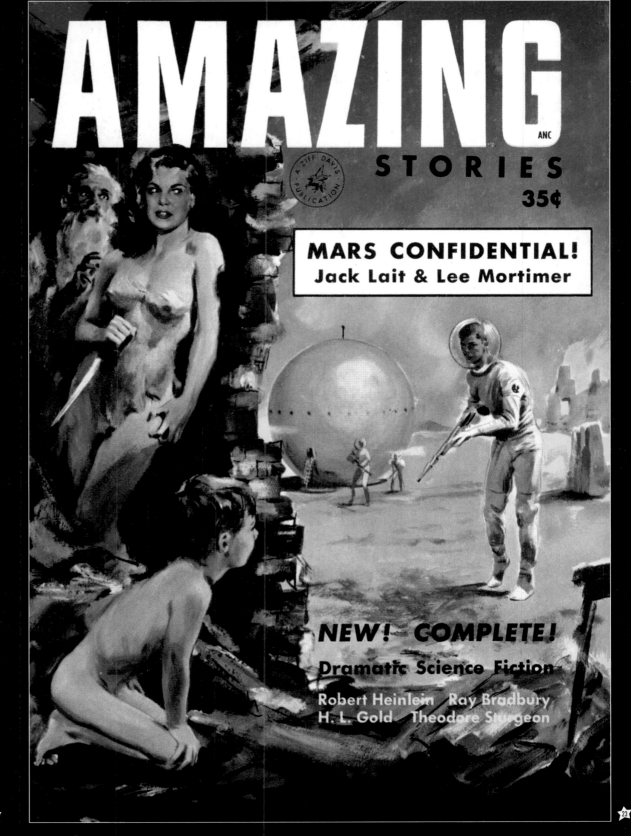

much income. It was a bad deal because with a guarantee, there was no incentive to do your best work. And it was bad personally because, in a sense, Palmer had bought you and there were times when he didn't let you forget it. At the weekly poker party at his home in Evanston, Palmer would point to the various authors at the table and tell them exactly how much he had paid for their first sale to him. Nobody complained and if Palmer cheated at cards, nobody objected.

It didn't happen very often but Palmer was as prone to frailty as the next man. And for one who had been at the bottom of the heap for so long, both financially and physically, a little strutting while he was at the top was forgivable. For Palmer himself, life had become very pleasant. He had carte blanche with the fiction division, he had married a beautiful woman and was inordinately proud of his children, straight-limbed and healthy.

With the advent of World War II and the resulting paper shortage, Ziff-Davis cut back the size— somewhat—and especially the frequency of their fiction magazines. It was more profitable for the company to spend its paper allotment on its slick technical magazines.

Both Palmer and Browne sat out the war—Palmer was badly crippled and Browne wore coke bottle glasses. They had the equivalent of one magazine to produce per month and filled their days with long lunches and endless games of pinochle. But Palmer grieved when David Wright O'Brien was shot down over Berlin. Palmer had considered him an older son, a younger brother.

Two momentous events happened in 1945. One, Palmer discovered the lunatic fringe and two, that appealing to it would sell magazines. "I Remember Lemuria," largely written by Palmer but based on a long letter from a Pennsylvania welder named Richard Shaver, related Shaver's experiences with the evil "deros" who lived in caverns deep underground and caused most of the bad things that happened on the surface.

It turned out that Shaver wasn't the only one who remembered Lemuria. The office was flooded with letters and circulation zoomed to 185,000—a figure for a science-fiction magazine that had never been achieved before and hasn't been equaled since.

The "Shaver Mystery," as it was called, made repeated appearances in the magazine, to the increasing discomfort of management—and the hostility of science-fiction fans. In their eyes, Palmer had "…drowned his Glory in a shallow cup and sold his reputation for a Song."

In 1948, Palmer started his own magazine, *Fate*, editing it on his lunch hour out of an office around the corner from Ziff-Davis. It dealt with odd and unusual happenings, especially with the "flying saucers," or UFOs ("unidentified flying objects") observed by businessman Kenneth Arnold in 1947 during a flight in his private plane.

★25

AMAZING STORIES
NOVEMBER 1963
ALEX SCHOMBURG

New editor Cele Goldsmith raised the standards, while working with a miniscule budget and little front-office support. Inside were Burroughs, Philip K. Dick, Harry Harrison, Piers Anthony, and Ben Bova —a stunning lineup.

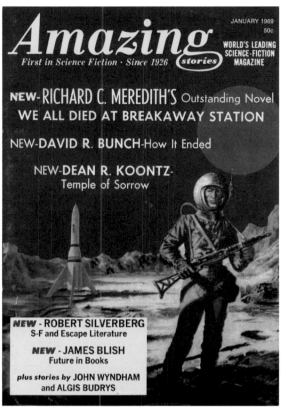

AMAZING STORIES
JANUARY 1969
UNKNOWN

A new publisher and a bewildering series of editors, including Barry N. Malzberg and Ted White, who kept the magazine afloat with quality reprints and top-notch new writers.

People who felt that science had left them with no say over the future of their own lives were more than willing to believe in phenomena for which science had ready explanations but no real proof. In 1949, Palmer founded a science-fiction magazine—*Other Worlds*—and left Ziff-Davis. Why let management make all the money?

It was the end of still another era—probably the most flamboyant of them all.

Ziff-Davis promptly called back Howard Browne to take over as editor (Browne had been on leave of absence to write mystery novels). Browne, who had never cared for science fiction, nevertheless had big plans for *Amazing Stories* and got permission from management to turn it into a large-size magazine with top writers.

Unfortunately, the advent of the Korean War raised fears of a paper shortage and the plans were cancelled. But Browne did get an okay to try his hand at an upscale fantasy digest titled simply, *Fantastic*. The result was probably the best-looking fiction digest ever published, with a five-color cover and stories by Walter Miller, Jr., Ray Bradbury, Isaac Asimov, and H.L. Gold and a short novel by Raymond Chandler, *Professor Bingo's Snuff*.

The second issue had two-color interior illustrations and stories by Roy Huggins (a Browne discovery for *Mammoth Mystery* who was to make his mark as a television screenwriter and producer), Theodore Sturgeon, and Fritz Leiber. The fantasy reprint was "Miriam" by Truman Capote.

It was the third issue of *Fantastic* that should have made the magazine's fortune. Featured was a short novel by, of all people, Mickey Spillane. A wraparound band announced "MICKEY SPILLANE" in huge letters and *The Veiled Woman*, his lead novel, in smaller ones. Rumor had it that Browne had largely written the story, that the original manuscript had been lost. Apologies were made to Spillane's agent but Spillane himself never complained—Browne was an accomplished mystery writer, and the story had an ending which was vintage Spillane.

For a while the magazine prospered with top talent. *Amazing Stories* had also become a class-act digest with two-color interiors and stories by Robert Heinlein, Ray Bradbury, Ted Sturgeon, H.L. Gold, and Richard Matheson. Browne was on a roll but, alas, not for long. The new *Amazing* and *Fantastic* were introduced right at the peak of the boom in science-fiction digests with more than forty titles clogging the newsstands. Three years earlier, Browne's new and improved magazines would have found a ready market. Now they had to struggle.

By the end of 1953, Browne's other digest magazines—*Conflict*, *The Seven Seas*, and *Tales of the Sea* (probably a retitling of the first) had folded. *Amazing* and *Fantastic* had been cut back from 160 pages to 128 and the two-color illustrations were gone. For a while, they held up editorially, though word rates had been slashed. But Browne was running on inventory bought in more optimistic days.

AMAZING STORIES
NOVEMBER 1982
MICHAEL WHELAN

Still another new publisher
and a new editor, George
Scithers, formerly editor
of *Asimov's*. The magazine
finally had a respectable
budget.

Browne stayed through the middle of 1956, then left for a television script-writing career with Roy Huggins (*77 Sunset Strip, Surfside 6, The Rockford Files*, etc.). The old "house" names reappeared though the writers behind the names now included Robert Silverberg, Harlan Ellison, Randall Garrett, etc. In 1958, editor Paul Fairman left to become a full-time writer and the trials and tribulations passed to Cele Goldsmith, who had been managing editor.

Science fiction was going through a sea change when Goldsmith took over—the "golden age" was long gone and so were most of the writers who had made it golden. But new writers appeared, new concepts explored, and most of it happened on Goldsmith's watch. In fact, a good deal of it happened because of her, despite front office indifference. The budget was small, the magazine thin, but still, Goldsmith worked wonders.

Gone was the hackwork that had filled the magazine's pages. Recognized authors' names began to replace the anonymous titles and blurbs that had graced the front cover. In 1959, there was a new serial by—surprise!—Doc Smith plus a new story by Isaac Asimov (a sequel to his first published story, "Marooned Off Vesta").

Cordwainer Smith appeared, then Poul Anderson and Ward Moore and a number of others. In 1960, the magazine was nominated for a Hugo. More class authors began to show up: Tom Disch (today a respected critic), Roger Zelazny, Ursula K. Le Guin, Fritz Leiber, Jr., Robert Sheckley, Brian Aldiss, J.G. Ballard, Philip José Farmer, Gordon Dickson, Leigh Brackett, Ben Bova, Arthur C. Clarke, Philip K. Dick, and a newly reinvented Edmond Hamilton, far removed from the "world wrecker" Hamilton of old.

Cele Goldsmith might have worked wonders with what she had, but she probably could have worked miracles if she'd had a little more, if management had been willing to beef up the magazines to make them competitive with other digests. But Bernie Davis, who had overseen the fiction division since the day Ziff-Davis had bought *Amazing*, was gone. There was nobody left in upper management to appeal to. From the days when the fiction magazines had been cash cows, they now made a tiny blip on the bottom line if they made any blip at all.

The firm's attention was on its slick paper money-makers, and the fiction division no longer fit in the lineup. *Amazing* (and *Fantastic*) were sold in 1965.

AMAZING STORIES
MAY 1991
TIM HILDEBRANDT

Kim Mohan was now the editor of the first all-slick, four-color monthly science-fiction magazine ever published. *Amazing* had had more ups and downs than any publication in the field but had now landed in the Big Time.

The new publisher added more pages, and editor Joseph Ross worked with Cele Goldsmith's inventory and bought new stories from Cordwainer Smith, Philip K. Dick, Poul Anderson (the first "Ensign Flandry" story), John Brunner, and Frank Herbert (author of *Dune*).

Then the publisher ran afoul of the Science Fiction Writers of America, who objected to his policy of reprinting stories without payment to the original authors. After two years, when the inventory of quality stories had run out and the publisher objected to spending money on new ones, Ross resigned.

Harry Harrison took over, more or less made peace with the SFWA, but resigned after five months when the publisher still hadn't phased out reprints. New editor Barry Malzberg lasted six months, to be replaced in turn by Ted White, a long-time science-fiction fan. He had written a few science-fiction stories and been a jazz critic for *Downbeat* and a first reader for *Fantasy and Science Fiction* before becoming editor of *Amazing*.

Like Goldsmith, White worked wonders with very little, adding personality to the magazine with a lengthy letters column, an equally lengthy editorial, and book reviews. Piers Anthony reappeared, as did Ursula K. Le Guin (*The Lathe of Heaven*), Bob Silverberg and John Brunner. *Amazing* won a Hugo nomination for Best Magazine in 1970, 1971, and 1972 and Ted White a Best Professional Editor nomination in 1973, 1974, 1975, 1976, and 1977. But the awards didn't help circulation, and in 1978 the magazine was sold once again.

Reprints returned—for a while—the new editor phased them out and authors like Greg Benford and Harlan Ellison and Roger Zelazny appeared. In 1982, the magazine was sold still again, this time to TSR

Vol. LXVI, No. 1 — $3.95

ALL NEW FORMAT, FEATURES, AND FICTION!

AMAZING STORIES

1-56076-287-X

Robert Silverberg
John Brunner
Kristine Kathryn Rusch
and
Kevin J. Anderson

Lawrence Watt-Evans
C. J. Cherryh
Robert Lynn Asprin
Arthur C. Clarke

Swimming the dark waters of the soul — $1.75 USA $2.25 CAN

AMAZING STORIES

AMAZING STORIES
NOVEMBER 1989
JANET AULISIO

The cover was a touching tribute to Albert Einstein who never wrote science fiction but whose theories inspired much of it.

AMAZING STORIES

FALL 1998
MARK ZUG

After several digest issues, *Amazing* had another new publisher and once again was a large-size slick with full color. The magazine could have shown Lazarus a thing or two. (Date shown on cover is a mistake.)

Editor Mohan encouraged new writers and published old favorites like Tom Disch, Barry Malzberg, Greg Benford, George Zebrowski, Frederik Pohl, John Brunner, Anne McCaffrey, Ursula K. Le Guin, Roger Zelazny, Barry Longyear, and Arthur C. Clarke—the contents page read like a Who's Who of best-selling authors. Cover artists included Tim Hildebrandt, Kelly Freas, Rick Berry, Ron Walotsky, Bob Eggleton, and David Mattingly. The four-color interiors were just as stunning, featuring newcomers like Rob Alexander and Pat Morissey.

And then…and then…

It was an old story. Circulation hadn't kept pace with increased costs. The magazine reverted to a digest and was finally discontinued.

That should have been the end of a magazine that had had more lives than the proverbial cat. It wasn't. The parent company was sold to another games publisher, Wizards of the Coast, and *Amazing Stories* was resurrected, not as a digest but once again as a large-size, slick-paper magazine with four-color interiors. Kim Mohan, the former editor, was also the new one.

There was, however, a significant difference between the new and the old magazine. The overline for the last issue in 1998 proclaimed: "*Babylon 5* Novel Excerpt." Mohan had acknowledged the vast appeal of science fiction on the screen and on television. Realizing that the best-selling science-fiction books were spin-offs from *Star Trek* and *Star Wars*, he decided if you can't beat them, at least meet them halfway. Mohan made the right decision.

There was still plenty of "sense of wonder" to go around.

Hobbies, a company best known for its "Dungeons and Dragons" role-playing game.

Amazing had another new editor—George Scithers, who had been editor of *Isaac Asimov's Science Fiction Magazine*—and a respectable budget. The magazine was beefed up, respectable word rates were paid, new artists appeared (including Michael Whelan, one of the top genre artists), but circulation continued to slide, hitting bottom in 1984. Scithers was replaced by Patrick Lucien Price in 1986 and then, in 1991, by Kim Mohan.

The magazine could not possibly have been profitable and TSR could have dropped it or sold it but what they did was …amazing. The company took a gamble. Effective with the May 1991 issue *Amazing* became a large-sized, slick paper magazine with four-color interior illustrations.

In one fell swoop, it had become the best-looking science-fiction magazine on the newsstand.

Vol. LXVII, No. 8

$3.95 U.S. / $4.75 Can. / £1.95 U.K.

The World's First Science Fiction Magazine

AMAZING®

STORIES

1-56076-458-9

Gail Regier

Pamela Sargent

George Zebrowski

Thomas M. Disch

AMAZING STORIES
NOVEMBER 1992
RICK BERRY

Rick Berry, the cover artist, had pioneered computer art with his cover
for William Gibson's novel *Neuromancer*. He had also done computer-

CHAPTER 3

NO, IT'S WONDERFUL!

Gernsback may have been pushed into bankruptcy through conspiring competitors, or he may have fallen into it through failure to pay his printing and paper bills. The former seems unlikely, but so does the latter—for a bankrupt, he certainly had no difficulty reestablishing paper and printing credit and was back in business within a month. Gernsback had recovered so quickly that his first issue of *Science Wonder Stories* for June 1929 competed on the newsstands with the June issue of *Amazing* that he had also edited (complete with cover by Paul), though his name was no longer on the masthead. There was another new title: *Air Wonder Stories*, a magazine of air stories of the future, as well as a *Science Wonder Quarterly*. And late in 1929, still another title: *Scientific Detective Monthly*. It did not, however, carry many stories that could be called "science fiction"

①

SCIENCE WONDER QUARTERLY
FALL 1929
FRANK R. PAUL

The first issue of Gernsback's new *Science Wonder Quarterly* featured one of its most prescient covers—a spacewalk with the astronauts tethered to the capsule, all of it against the gold of space. Gold?

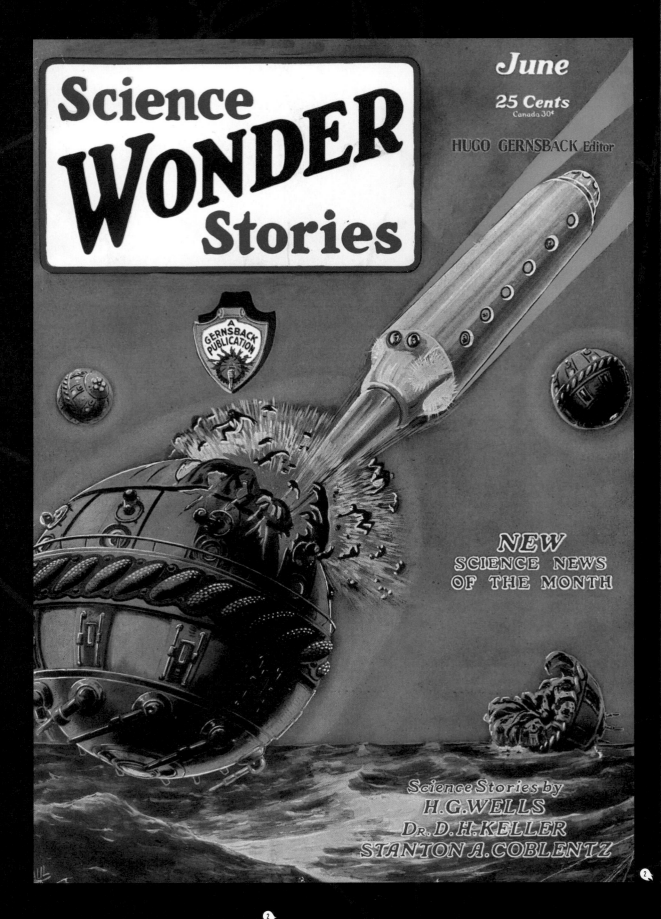

②

SCIENCE WONDER STORIES
JUNE 1929
FRANK R. PAUL

Gernsback had lost control of *Amazing Stories* two months before but was back on the newsstands not

—a phrase now used by Gernsback instead of "scientifiction" (a corruption of "scientific fiction," a term identified with *Amazing Stories*).

Gernsback had always stressed the connection between science and his fiction magazines; they weren't just pure entertainment, they were also meant to enlighten and educate. Gernsback's well-qualified managing editor, replacing the venerable T. O'Conor Sloane, Ph.D., was David Lasser, who had written a book on rocketry and was to become the first president of the American Rocket Society. Sloane might have doubted the possibility of space travel but Lasser certainly didn't.

Gernsback soon discovered, probably to his acute disappointment, that the word "science" didn't sell his fiction magazines. It was reduced in size, then appeared in pale pastels and by the twelfth issue had disappeared entirely from both the monthly and the quarterly. *Air Wonder Stories* disappeared along with it, being combined with its companion as simply *Wonder Stories*. After five issues, *Scientific Detective* dropped the word "Scientific" and became *Amazing Detective Tales*, then vanished.

Gernsback had had the field to himself with *Amazing Stories*. Now he not only had competition from his old magazines, he also faced a newcomer whom he undoubtedly resented. Clayton Publications, a major pulp chain (*Ace-High*, *Danger Trail*, *Ranch Romances*, etc.), had started *Astounding Stories of Super-Science* (January 1930) in the standard pulp format. It cost a nickel less, paid its authors considerably more, and wasn't the least interested in teaching its readers much about science or anything else.

Wonder Stories went through a bewildering series of size and price changes trying to compete—from large size to pulp size, back to large size and then pulp again. The price was as variable as the paper stock, which ranged from pulp to slick to a high-quality book paper. It was either a quarter or fifteen cents, depending.

The last issue of *Wonder* was April 1936, though Gernsback didn't give up without a fight. He had a scheme for bypassing the newsstands, and their ruinous returns, altogether. Readers had only to clip out a coupon, mail it to the magazine, and they would get the next issue with a bill for fifteen cents, payable in coin or stamps. A pay-as-you-go subscription plan, it was dead on arrival.

It was eleven years to the month after Gernsback had founded *Amazing Stories*. The magazine was sold to one of the larger pulp chains and beginning with the August 1936 issue became *Thrilling Wonder Stories*, a companion of *Thrilling Mysteries*, *Thrilling Adventures*, etc.

(Gernsback was left with *Everyday Science and Mechanics*, his radio magazine—eventually to be retitled *Radio Electronics*—and *Sexology*, sort of a combination Playboy Advisor with somewhat mechanistic and strictly non-erotic how-to-do-it illustrations. Gernsback would make a small fortune with the three of them.)

During its seven years, the Gernsback *Wonder* was not without its high points. Gernsback didn't rely on fiction reprints for the monthly, though he reprinted science articles from the French and German, and the *Quarterly* was fond of interplanetary novels in translation.

In the monthly, Gernsback printed David H. Keller with great regularity (ten of the first twelve issues), as he did Clark Ashton Smith (one of the Big Three for *Weird Tales*, along with H. P. Lovecraft and Robert E. Howard). Smith's "The City of the Singing

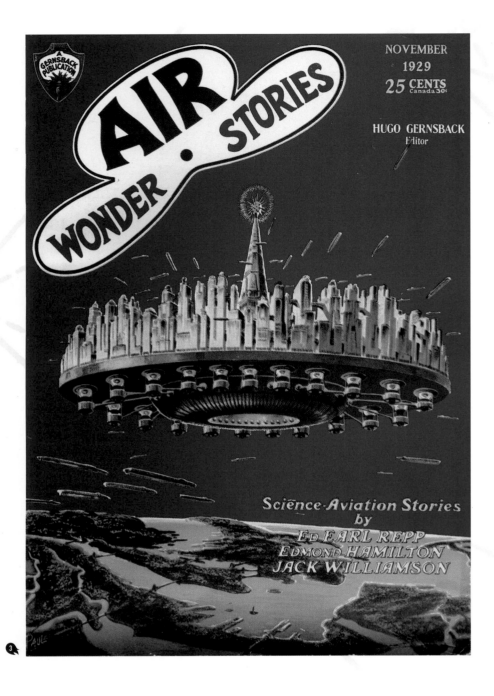

AIR WONDER STORIES
NOVEMBER 1929
FRANK R. PAUL

Seventy years ago, *Air Wonder* featured a story by
Jack Williamson. As of this writing (1999), author
Williamson is still writing science-fiction stories
and novels.

WONDER STORIES
SEPTEMBER 1930
FRANK R. PAUL

"Science" didn't sell
magazines, so it was
dropped from the title.
The new *Wonder Stories*
combined both *Science
Wonder* and *Air Wonder*
in the same magazine.

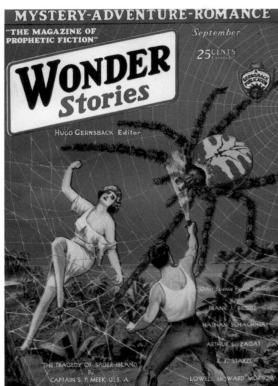

Flame" became a classic, readers crediting it with
having a true "sense of wonder."

Another writer with a firm grip on a "sense of
wonder" was Laurence Manning, who with Fletcher
Pratt collaborated on "The City of the Living Dead,"
another classic. In the story, a person's nerve endings
are hooked up to machinery that produces "adventures" to suit their desires. For all practical purposes,
the popular "adventures" are real. Those who buy
them are willing to trade in their real lives for fantasy
ones. It was a theme that would appear many times
in science fiction.

Eighteen-year-old P. Schuyler Miller was published
in 1930 with "The Red Plague." Joining the barely-old-
enough-to-shave crowd in 1931 was sixteen-year-old
Frank K. Kelly with "The Light Bender." (Kelly
retired from writing science fiction at the jaded old
age of twenty-one to become a newspaperman in
Kansas City, where he met Harry S. Truman and became a speech writer for him in the 1948 elections.)

Gernsback (obviously) embraced science-fiction
fans who had literary aspirations, buying Raymond
A. Palmer's first story, "The Time Ray of Jandra," for
a 1930's issue. (Palmer had also won an essay contest
in *Science Wonder Quarterly* for "What I Have Done
to Spread Science Fiction.")

Palmer was one of the first science-fiction fans but
hardly the last to play a pivotal role in Gernsback's
publishing life. In 1933, David Lasser left the magazine, and Gernsback cast about for a new managing
editor. Having seen a copy of a fanzine titled *The
Fantasy Fan*, he asked its editor to visit the office.

Charles D. Hornig was seventeen years old and still
in high school. Nevertheless, a startled Gernsback
hired him—the youngest editor of a professional
science-fiction magazine either before or since.

Hornig got his high school diploma attending night school, while editing *Wonder* during the day.

Hornig was not without a certain expertise and soon launched on a search for new concepts—not exactly an innovative policy since F. Orlin Tremaine, the editor of *Astounding*, had already announced a series of "thought variants." But for a "literature of ideas," as science fiction touted itself to be, new concepts would become the editor's Holy Grail.

It wasn't long before Hornig's policy paid off and in a very big way. The July 1934 *Wonder* ran what was arguably the magazine's most popular story, "A Martian Odyssey" by Stanley G. Weinbaum. It was the first story in which "aliens" were truly alien, impossible to understand by human standards—yet presented in such a way that they were likeable.

Weinbaum sold five more stories to *Wonder* though he, too, was eventually seduced by *Astounding* with its higher rates of pay. Weinbaum had a background in the sciences and a strong desire to be a writer. He produced a romance novel, an operetta, and a sheaf of poetry before turning to science fiction. He had read it since the early days of *Amazing* and, like so many writers before and after, must have thought: "I can write something as good as this."

Weinbaum wrote something better.

It didn't take long for Weinbaum to become the equivalent of a science-fiction rock star. Readers of both *Wonder* and *Astounding* raved about his stories—well-written and conceptually new. One of them, "Pygmalion's Spectacles," concerned a young man who tries on special glasses invented by a professor who had been trying to sell them to film producers. Once our hero puts them on, he lives a life on what seems to be another world—only the

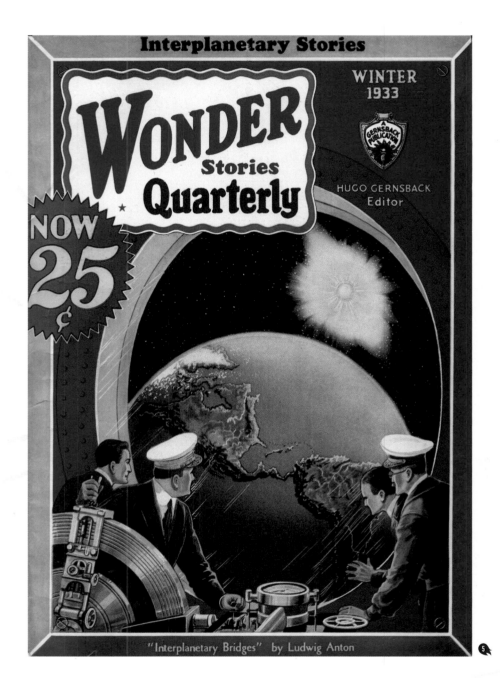

WONDER STORIES QUARTERLY
WINTER 1933
FRANK R. PAUL

It was 1933 and the depths of the Depression. Magazines that cost fifty cents weren't that popular—neither were magazines that sold for a quarter.

Gernsback, realizing the audience for science fiction was young and vocal and willing to proselytize for its favorite fiction, urged his readers to organize local chapters. The magazine was now pulp size.

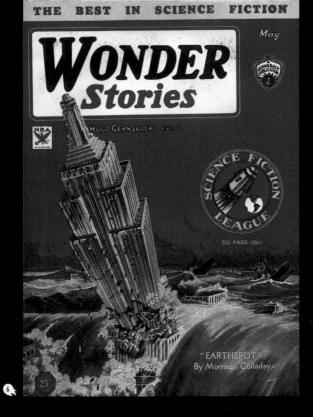

spectacles affect more than just his seeing. What he sees he can also touch and feel, smell and taste. What Weinbaum described, of course, was another version of Star Trek's "holodeck."

Stanley G. Weinbaum wrote twenty-two science fiction stories in a career that lasted all of fifteen months. When he died of cancer, *Astounding* published an obit. So did *Wonder*—in the last issue Gernsback published.

One other major innovation that Hornig and Gernsback started was the Science Fiction League. Gernsback had never really capitalized on the enthusiastic readership of *Amazing Stories* when he was editor. He *had* started the Short Wave Radio League and now came up with the Science Fiction League, both as a rallying point for the readers and as a circulation builder.

Interested fans could apply for membership and receive a certificate, stationery, and badges and even a charter for a club if three or more readers asked. The magazine in turn would report on the newly formed chapters, fan activities, etc. All well and good, but it was a commercially sponsored enterprise and many fans were nothing if not independent.

One of the first to stray, partly in objection to *Wonder*'s payment-on-lawsuit story policy, was Donald A. Wollheim, whose first fiction sale—"The Man From Ariel"—had been published in a 1934 issue of *Wonder*. Along with several friends, Wollheim formed the International Scientific Association (ISA) in competition with the Science Fiction League. Predictably, he and his friends were drummed out of the League.

The League itself eventually died but Wollheim became a noted writer, anthologist, editor of a number of magazines, and eventually editor of one of the early paperback lines devoted to science fiction, Ace Books. Science-fiction clubs didn't die with either the League or the ISA but continued to proliferate and prosper on a city-by-city basis across the country.

What publishers didn't realize at the time was that the inmates were organizing to take over the asylum.

The new editor of *Thrilling Wonder Stories* was another fan—Mort Weisinger, former associate editor of an early fan magazine called *The Time Traveller*. Managing editor of *The Time Traveler* was Julius Schwartz who, along with Weisinger, formed the first literary agency to specialize in science fiction. Schwartz later edited *Batman* and *Superman*, and in his senior years became Goodwill Ambassador for DC Comics.

The contributing editor to *The Time Traveller* was Forrest J. Ackerman, who became known as science

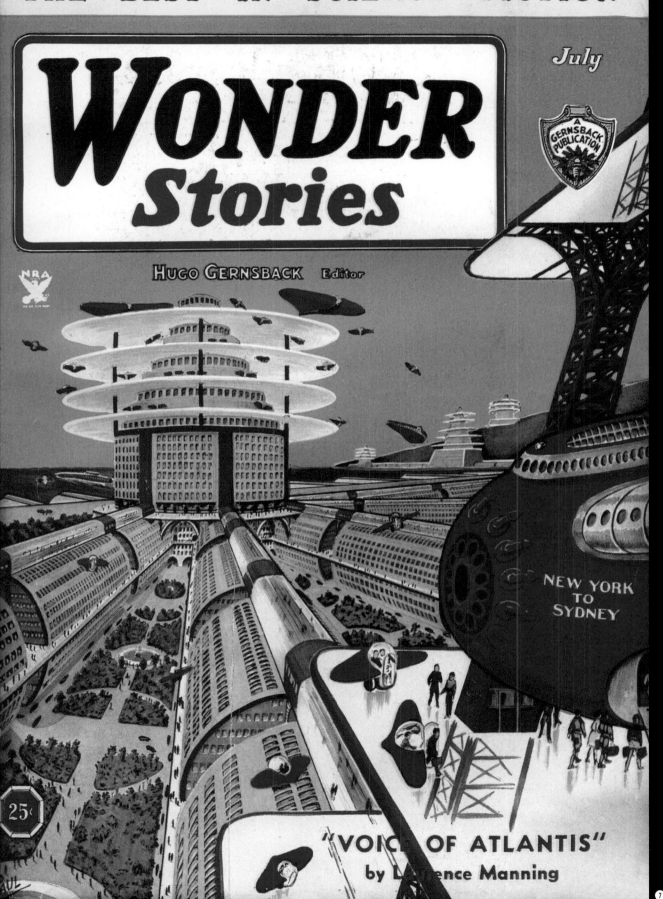

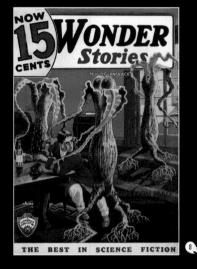

WONDER STORIES
JUNE 1935
FRANK R. PAUL

Gernsback dropped the price to fifteen cents but it was too late to help. Man-eating plants were no help either.

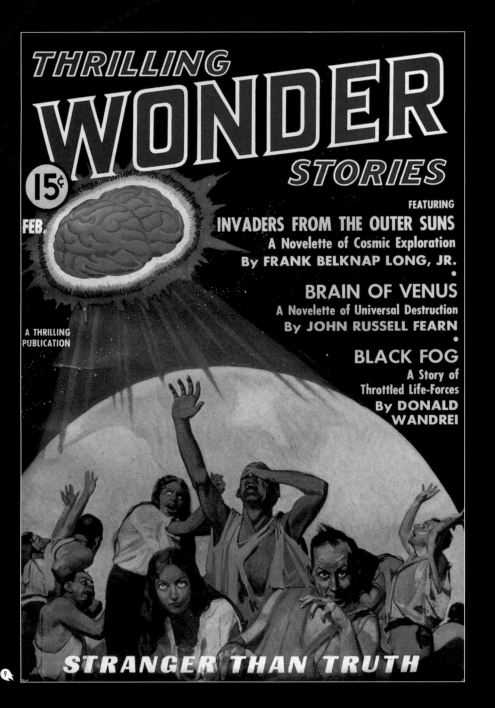

THRILLING WONDER STORIES
FEBRUARY 1937
HOWARD V. BROWN

The magazine was now part of a large pulp chain. The fiction became oriented more toward action-adventure than science.

fiction's Number One Fan and later edited *Famous Monsters of Filmland.* (In 1929 Ackerman won a contest in the *San Francisco Chronicle* for his story "A Trip to Mars." When Ackerman was approached to join a Bay Area science-fiction club, members were surprised to discover that their new initiate was only thirteen years old.)

Weisinger's approach to science fiction was much the same as Palmer's several years later—he aimed the magazine at the teenage market, even including a black-and-white comic strip, "Zarnak," which was dropped after eight issues. In 1939, the magazine published the winning story in its short-story contest, "The Broken Axiom," by Alfred Bester, later famous for his novels *The Stars My Destination* and *The Demolished Man,* voted among the top science-fiction novels of all time.

John W. Campbell, Jr., appeared in *Thrilling Wonder,* as did Eando Binder (for Earl and Otto, later Otto alone). Among the more popular stories were those by Arthur K. Barnes about "Gerry Carlyle," a female interplanetary big-game hunter, and Henry Kuttner's series about "Hollywood on the Moon."

In the anniversary issue for June 1939, the magazine ran Stanley G. Weinbaum's *The Dawn of Flame* posthumously, as well as stories by Doc Smith and John Coleman and Hulbert Burroughs (the sons of Edgar Rice Burroughs). A year later, unnoticed by historians, *Thrilling Wonder* ran the first movie "tie-in" by a science-fiction magazine. The film was Paramount's *Dr. Cyclops* and was featured in a painting on the cover. Inside, stills from the movie helped illustrate the "novelization" by Henry Kuttner.

World War II was not kind to *Thrilling Wonder.* Reduced in number of pages and frequency, it lost many of its writers to the draft and the war effort and

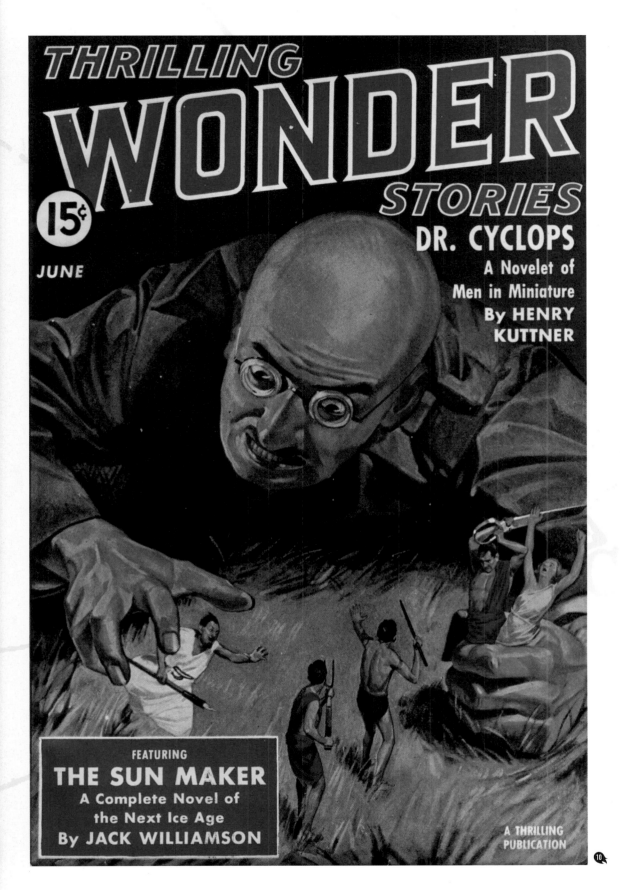

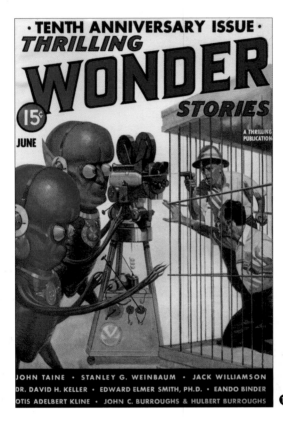

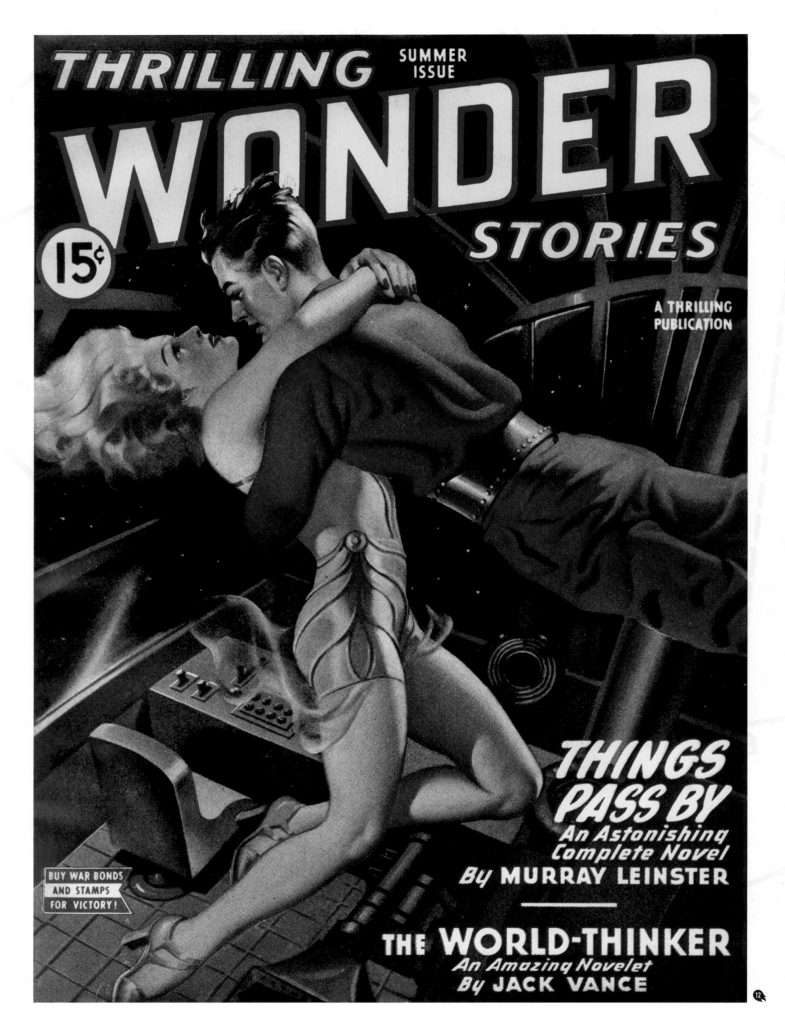

 THRILLING WONDER STORIES

SUMMER 1945

EARLE K. BERGEY

With most of its regular readers at war, the magazine's departments were dumbed down to appeal to kids too young for the draft. The letter column, run by "Sergeant Saturn" and featuring futuristic "lingo," was an embarrassment to all concerned.

THRILLING WONDER STORIES
AUGUST 1949
EARLE K. BERGEY

The magazine had gone upscale with a vengeance—writers included Bradbury, Arthur C. Clarke, A. E. van Vogt, John D. MacDonald, and Murray Leinster. An all-star issue.

made the editorial judgment that it had lost many of its older readers as well. A fictional "Sergeant Saturn" took over the magazine's columns using "space lingo" to try and create a camaraderie with readers not yet old enough for the Army. Naturally, he was resented. In 1945, what was left of the old Science Fiction League finally bit the dust.

After the war, things improved immeasurably—favorite writers were back, among them Murray Leinster, Henry Kuttner, and Catherine L. Moore (they married each other in 1940), plus Ray Bradbury with a number of stories that later appeared in his seminal collection, *The Martian Chronicles*.

The years 1946 and 1947 were boom years for the pulps. The circulation of the two biggest chains, *Thrilling* and *Popular*, had never been higher. *Popular* even took full page newspaper ads extolling the advertising possibilities to be found among "the people who live on Popular street."

Thrilling Wonder had acquired a number of companion magazines, and they were all doing well (*Startling Stories*, *Fantastic Story Magazine*, *Space Stories*, and even a *Wonder Story Annual*). The fiction in the magazine had matured with its audience and featured adult stories by Philip José Farmer ("Mother") and Edmond Hamilton's realistic story of space exploration, "What's It Like Out There?" Hamilton had written it in the early 1930s but never submitted it, figuring—rightly—that the magazine audience was too young for it then. It came as something of a shock to readers that Hamilton, the author of numerous potboilers and the creator of "Captain Future," had been a skilled craftsman all along.

There was growing competition from paperbacks, and digest science-fiction magazines had begun to proliferate. Nevertheless, nobody would

THRILLING WONDER STORIES
APRIL 1943
EARLE K. BERGEY

The cover, with its overtones of alien menace, was one of the more effective ones by artist Bergey.

THRILLING WONDER STORIES
NOVEMBER 1953
WALTER POPP

The pulps were running out of steam, and it wouldn't be many more issues before *Thrilling Wonder Stories* vanished with the rest of them.

WONDER STORIES

FEATURING:
RAY BRADBURY
JOHN D. MACDONALD
ARTHUR C. CLARKE
FREDRIC BROWN
KURT VONNEGUT, JR.
WALT SHELDON
MARGARET ST. CLAIR
ANTHONY BOUCHER

35c

AN ANTHOLOGY OF THE BEST IN SCIENCE FICTION

WONDER STORIES
1957 ANNUAL
RICHARD POWERS

The last gasp—a reprint, digest-sized annual. The list of authors included John D. MacDonald, Ray Bradbury, Arthur C. Clarke, Fredric Brown, Anthony Boucher, and Kurt Vonnegut, Jr. And once again, a touch of gold in the logo.

have predicted disaster was just around the corner. But the circulation of the pulp chains had begun to sag in the late 1940s and by 1955 it was all over.

Thrilling Wonder Stories decreased in size and frequency, eventually was combined with *Startling Stories* and *Fantastic Story Magazine*, and then was discontinued. Oddly, science fiction had never been more popular—during the mid-1950s there were more than forty science fiction digests, innumerable science fiction paperbacks and dozens of films.

There were many reasons for the decline of the pulps, but a major one was the package itself, not necessarily the contents. If anything, the stories appearing in *Thrilling Wonder* and its companion magazines were equal to or superior to those found in many of the digests. But the pulps themselves hadn't changed since the turn of the century. They were too large, too bulky, shed little bits of paper over the consumer, and couldn't be carried in one's pocket. Many of them tried to modernize with more adult fiction, trimmed edges, and dignified title designs but it was too late.

The pulps went the way the LP phonograph record and the eight-track audio tape would go in later years and for the same reason.

The music was still great but the package was inconvenient.

THRILLING WONDER STORIES

SCIENCE FICTION BY TOP WRITERS

FEATURING

THE TRANSPOSED MAN
by Dwight V. Swain

MISSION TO MIZAR
by Kendell Foster Crossen

NOV. 25c

A THRILLING
PUBLICATION

There had been one science-fiction magazine in 1926. By the middle of 1929 there were suddenly five, all of them brain children of Hugo Gernsback. This sudden expansion didn't go unnoticed by the regular pulp publishers. Top management, as well as the editors, watched very closely the comings and goings of the different titles on the newsstand. William Clayton, publisher of the Clayton line of magazines (*Ace-High*, *Danger Trail*, *Ranch Romances*, *Cowboy Stories*, etc.) was one of them. So was Harry Bates, one of his ablest editors. Clayton was publishing thirteen titles at the time and was acutely aware that publishing three more could be done on the cheap. A printing form with sixteen covers would cost little more than thirteen and would save

ASTOUNDING

THE CLASS ACT

CHAPTER 4

ASTOUNDING STORIES OF SUPER-SCIENCE
JANUARY 1930
H. W. WESSOLOWSKI

The first issue of the first true "pulp" science-fiction magazine. Clayton Publications, which also published *Ace-High Magazine* and *Cowboy Stories*, preferred action-adventure to science and technology.

on paper, the cost of press time for three more titles would be minimal, and editorial tasks could be handled by editors already on staff.

Clayton's first suggestion, according to Bates, was for a magazine to be titled *Torchlights of History*. Bates, of course, would be the editor. Rather than face editing the disaster that *Torchlights* might well become, Bates came up with *Astounding Stories of Super-Science*. He had watched the success of *Amazing*, read a copy or two, and was appalled at what he considered the low quality of the fiction when judged by the usual pulp standards.

Astounding Stories of Super-Science was on the newsstands with the January 1930 issue. It was the first real science-fiction *pulp*, featuring stories full of action and with a minimum of science.

Bates acknowledged that his major problem was finding science-fiction writers who could write pulp stories, or pulp writers who could write science fiction. He devoted a good deal of time to rewriting stories by the latter to squeeze in at least a little science. For the former, he picked up several writers who had written science fiction for *Argosy* and *All-Story*—Ray Cummings, Murray Leinster, and Victor Rousseau.

Later he added Edmond Hamilton, Jack Williamson, and "Anthony Gilmore," author of the popular shoot-em-up "Hawk Carse" stories. Clayton loved the stories, not suspecting that "Anthony Gilmore" was Harry Bates in collaboration with his assistant editor, Desmond Hall.

Astounding never made a profit for Clayton. It had high editorial costs, paying two cents a word in a field where half a cent or less was standard. *Astounding* would undoubtedly have edged into the black with an issue already in the planning stages.

ASTOUNDING STORIES
JANUARY 1932
H. W. WESSOLOWSKI

The image of a huge ape climbing a
skyscraper while holding a human
hostage was to resurface in the movie
King Kong released a year later.

Bates had acquired the rights to Doc Smith's
Triplanetary and intended to publish the first half in
one issue. He never had the chance. The Clayton chain
slipped into bankruptcy in 1933, and *Astounding*
was sold to Street & Smith, one of the oldest of the
pulp chains and one that had a huge advantage over
the others—it printed its own magazines as well as
published them, which meant their break-even was
much lower. (*Triplanetary* would appear some
months later in *Amazing*.)

The Clayton *Astounding* had lasted for thirty-
four issues, through several minor title changes but
relatively little in the way of notable stories. As it
turned out, the past was prologue, the main act had
yet to begin.

Neither Bates nor Desmond Hall vanished from the
scene with the sale of *Astounding*. Hall went along
with the magazine as assistant editor to F. Orlin
Tremaine, another editor for Clayton who had gone
over to Street & Smith but had never worked with
Astounding. (Some writers in later interviews credited
Hall as the real force behind the Street & Smith
Astounding). Bates was to have his day in the sun
with the sale of several outstanding stories to the
new *Astounding*, including "Farewell to the Master"
(October 1940). When the publisher was approached
for the film rights years later, a surprised Street &
Smith suggested one hundred fifty dollars as a price.
When Bates heard about it and asked for his cut, he
was given half, seventy-five dollars, probably the
cheapest price ever paid an author for story rights to
a movie that was to become a classic— *The Day the
Earth Stood Still*.

There was little about the first issue of the Street
& Smith *Astounding* to even suggest it was a science-

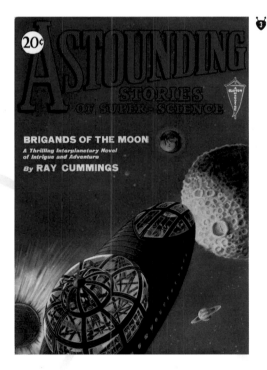

 ASTOUNDING STORIES OF SUPER-SCIENCE
MARCH 1930
H. W. WESSOLOWSKI

By the third issue, *Astounding*
had embraced the rocket ship in
outer space—a staple in covers
for science-fiction magazines.

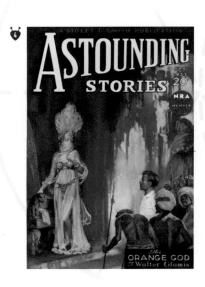

ASTOUNDING STORIES
OCTOBER 1933
HOWARD V. BROWN

A new publisher with no conception
of what comprised science fiction—
no aliens, no rocket ships, no robots.
What were they thinking of?

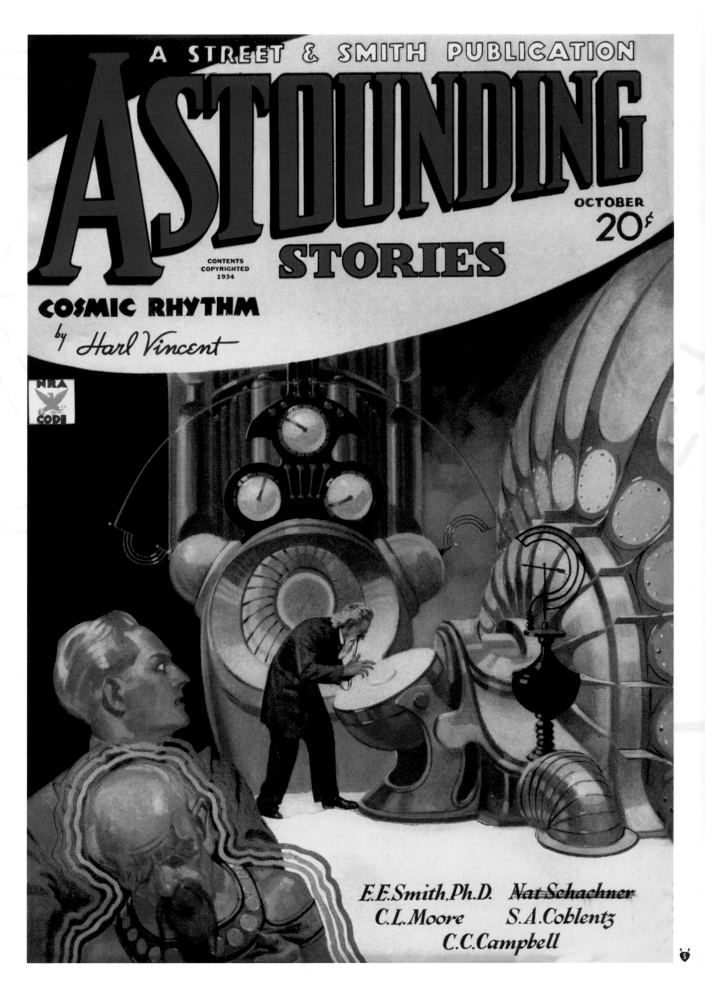

ASTOUNDING STORIES
OCTOBER 1934
HOWARD V. BROWN

Author Nat Schachner—crossed off on the cover by an
angry reader—didn't appear inside, but "Doc" Smith and
C. L. Moore both did. Smith was already a giant in the field
and C(atherine) L. Moore became one.

fiction magazine. The cover, well painted by Howard V. Brown, showed Our Hero surrounded by natives of some sort confronting the high priestess of God-knew-what. It could have been the cover for any of a dozen adventure magazines.

Inside were three novelettes by recognizable authors—Donald Wandrei, the ever-popular Anthony Gilmore, and Nat Schachner. The eight short stories were probably gleaned from the inventories of other Street & Smith magazines. There was no letter column, no editorial explaining the magazine's sudden reappearance. The only plus was that you got 144 pages for twenty cents, a nickel less than the competition. The minus was, you didn't get much.

The second issue was a wash as well, with the cover featuring still another priestess. The third issue was decidedly better. There was no priestess on the cover and there was a combination letter column/editorial ("Brass Tacks") explaining that the featured story by Nat Schachner was a "thought-variant" and that there would be a new one in every issue.

With January 1934, *Astounding* was up and running. The cover, illustrating Donald Wandrei's "Colossus," was all black with a yellow semi-transparent one-man spaceship roaring off to the left—one of the best covers a science-fiction magazine would ever publish.

The February issue featured a rah-rah welcome by the editor, and with March the number of pages jumped to 160 for the same price. April had the first part of *The Legion of Space* by Jack Williamson plus "A Matter of Size" by former editor Harry Bates. Bates may not have been the best science-fiction editor going, but he was certainly a better-than-average writer.

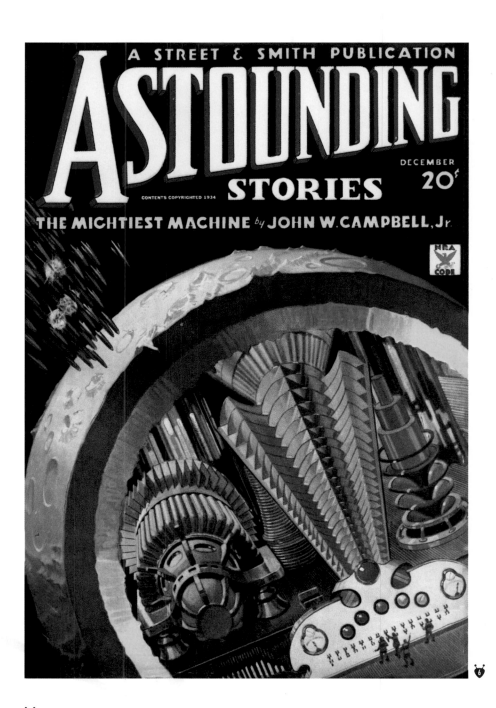

ASTOUNDING STORIES
DECEMBER 1934
HOWARD V. BROWN

John W. Campbell, Jr., was later to become the editor. Artist Brown picked up his skill in drawing machinery from an apprenticeship painting covers for Hugo Gernsback's *Science and Invention* in the 1920s.

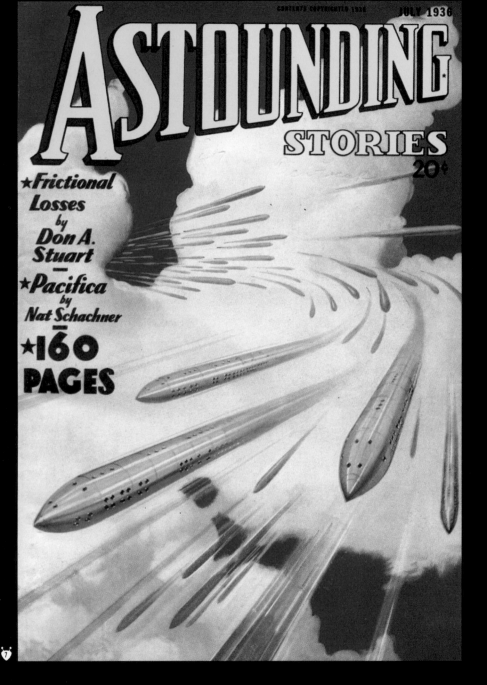

CONTENTS COPYRIGHTED 1936   JULY 1936

ASTOUNDING
STORIES
20¢

★ Frictional
Losses
by
Don A.
Stuart

★ Pacifica
by
Nat Schachner

★ 160
PAGES

ASTOUNDING STORIES
JULY 1936
HOWARD V. BROWN

The magazine had trimmed its edges in an effort to become
something more than a "pulp" magazine. Future editor
Campbell was writing a monthly science article under his
own name plus fiction as "Don A. Stuart."

By the end of the year, *Astounding* had gutted the competition. Among the other authors featured were Doc Smith (*The Skylark of Valeron*), John W. Campbell, Jr. (*The Mightiest Machine*), Murray Leinster, Jack Williamson, and a newcomer named "Don A. Stuart" (a pen name for Campbell). With "Twilight," a mood story by Stuart, Campbell was phasing out his super-science tales in favor of something a good deal more literary.

In 1935, *Astounding* added the last remaining superstar of the field—Stanley G. Weinbaum. The magazine was now the undisputed leader in content as well as circulation. Editor Tremaine dreamed of publishing the magazine on a semi-monthly basis, and in his editorial column shilled for new readers with all the enthusiasm of a country preacher bringing in the sheaves. The cover story for January featured "Star Ship Invincible" by Frank K. Kelly, who then retired from writing science fiction at age twenty-one. The shocker for 1936 was H.P. Lovecraft, the dean of *Weird Tales*, who showed up with *At the Mountains of Madness* and "The Shadow Out of Time."

Oddly, Tremaine was even more dedicated to science than Gernsback had been. Regular science articles were featured, and in the December issue Tremaine announced that the letter column, "Brass Tacks," would be discontinued in favor of "Science Discussions." In his editorial, Tremaine wrote: "We must plan so that twenty years hence it will be said that *Astounding Stories* has served as the cradle of modern science. It must be said that the great and near great in science first nurtured and presented their thoughts and theories through the 'Science Discussions' pages."

That was stretching it more than just a bit, but it was an attitude that the magazine and many of its readers never lost.

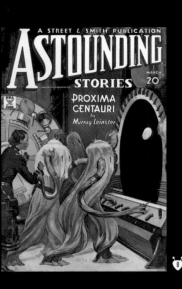

ASTOUNDING STORIES
MARCH 1935
HOWARD V. BROWN

Howard V. Brown could paint aliens with the best of them, but these looked like animated shredded wheat.

ASTOUNDING SCIENCE-FICTION
APRIL 1938
HOWARD V. BROWN

A new title ("stories" had become "science-fiction"), a new editor—John W. Campbell, Jr.—and new writers like L. Sprague de Camp and Lester del Rey. Plus Raymond A. Palmer, who became editor of *Amazing* two months later.

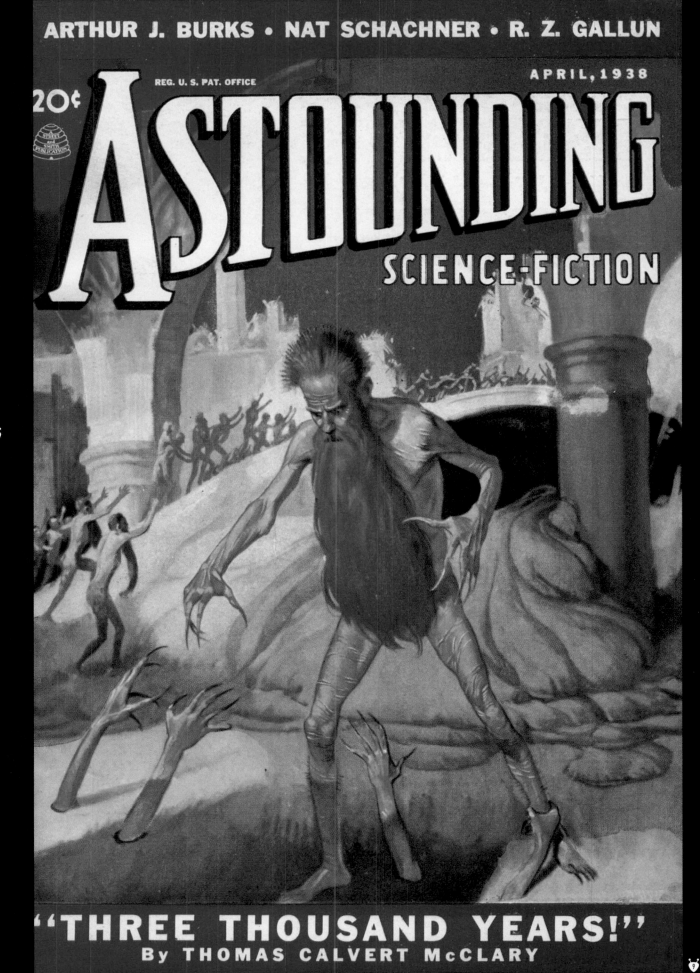

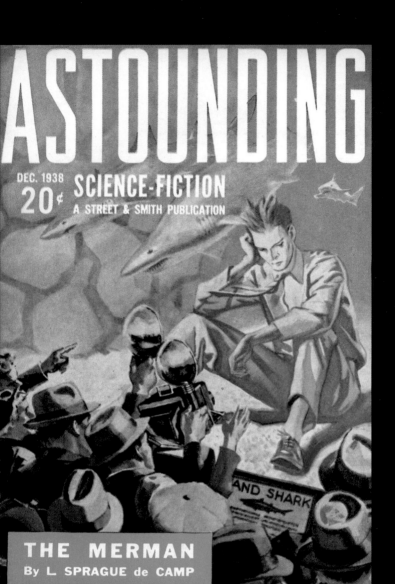

ASTOUNDING SCIENCE-FICTION
NOVEMBER 1939
HUBERT ROGERS

"Doc" Smith was one of the most
popular authors in *Astounding*—
and *Gray Lensman* one of its most
popular serials.

became the editor of *Amazing Stories*. A new department, "The Analytical Lab," a rating of the stories by reader vote, began in May, along with the first installment of Williamson's *The Legion of Time* (Campbell called it a "mutant" story, his version of Tremaine's "thought variant," because it was based on a new concept). Campbell's prediction in his editorial that month: "The discoverer of the secret of atomic power is alive on Earth today."

In July, the magazine ran the most controversial article it would ever publish—L. Sprague de Camp's "Language for Time Travelers." Travel into the future for a thousand years and you'll find that "your" language (whatever it is) will have changed a lot since the last time you spoke it, a thousand years before. Also in the issue: The first science-fiction story by L. Ron Hubbard, "The Dangerous Dimension."

August was remarkable in ways that Campbell never suspected. Inside was "Who Goes There?" by "Don A. Stuart." Campbell was appropriately modest and refrained from calling it a "mutant" story though it certainly was.

The story dealt with an Antarctic expedition's discovery of an alien frozen in the ice. The scientists defrost it and then discover it's intelligent, vicious, malevolent—and can assume the appearance of any one of them. Problem: How can they tell the real from the fake when it comes to determining who is what?

The story was set in modern day, it had an entirely new concept for science fiction—that of the "shapeshifter"—and the monster was a threat to the entire world. The story was a far cry from either Campbell's super-science tales or the usual mood stories turned out by "Stuart." The writing was mainstream, the theme pure horror. "Who Goes

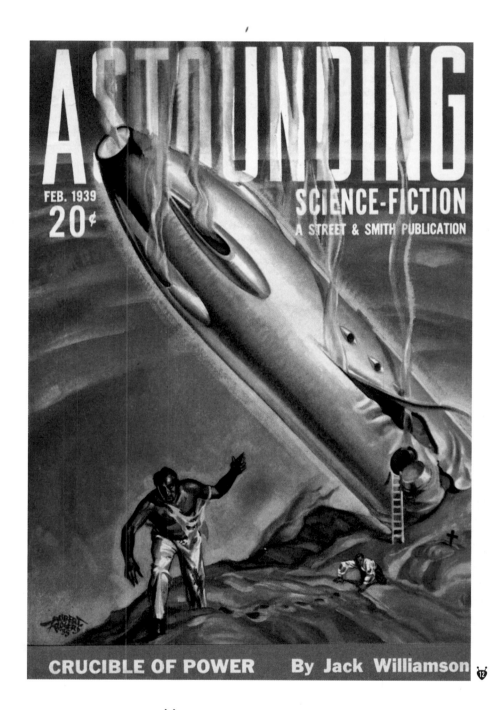

ASTOUNDING SCIENCE-FICTION
FEBRUARY 1939
HUBERT ROGERS

A new cover artist with a dramatic approach—the first time a crashed rocketship had been featured with the survivors staggering away.

ASTOUNDING SCIENCE-FICTION
OCTOBER 1940
HUBERT ROGERS

Slan was van Vogt's most popular serial. On the inside was former editor Harry Bates' story "Farewell to the Master," filmed as the classic *The Day the Earth Stood Still.*

ASTOUNDING SCIENCE-FICTION
JANUARY 1941
HUBERT ROGERS

"Anson MacDonald" was a pseudonym for author Robert A. Heinlein.

The cover story was about a wacky future in which corporations were more important than nations and duels were held between opposing businessmen rather than stock-option battles—probably an improvement over today.

There?" was the first real science-fiction thriller published since Wells' *The Invisible Man.*

("Who Goes There?" was filmed in 1951 as *The Thing From Another World* and became an instant classic. It was filmed again in 1982 as *The Thing.*)

September saw the start of a three-part serial by Hubbard, *The Tramp,* and December a new front cover title design. The comet tail was gone, the new sans serif type much more dignified and modern. The cover painting (by Charles Schneeman) was of a man sitting in a tank of water who was obviously having no trouble breathing it. A perfect cover for "The Merman" by L. Sprague de Camp.

Probably not even Campbell himself was fully aware of what was happening, but the Golden Age of *Astounding* was about to begin. It needed only five additional pieces for the miracle to occur.

The cover for the February 1939 issue was painted by a Canadian artist, Hubert Rogers, who had been a regular for the old *Adventure* and for a number of Street & Smith pulps. It illustrated "Crucible of Power" by Jack Williamson and showed two injured crewmen crawling away from a wrecked spaceship on Mars—realism seldom seen on a science-fiction magazine.

Hubert Rogers, who was to become the pre-eminent cover artist for *Astounding,* was the first of the missing pieces. Four more soon followed.

July featured the first story by A. E. van Vogt ("Black Destroyer"), as well as the first story—for *Astounding*—by Isaac Asimov ("Trends"). August provided the most important piece. It introduced thirty-two-year-old Robert Heinlein with a story titled "Life-Line."

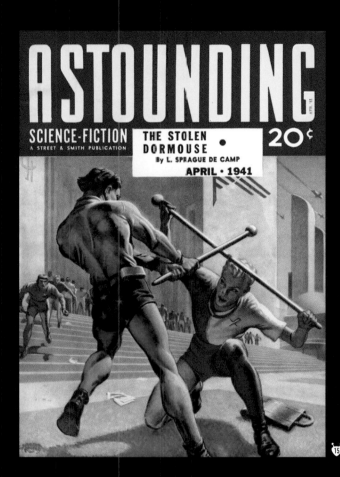

Van Vogt was to write stories with totally new concepts and more than their share of the "sense of wonder." Asimov would write the enormously popular "Foundation" science-fiction series. Heinlein would become the most revered of all modern science-fiction writers. More than any other, he could make the future seem so real you could walk around in it. Heinlein was a "hard science" man, but he also viewed sociology and politics as sciences and extrapolated stories from them as well. His influence on the field persisted to the end of the century, when promising new writers were introduced by publishers as "the new Heinlein."

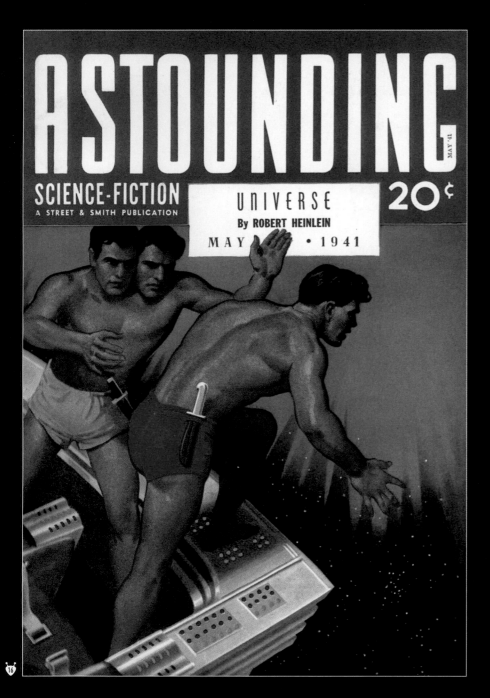

ASTOUNDING SCIENCE-FICTION
MAY 1941
HUBERT ROGERS

"Universe" was a "generation ship" story and established
a sub-genre all by itself. But the first such genre story was
Don Wilcox's "The Voyage That Lasted Six Hundred Years"
published in *Amazing Stories* the year before.

September had another cover by Rogers and showcased Theodore Sturgeon's "Ether Breather." If
Heinlein was the brains of science fiction, Sturgeon
would become its heart. He could handle new concepts, but his best stories were character driven; he
was a writer with compassion to spare. Sturgeon was
the last piece.

And that was how it all began. One small change
at a time and then, within three issues, *Astounding*
published the first stories of the writers who were at
the core of the Golden Age.

The magazine already had Doc Smith, Williamson,
Simak, de Camp, del Rey, and Hubbard. With the
four new additions, no other science-fiction publication on the newsstand could touch *Astounding*.

In March 1939 the first issue of Campbell's
Unknown appeared, a magazine devoted to the weird
and the fantastic but with a twist. It was fantasy in
a fright wig, ghouls with a sense of humor. The first
issue featured Eric Frank Russell's *Sinister Barrier*,
based on the premise that the human race is…
property. Campbell followed it with a remarkable
string of novels by L. Ron Hubbard, L. Sprague de
Camp, Jack Williamson, and others.

The next two years were blowout years for *Astounding*.
If This Goes On…, a two-part serial by Heinlein;
Final Blackout, a three-parter by Hubbard and his
best science-fiction novel; *Slan*, a four-part serial by
van Vogt about future mutants and probably his best
work (fans immediately coined the phrase "Fans are
Slans!" and a commune in Michigan became known
as "Slan Shack"). Add to them "Farewell to the
Master" by former editor Harry Bates (filmed as the
classic *The Day the Earth Stood Still*); *Sixth Column*
by "Anson MacDonald" (Heinlein in false face);

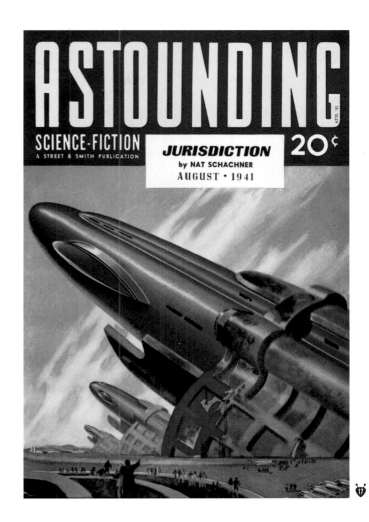

"Microcosmic God" by Theodore Sturgeon; "Universe" by Heinlein; "Solution Unsatisfactory" by "Anson MacDonald;" "Liar" by Asimov (that introduced the "three laws of robotics," which Asimov claimed Campbell had given him and Campbell just as adamantly said were Asimov's own idea); *Methuselah's Children*, another serial by Heinlein; *Second Stage Lensman* by Doc Smith; and perhaps especially, "Nightfall," by Isaac Asimov.

"Nightfall" repeatedly has been voted as one of the best science-fiction stories ever written. Asimov postulates a world that orbits a collection of six suns so there is no such thing as "night," or total darkness —except for once every two thousand years when the six suns suffer a total eclipse. The inhabitants are faced with horror and a sense of impending doom as darkness gradually covers the planet. They fear going mad—and do, but not because of the darkness. Their system is in the middle of a globular star cluster and when the last sunlight fades, for the first time they see the stars—all thirty thousand of them.

Campbell worked closely with all his writers, suggesting ideas and concepts and variations on themes they might have suggested. Asimov was one of those he worked closely with, not alone on "Nightfall" but on his robot stories and the creation of the "Foundation" series, based loosely on the fall of the Roman Empire.

The son of a candy-store owner, Asimov discovered science fiction by reading the magazines the store carried. He sold his first story to the Palmer *Amazing Stories*, but it was *Astounding* with which he was most closely associated in his early years. He earned a Ph.D. in chemistry at Columbia University and joined the Boston University School of Medicine as an associate professor of biochemistry, resigning in

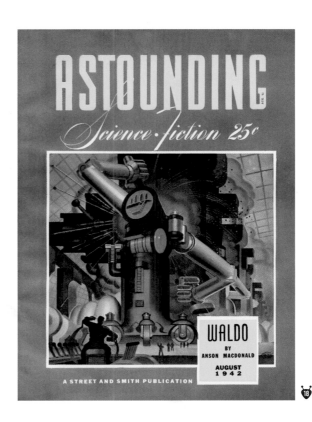

Most of the pulps, faced with the wartime paper shortage, reduced pages and frequency of publication. *Astounding* remained a monthly—but had shrunk in size to a digest magazine.

1958 to become a full-time writer—which is an understatement. Most writers write to live; Asimov lived to write. Later in life he lent his name to *Isaac Asimov's Science Fiction Magazine*, for every issue of which he wrote an editorial for as long as he lived.

He was immensely prolific, writing more than 400 books in his lifetime. As a science popularizer he was in the same league with Carl Sagan. Next to Heinlein, he was the most respected science-fiction writer of modern times. He was also, in the best aspect of the word, the most loved.

With January 1942 *Astounding* became a large-size magazine similar to the first issues of *Amazing* and *Wonder*. It was 130 pages for twenty-five cents and

reflected Campbell's consistent efforts to make the magazine something more than a "pulp" magazine, despite the paper it was printed on.

The changeover could not have come at a worse time. The January issue went on sale during the month of December 1941, the same month the United States entered World War II.

For most of 1942, nothing changed. Heinlein was present with a serial, *Beyond this Horizon* (by "Anson MacDonald") and a short novel, *Waldo* (also by "MacDonald"). Jack Williamson was present, both as himself and as "Will Stewart," van Vogt contributed "Asylum" and "The Weapon Shop" and would show up again in early 1943 with "The Weapon Makers." But Rogers' cover for *Waldo* for the August issue was his last for the duration.

The June issue was notable for "Bridle and Saddle," the cover story by Isaac Asimov. It was the second of many that would make up the Foundation series. (The first in the series, "Foundation," had run in May.)

The large-sized *Astounding* lasted four issues into 1943, then retreated to pulp size. Heinlein was in war work, so were Asimov and L. Sprague de Camp. Theodore Surgeon had gone into the service, as had Jack Williamson.

With the November issue Street & Smith made a decision that would effect the science-fiction field through the end of the century. The paper shortage was forcing publishers to either cut pages or cut back on the frequency of publication.

Street & Smith did neither. Instead, it made *Astounding* a digest.

For readers already suffering withdrawal symptoms because of the disappearance of their favorite authors, it was a blow. But at least they didn't have to wait two or three months for a new issue. And somehow Campbell found new writers to replace the old. They might not have had the conceptual sense of a Sturgeon or the realism of a Heinlein, but they were head and shoulders above the competition.

New (and old) writers included Anthony Boucher —in a few years to become the editor of the first substantial competition to *Astounding*, Lewis Padgett (Kuttner plus wife C. L. Moore), Hal Clement, Raymond F. Jones, George O. Smith, Fritz Leiber, Jr., Clifford Simak, Murray Leinster, P. Schuyler Miller (who would later become the magazine's book reviewer), Malcolm Jameson...

Sturgeon took time out from the war to contribute "Killdozer" for a 1944 issue, a minor classic about a bulldozer with a vicious personality. In December came C. L. Moore's poignant story of a dancer, badly disfigured in a fire, who is given a new body of chrome and steel ("No Woman Born"). She can dance even better than before but she is no longer quite... human. You could hear "...the distant taint of metal already in her voice."

The most important story to be published that year was one rated last by the readers but first by the Military Intelligence men who dropped in to see editor Campbell shortly after publication. Cleve Cartmill's story, "Deadline," tells of a Seilla ("allies" spelled backwards) agent parachuting into enemy Sixa (try again) territory to defuse an atomic bomb.

In all its more important details, the description of the bomb was right on, and the agents wanted to know who at the Manhattan Project had talked. Nobody had, but a stunned Campbell had to talk fast to convince the agents it had all been coincidence and most of the details had been printed elsewhere several years before.

The war was over and so was the paper shortage. But *Astounding* opted to remain a digest—the first and only one in the field.

The very fact of the agents' visit convinced Campbell that the country was working on an atomic bomb and the only real secrets were where it would be tested and when and where it might be dropped. The circulation department could have helped him out with the first—distribution of the magazine had become strangely skewed. For example, hundreds of copies were being sold in the little New Mexico town of Alamogordo...

World War II ended with the dropping of the atomic bomb on Hiroshima and Nagasaki, and science-fiction readers and writers felt vindicated. In the last issue for 1945, one reader wrote that we would be on the moon by 1960—in reply Campbell pushed it up to 1950. And Theodore Sturgeon wrote a soliloquy about "Who reads that crap?"—meaning

ASTOUNDING SCIENCE FICTION
MAY 1947
HUBERT ROGERS

Artist Rogers returned with one of his best covers, but the small size of the magazine made it less effective.

ASTOUNDING SCIENCE FICTION
JANUARY 1949
HUBERT ROGERS

The cover was a distinct throwback to the poster covers of the early *Doc Savage* and *The Shadow* magazines. But it was a radical departure for artist Rogers.

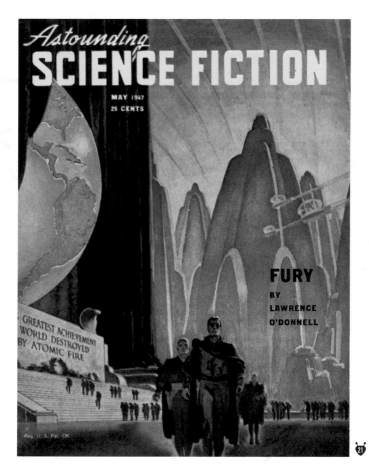

ASTOUNDING SCIENCE FICTION
NOVEMBER 1949
HUBERT ROGERS

A brief return to the Golden Age featuring authors Heinlein, Asimov, Sturgeon, van Vogt, del Rey, and de Camp. The issue was based on a "wish fulfillment" letter from a reader.

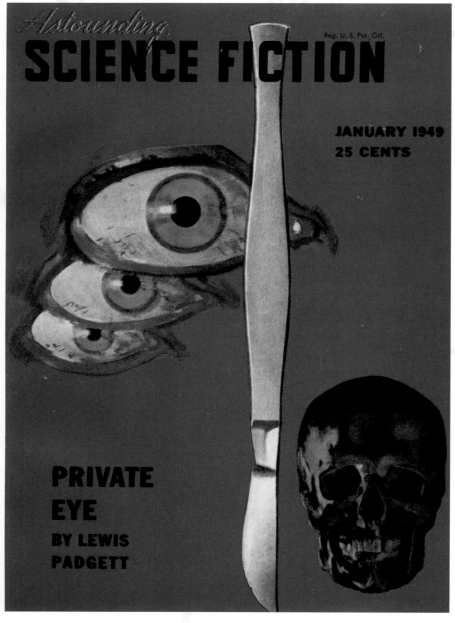

ASTOUNDING SCIENCE FICTION
FEBRUARY 1950
HUBERT ROGERS

An evocative portrait cover by Rogers for the last *Astounding* serial by regular author L. Ron Hubbard.

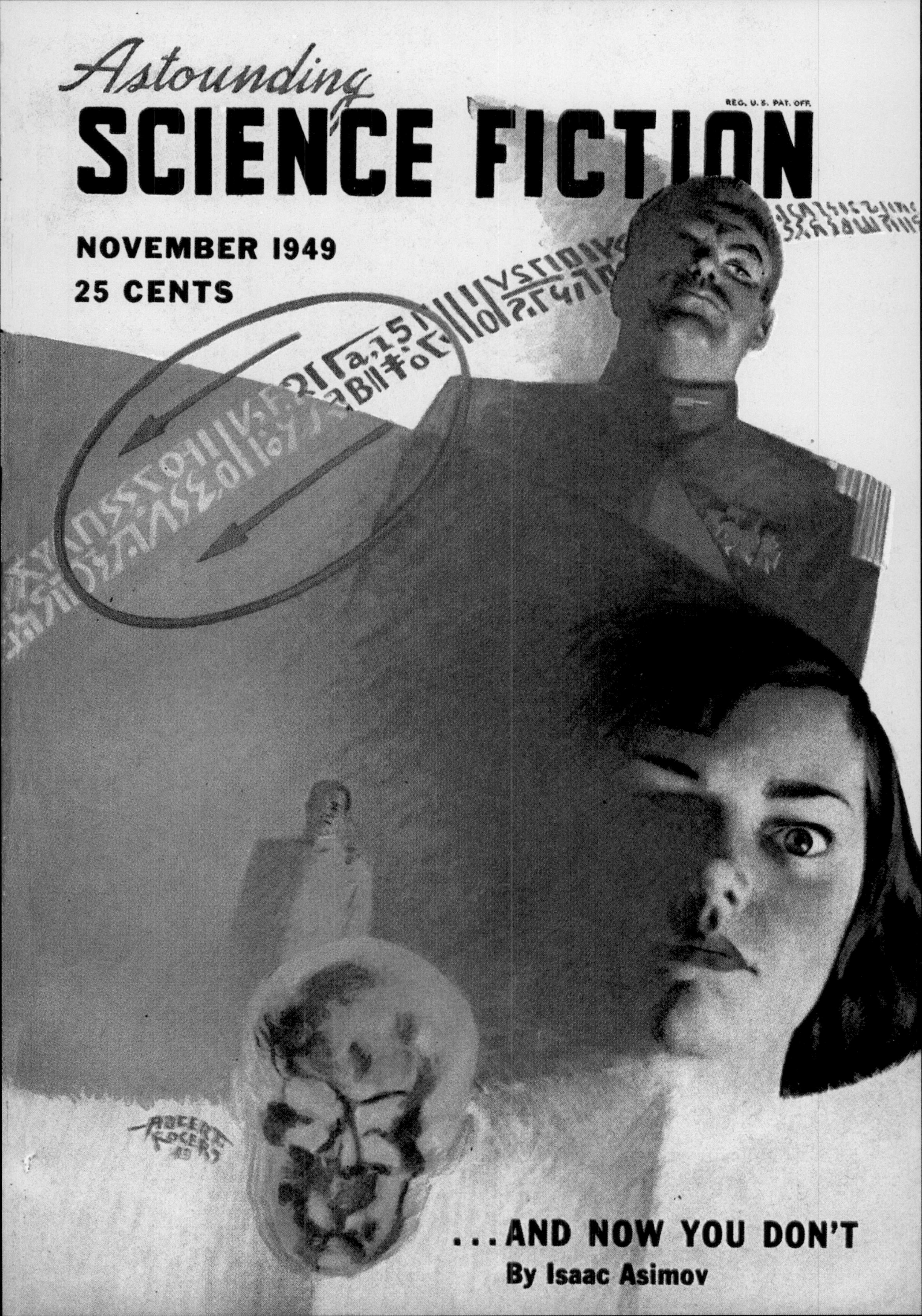
Astounding
REG. U. S. PAT. OFF.
SCIENCE FICTION
NOVEMBER 1949
25 CENTS
...AND NOW YOU DON'T
By Isaac Asimov

ASTOUNDING SCIENCE FICTION
FEBRUARY 1956
KELLY FREAS

By the mid-1950s, Kelly Freas had become
a regular cover (and interior) artist for
Astounding. Sadly, *Double Star* was
Heinlein's last serial for the magazine.

science fiction—and answered it with all the passion of a man who'd spent a sizable fraction of his life writing it.

With the dropping of the Bomb, science fiction had become more than just entertainment.

It had finally become Important.

The war was over, but not everybody was mustered out immediately. *Astounding* gradually altered the title, reducing "Astounding" and enlarging "Science Fiction." From a distance, that was what you saw first.

Sturgeon was back in 1947 with a major classic—"Maturity." The other standout for the year was by Arthur C. Clarke. "Rescue Party" dealt with an attempt by members of a Galactic Union to rescue the inhabitants of Earth, doomed because the sun is about to go nova. Unable to find them, they discover that the "primitive" inhabitants had launched a century-long migration to the stars years before using relatively primitive rockets. It occurs to the members of the Union that when they finally meet the race with such a strong drive to survive, they had better be nice to it. The story was vintage Clarke.

The magazine had caught its second wind. Rogers came back to do covers, along with a newcomer expert at astronomical scenes—Chesley Bonestell. Williamson was back with "With Folded Hands," the first part of his novel *The Humanoids*. A new author, William Tenn, showed up with "Child's Play." A "Bild-A-Man" set is delivered to a Sam Weber some 200 years too soon. Fascinated by the manual's instructions on "how to twin yourself and your friends," Weber duplicates himself. And then the "census taker" from the future shows up to take back the set and put all the chemicals back in their tubes, which means "dismantling" the twin. Naturally, he

Van Vogt was present with two novelettes in successive issues, Hubbard had a three-part serial, *The End Is Not Yet* and the year closed out with Doc Smith's *Children of the Lens*. The only author missing was Robert A. Heinlein who was busy launching a series of juveniles and writing short stories for the *Saturday Evening Post*—the payment for any one of which would equal what he might get for a serial in *Astounding*.

If it wasn't the Golden Age, it was something very close to it. The paper was slicker, the covers far more dramatic than during the war. Edd Cartier, the premier illustrator for *Unknown Worlds*, now joined Hubert Rogers in doing interiors.

It had now been ten years since Campbell had taken over *Astounding*. In 1947 the Fifth World Science Convention was held in Philadelphia and John W. Campbell, Jr., was the guest of honor.

The standout issue in 1950 was May, not for its fiction but for an article by L. Ron Hubbard titled "Dianetics." Campbell called it an "introduction to a new science."

Astounding was the ideal launching pad for such a piece. Campbell strongly believed in unconventional thinkers who he thought would reshape the

Astounding before him, Campbell had always hoped the magazine would serve as an arena in which scientists could present their theories and debate them. It should have come as no surprise that Campbell would broaden his concept of "science" and print a lengthy article by Hubbard on a new form of psychotherapy, one in which—at the time of printing—Campbell strongly believed.

For the first time, real competition showed up with the launching in late 1949 of *The Magazine of Fantasy* (soon to be retitled *The Magazine of Fantasy and Science Fiction*), edited by one-time contributor Anthony Boucher and anthologist J. Francis McComas. More competition would show up with the October 1950 *Galaxy*, edited by still another former contributor, H.L. Gold. Both magazines had more flexible editorial policies than *Astounding*, and *Galaxy* paid more.

Still, *Astounding* managed to retain its lead. In 1949, when Street & Smith discontinued their chain of pulps (*The Shadow*, *Doc Savage*, *Detective Story Magazine*, etc.), *Astounding* was the only one saved from the axe. It was, as Campbell once said, a gold mine—even though a small one. That year, Campbell's gift to his faithful readers was the issue for November that featured the beginning of...*and Now You Don't*, a three-part "Foundation" serial by Isaac Asimov, a novelette by Sturgeon, short stories by del Rey, van Vogt and de Camp, and the start of a two-part serial, *Gulf*, by Robert A. Heinlein. The cover, of course, was by Hubert Rogers. All of it had been suggested the year before by a reader who, as a gag, had written in commenting on the issue of November 1949. Campbell couldn't resist making the reader's "prophecy" come true.

ASTOUNDING / ANALOG SCIENCE FACT & FICTION
JUNE 1960
JOHN SCHOENHERR

When you change the title of a magazine that's been continuously published (more or less) since 1930, you do it very cautiously. It took months for *Astounding* to morph into *Analog*.

ASTOUNDING SCIENCE FICTION
FEBRUARY 1959
KELLY FREAS

A satirical action-adventure cover by artist Freas showing a pirate holding a futuristic "blaster" and clutching a slide rule between his teeth rather than a dirk.

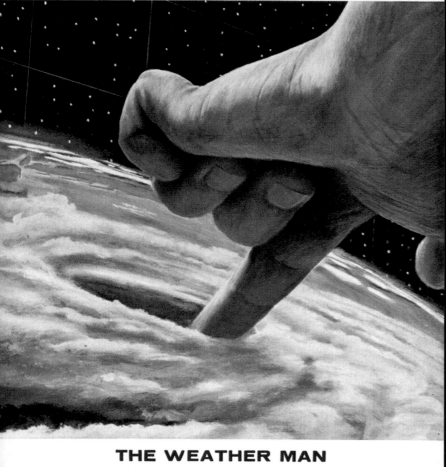

THE WEATHER MAN
A novelette by Theodore Thomas

ANALOG SCIENCE FACT - SCIENCE FICTION
JUNE 1962
JOHN SCHOENHERR

Astounding was now officially *Analog*. Along the
way, the price had been raised and sixteen pages
of slick paper added—a taste of things to come.

So *Astounding* now had competition. If the situation
affected *Astounding*, it wasn't all that obvious.

The cover for July 1950 was a still from George
Pal's movie *Destination Moon* accompanying an
article by Robert A. Heinlein, the screenwriter,
telling how the movie was made. (It was the most
technically accurate "space" movie made up to that
time, a true predecessor to *2001: A Space Odyssey*).
The next year Campbell did another movie tie-in for
still another George Pal movie, *When Worlds Collide*.
The cover illustrating the movie was a painting
by Chesley Bonestell, and the magazine had a wrap-
around band promoting the tie-in. *Astounding's*
circulation was now 110,000—and rising.

By the mid-1950s there were more than forty
different science-fiction digests on the newsstand
but by the end of the decade, only a dozen.
Astounding was unperturbed. Its circulation was
high, it continually discovered new authors. And it
kept going through incremental changes that, in
Campbell's mind, would make it an even better
magazine. The title changed (ever so gradually) to
Analog Science Fact & Fiction, and new artists were
added—including one of the biggest stars of all,
Kelly Freas, who would win a total of ten Hugos for
Best Professional Artist of the Year.

In 1963, Campbell fulfilled what must have been
a long-standing dream. *Analog* once again became
a large-size magazine. Condé Nast Publications had
bought the old Street & Smith firm (they wanted
its slick fashion magazines), and *Analog* went along
as part of the package. The new owner was a huge
publishing company with a large "presence" on the
newsstands. Campbell was quick to take advantage
of it.

ANALOG SCIENCE FACT – SCIENCE FICTION
MARCH 1965
JOHN SCHOENHERR

Frank Herbert's "Dune" was the most popular serial to run in *Analog*. Acclaimed by readers, it became a classic, spawning five sequels and a film. This cover by Schoenherr depicting the "sandworm" symbolized the series. The magazine was once again large size.

The world had become a vastly different place from what it had been when Campbell took the editor's chair. Atomic energy plants were a reality, so was a space program. Campbell was betting that the public no longer viewed science fiction as "that crazy stuff," and he wanted to make the connection between fiction and fact in the magazine. He had once edited a slick science magazine for a few issues—Street & Smith's *Air Trails and Science Frontiers*. It wasn't successful, but perhaps it had simply been too soon.

Now Campbell had another chance. The new *Analog* was large-sized with sixty-four pages of good quality "book" paper in the middle and sixteen pages of slick paper fore and aft for the articles and, hopefully, the advertising. The idea was that advertisers for *Scientific American* would ship their ad plates to the new *Analog* with no changes needed.

It was a good idea but it didn't work. Condé Nast gave it their best shot for twenty-five issues. The first of the new *Analog*s was dated March 1963; the last March 1965. It wasn't yet time for an advertising-supported science-fiction magazine, though a contributing factor might have been that fictionally, except for two exceptions, the two years had been dull.

But the two exceptions were…exceptional. Frank Herbert, whose serial *Under Pressure* had been well received ten years before, reappeared in December 1963 with his three-part serial, *Dune World*, and then a five-part sequel, *The Prophet of Dune*, in January 1965, both of them with evocative covers by Schoenherr. Twenty-five years later the novel *Dune* (both serials combined) was rated by readers of *Locus* (the *Publishers Weekly* of the science-fiction world) as the best science-fiction novel ever published. (It was filmed, unsuccessfully, by David Lynch in 1984.)

It wasn't downhill for *Analog* after that, it was just… stable. The magazine was the largest and best produced of the digests; it had a solid line of cover artists. New authors continued to be discovered, including Ben Bova (who would later become editor), Stanley Schmidt (ditto), Anne McCaffrey with the first of her "Dragonrider" novels, James Tiptree, Jr., and others. Old reliables like Hal Clement, Murray Leinster, Poul Anderson, Mack Reynolds and Harry Harrison were frequently present.

Campbell rode his enthusiasms to the end, though his thoughts and speculations ended up more in editorials than in suggestions to writers. There was the Dean Drive, the Hieronymous machine, his fascination with psi abilities… His editorials became longer, sometimes almost cranky or chiding and frequently political in tone. Most of his original

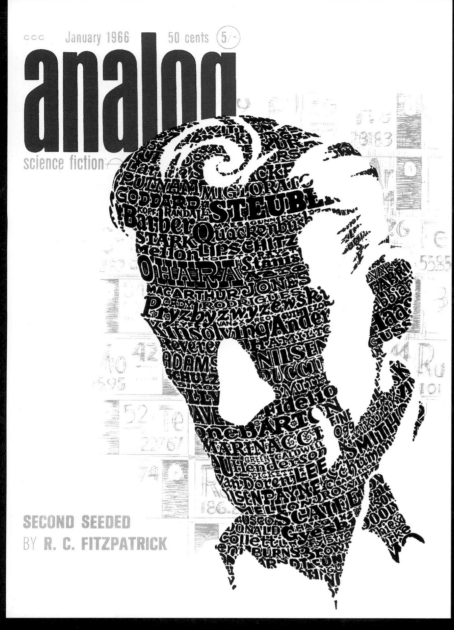

On the magazine cover:

CCC January 1966 50 cents 5/-

analog
science fiction

STEUBL...

SECOND SEEDED
BY R. C. FITZPATRICK

**ANALOG SCIENCE FICTION –
SCIENCE FACT**
JANUARY 1966
KELLY FREAS

The grand experiment had failed months before, and *Analog* was a digest once more—though still the leader of the field. The black-and-white cover by Freas was one of the most unusual *Analog* ever printed.

Golden Age authors were now writing hardback best sellers, had defected to other, less demanding magazines, or had given up writing altogether.

And then, in the middle of 1971, John W. Campbell unexpectedly died.

His legacy was a simple one. Campbell considered science fiction important not because it was predictive (though it frequently was) but because it encouraged curiosity and speculation—the first steps in solving any problem or making any social or scientific advancement. *Astounding* (later *Analog*) was more than just an entertainment magazine, it was Important, and Campbell had spent most of his life trying to make it even more Important.

Campbell was something of a frustrated scientist and also something of a tinkerer—he'd built his own hi-fi system from scratch—and came from an era in which there was a home workshop in almost every garage, many people built their own radios, and many more repaired their own cars. He would have agreed wholeheartedly with Ray Bradbury who remarked during an interview on the Larry King radio show that "America was built in garages."

Campbell largely distrusted corporate or government science and championed the individual who came up with a major "invention," no matter how crackpot. In an editorial early in his career, Campbell had written that the inventor of atomic power was living somewhere in the world even as he wrote.

Unfortunately, Campbell never wrote an editorial suggesting that somewhere in the world, in some garage or attic, there was a young tinkerer who would invent a device that would totally change how the world lived, how it managed its commerce and its communications, and that such a device would prove to be far more important than atomic power.

If he had written such an editorial, he might have been astonished to see it come true so soon and so completely.

He would have loved to have met Steve Jobs and Steve Wozniak and Bill Gates.

Campbell's successor was Ben Bova who had worked as a technical editor and science writer and written a number of science-fiction stories himself. His long term goal was to be a full-time writer. His editorship of *Analog* was a detour along the way—a detour that lasted for seven years and earned him six Hugos as Best Professional Editor. He was exactly what *Analog* needed.

Campbell had been editor of *Astounding/Analog* for thirty-four years and a certain amount of plaque had built up in its arteries. Bova blew the cobwebs

**ANALOG SCIENCE FICTION /
SCIENCE FACT**
MARCH 1976
VINCENT DI FATE

Artist Di Fate started
drawing interior illustrations for *Analog* in 1969
and eventually became
the magazine's star cover
artist.

ANALOG SCIENCE FICTION / SCIENCE FACT
JULY 1979
ROBERT MCCALL

A rare instance in which "science fact" domi-
nated the cover. Had it been ten years already?

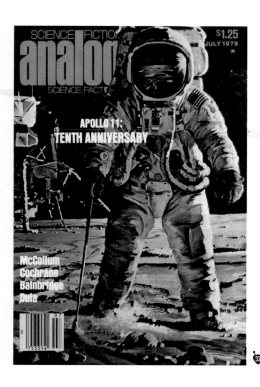

out of the corners and opened up the magazine to contributors Campbell might never have considered, some of whom became best sellers in the field by the end of the century.

Bova's writers—some were discoveries, some old-timers in the magazine—included David Brin (who was to write the best-selling novels *Startide Rising* and *The Uplift War* and sell *The Postman* to film), Joe Haldeman, John Brunner, George R.R. Martin, Jerry Pournelle, Gene Wolfe, Anne McCaffrey, Stanley Schmidt, Greg Benford, Orson Scott Card, Joan and Vernor Vinge, Spider Robinson, Robert Silverberg, Greg Bear, and many more.

Bova's major coup was *Children of Dune*, a four-part serial by Frank Herbert and the fourth in the magazine versions of the "Dune" series. Campbell had let the third in the series—*Dune Messiah*—get away from him; Bova didn't make the same mistake. (*Dune Messiah* was published by *Galaxy*.)

For cover artists, Campbell had relied heavily on John Schoenherr and especially Kelly Freas. Bova opened up his covers to Rick Sternbach, Dean Ellis, Alex Schomburg (who had been around since the days of Hugo Gernsback), and especially Vincent Di Fate who showed more than just a knack for rocket ships and outer space—his covers had a distinct and very modern "sense of wonder." (Di Fate would later become president of the Society of Illustrators.)

Bova gave up the editorship of *Analog* at the end of 1978 to become fiction editor of the new *Omni* magazine, then Executive Editor, and a few years later a full-time novelist and one of the leading writers of "hard science fiction." His successor was Stanley Schmidt, Ph.D., a sometime contributor to the magazine and a professor of physics. It was Schmidt's turn to become Keeper of the Flame and he did so

admirably. When *Analog* was finally sold to Davis Publications in fall 1980, the magazine didn't miss a beat.

Schmidt did an excellent job with new writers as well as holdover writers from Bova. He started with a bang: John Varley's four-part serial of *Titan* (nominated for both a Hugo and a Nebula). His roster of writers included Timothy Zahn, Larry Niven, George Zebrowski, Harry Turtledove, Lois McMaster Bujold, Laura Mixon, Steven Gould (he and Mixon would later marry and start writing in tandem as well as separately), Kevin J. Anderson, and James P. Hogan.

The art department became even more open to new cover artists including Tom Kidd, Doug Beekman, Janet Aulisio, David Hardy, Jim Burns, Stephen Youll, and Nicholas Jainschigg.

In 1992, the magazine was sold to Dell magazines. By this time, Schmidt's job had become harder, as it had for all science-fiction magazine editors.

In the 1990s, the real money lay in writing hardcover books, and most of the publishers didn't want them appearing in magazines first and possibly siphoning off readers. Longer stories (which could be expanded into novels) and serials by better known authors became scarce. Talented writers of short stories could be nurtured and published, but the chances were that they, too, would soon turn to novels.

But Schmidt and his fellow editors kept diligently at their craft, and the magazines remained a keystone of science fiction. As this book goes to press *Analog*, under the capable editorship of Dr. Schmidt, continues to be published—the last bastion of the "hard science-fiction" story so beloved by John W. Campbell and the magazine's thousands of technically oriented readers.

ANALOG SCIENCE FICTION / SCIENCE FACT

MARCH 29, 1982

VINCENT DI FATE

Clarke, author of *2001* and inventor of the communications satellite, returned to the magazine that published his first story thirty-six years before. The article was a reprint of a Clarke speech at a UNESCO meeting in Paris.

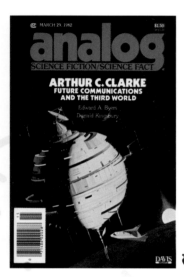

ANALOG SCIENCE FICTION & FACT

FEBRUARY 1992

BROECK STEADMAN

The cover looked like a rare photo-art combination. Forward, into the future!

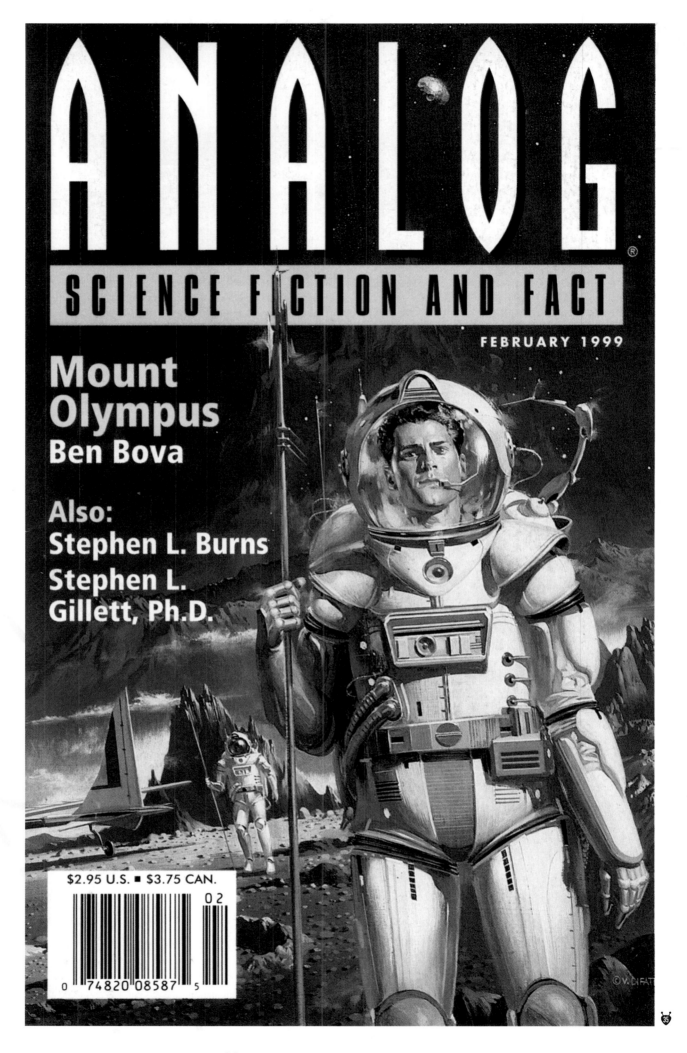

ANALOG SCIENCE FICTION AND FACT

FEBRUARY 1999

VINCENT DI FATE

The issue of *Analog* nearest the closing date of this book. One of the oldest magazines in America—published continuously since 1930 (barring a short hiatus in 1933)—*Analog* is a tribute to science and the imagination.

STELLAR COMPANIONS
AND DWARF STARS
CHAPTER 5

Many magazines had always published a certain amount of science fiction, both before and after the birth of *Amazing Stories*. *Argosy*, *The All-Story*, and *Blue Book* were general pulps that published a variety of material, though science fiction—especially if it was by Edgar Rice Burroughs—usually got a cover position. Edmond Hamilton, noted for his space operas later in the science-fiction magazines of the 1930s, appeared with similar stories in the late 1920s *Weird Tales*—a magazine devoted to "ghoulies and ghosties and long-leggety beasties and things that go bump in the night." Later, the magazine even sponsored a club which sent you a membership card and printed your name and address so other readers could contact you. (Hugh Hefner joined in 1943, cheerfully admitting to it in later years.) An early competitor to *Amazing* was *Miracle Science and Fantasy Stories*. Harold Hersey, the publisher, had been editor of the short-lived *Thrill Book* (sixteen issues in 1919) which was

The cover by Bok—symbolic of the war that had just begun—was complete with bomb shelter and two victims who might have been consumed in the later fire bombing of Dresden.

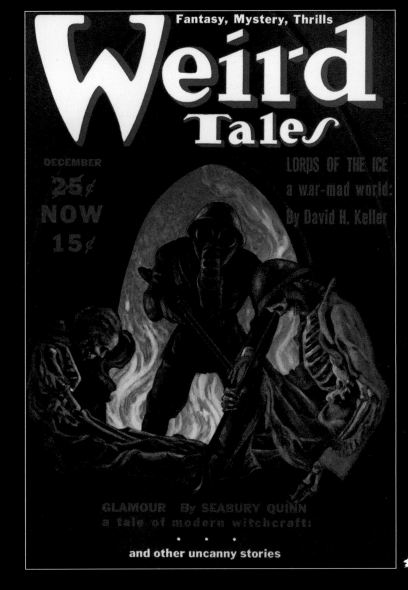

Fantasy, Mystery, Thrills

Weird Tales

DECEMBER
25¢
NOW
15¢

LORDS OF THE ICE
a war-mad world:
By David H. Keller

GLAMOUR   By SEABURY QUINN
a tale of modern witchcraft:
• • •
and other uncanny stories

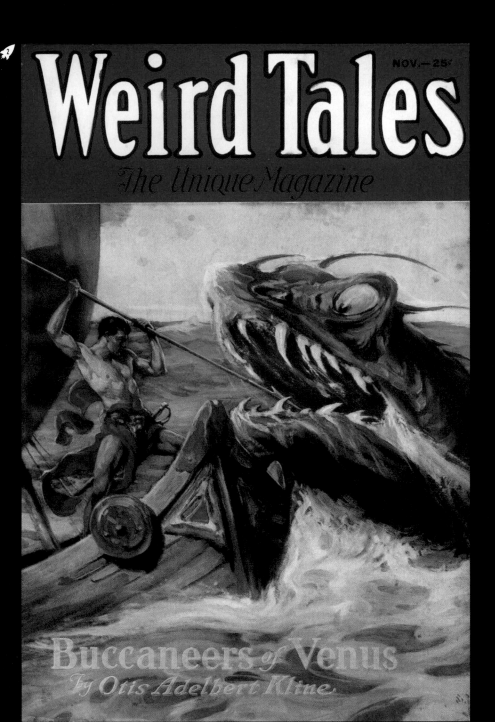

WEIRD TALES

NOV.—25¢

The Unique Magazine

Buccaneers of Venus
by Otis Adelbert Kline

WEIRD TALES
NOVEMBER 1932
J. ALLEN ST. JOHN

Otis Adelbert Kline was one of the many imitators of Edgar Rice Burroughs; his series on Venus was written first, but Burroughs beat him into print with his own *Pirates of Venus* in *Argosy* two months before.

Weird Tales

The Unique Magazine

THE STAR-STEALERS
by EDMOND·HAMILTON

FEBRUARY 1929
HUGH RANKIN
25¢

WEIRD TALES
FEBRUARY 1929
HUGH RANKIN

Even *Weird Tales*, the home of "ghoulies and ghosties and long-leggety beasties and things that go bump in the night," published an occasional science-fiction story.

sometimes mentioned as the first science-fiction magazine. But the science-fiction and fantasy content was much too low; the bulk of the magazine was devoted to adventure stories.

Miracle Science and Fantasy lasted two issues. The covers and interior illustrations were by Elliott Dold, who had drawn interiors for *Astounding* and painted the covers for a number of other pulps. Both Elliott and his brother, Douglas, contributed stories. (Douglas, sometimes credited with editing *Miracle*, was blind.)

In 1938, the first major explosion in the science-fiction field occurred. *Amazing* was a success under the Ziff-Davis banner, *Thrilling Wonder* was doing fine, and, of course, *Astounding* ruled the roost. Red Circle Magazines, a secondary chain noted primarily for their weird-horror pulps, launched *Marvel Science Stories* and followed it in 1939 with *Dynamic Science Stories*, which lasted two issues.

Marvel lasted for fifteen, counting issues before and after World War II. For two of them, it was retitled *Marvel Tales* and featured such non-science-fiction stories as "Lust Rides the Roller Coaster" and "Fresh Fiancés for the Devil's Daughter."

There was a *Dynamic Science Fiction* published after World War II, but another publisher had hijacked the adjective.

Blue Ribbon Magazines introduced *Science Fiction* and *Future Fiction* in 1939 and 1940 respectively. The publisher was a friend of Hugo Gernsback, and Gernsback wrote an editorial for the first issue of *Science Fiction*. Gernsback's old editor of *Wonder*, Charles D. Hornig, edited both magazines. As might be expected, the first few issues of *Science Fiction* ran covers by Frank R. Paul.

One of the more popular entries in the science-fiction sweepstakes was *Planet Stories*, which featured space operas, aliens, and priestesses on other planets. Present were such sterling stories as "War Gods of the Void," "The Dragon-Queen of Jupiter," and "The Rocketeers Have Shaggy Ears."

Astounding could aim for the more mature audience; *Planet Stories* was happy with the curious teenager who dreamed of rocketships and lusty priestesses when he went to bed at night. Oddly, the magazine also had a taste for literature and printed "The Million Year Picnic," "Mars Is Heaven," "Rocket Summer," and other stories by Ray Bradbury that later appeared in his collection, *The Martian*

MARVEL SCIENCE STORIES
AUGUST 1938
NORMAN SAUNDERS

The first issue of more solid competition to the Big Three. Saunders—who had painted covers for almost every pulp genre—showed a flair for futuristic machinery as well as half-naked women with metal bras.

Chronicles. Late in its existence, *Planet Stories* published Bradbury's "The Golden Apples of the Sun" and reprinted—the magazine's only reprint—his "A Sound of Thunder," which had appeared in *Collier's* (a major slick-paper magazine) a year-and-a-half before.

The magazine was also fond of Leigh Brackett who honed her skills in science fiction by writing such memorable tales as "Queen of the Martian Catacombs" and "Black Amazon of Mars" (both featuring her popular character, Eric John Stark). She even teamed up with Ray Bradbury on "Lorelei of the Red Mist."

Brackett went on to write screenplays for the Howard Hawks' movies *The Big Sleep* and *Rio Bravo*, and her science-fiction skills were on display in her script for *The Empire Strikes Back*. It was the only science-fiction script she ever wrote and earned a posthumous 1980 Hugo.

Along with the rest of the science-fiction pulps, *Planet* died in 1955. Within the limits it set for itself, it had done remarkably well. It was acknowledged as the home of space opera, though it strayed occasionally to publish some genuinely literary stories. It had an exciting and reader-involving letter column and sported a series of excellent action covers by Allen Anderson, Jerome Rozen, Parkhurst, Kelly Freas, Leydenfrost and occasional entries by Finlay, Bok, and Paul. (One cover was even credited to author Algis Budrys, but that had to have been an editorial glitch.) On the collector's market, issues of *Planet* now bring a premium.

The Futurians, a politically "left-tinged" fan group (several of its members were Communists at a time when to be a Communist was not all *that* bad—the

party was legal and thoroughly anti-Fascist), were now to play a prominent role in science fiction.

The New York World Science Fiction Convention —attendance: all of 200—had been held in 1939 and attendees came from throughout the United States. (As predicted, the inmates were taking over the asylum.)

Not present were the Futurians who had been blacklisted because of a squabble with the sponsoring group, New Fandom. Those of the Futurians who were professionals—like Isaac Asimov—were allowed in, however. Strangely, within a year or two almost all of the Futurians would be professional science-fiction writers and editors.

The first was Robert A. W. Lowndes who took over from Charles Hornig at *Science Fiction and Future Fiction*. Hornig had departed for California where he thought he had a better chance of registering as a conscientious objector (the draft was now in full force). Lowndes, who had offered to do the job for even less than what Hornig was earning, was to make a career for himself as the best editor in the field to put out decent-looking magazines on a minuscule budget, whether they were pulps or digests.

The second Futurian to achieve editorial fame was Frederik Pohl, destined to have a major role in science fiction as writer and editor. The Futurians were young, for the most part politically active, and science fiction played a hugely important role in their lives. With the later addition of women to the group, it became something of an incestuous organization—there were marriages, divorces, and remarriages, all within the group. For a time there was even a communal living arrangement.

(After the war, Pohl became a member of New York's Hydra Club, composed primarily of

DYNAMIC SCIENCE STORIES
{"image_fingerprint":" accepting as FEBRUARY 1939 and FRANK R. PAUL block"}

{}

FEBRUARY 1939
FRANK R. PAUL

A companion magazine for *Marvel* with a cover by former *Amazing* and *Wonder* artist Frank R. Paul. Lloyd Eshbach, featured on the cover, founded the specialty book publishing house Fantasy Press after World War II.

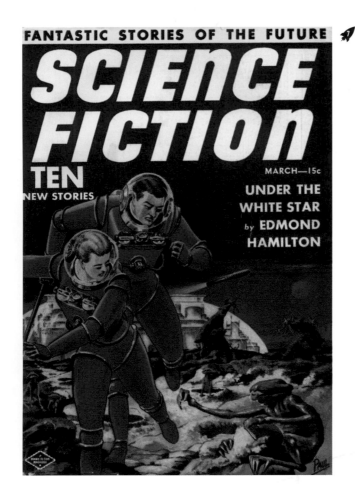

SCIENCE FICTION

MARCH 1939
FRANK R. PAUL

Another first issue
with a cover by Paul
and a story by another
old-timer, Edmond
Hamilton. It wasn't a
Gernsback magazine
but had an editorial
by Hugo who was a
friend of the publisher.

professional writers and their wives and girlfriends,
which was an even more incestuous group than the
old Futurians. One young sociologist spent several
months studying the shifting relationships within
the group and then gave up.)

Pohl became the editor of the only ten-cent
magazine in the field—*Astonishing Stories*—and its
fifteen-cent bigger brother, *Super Science Stories*, at
the age of nineteen. Pohl could pay half-a-cent a
word (against *Astounding's* penny), which was par
for most of the competition. By skimping here and
there, Pohl even managed to buy an occasional story
from Heinlein or L. Sprague de Camp. Campbell's
objections to sex in almost any form also helped—
stories he rejected because of their "racy" content
could usually find a home with Pohl.

And Pohl had a secret weapon. If he really
needed stories on the cheap, there were always the
Futurians—most of whom wanted to be writers and
many of whom were quite good.

After World War II, during which he served over-
seas, Pohl became an agent. His science-fiction agency
was hugely successful, but despite that, he ended up
owing almost everybody when the agency finally
closed (he eventually paid down the total debt of
approximately $30,000). At a convention in Chicago,
meeting one of his impoverished former clients to
whom he owed money, he pulled out his wallet and
paid the author two hundred dollars on account. They
were the first hundred dollar bills the author had
ever seen, and he couldn't thank Pohl enough.

The only editor who did more with less than
either Pohl or "Doc" Lowndes was Donald A.
Wollheim, who edited *Stirring Science Stories* and
Cosmic Science-Fiction in 1941. Albing Publications,
the publisher, was a father and son team who operated

FUTURE FICTION

MARCH 1940
H. W. SCOTT

A companion magazine to *Science Fiction*. Cover artist Scott
was much better known for his western and mystery covers.

from a desk in an ad agency. Wollheim ran Pohl one better when it came to a budget. He didn't have any—though father and son offered to pay him a salary effective with the third issue if the magazines were successful. Once again, it was the Futurians to the rescue; many of them contributed stories out of friendship and for the experience. Wollheim himself wrote a good deal of his own material, as well as for other magazines. (Wollheim's short story, "Mimic," was filmed in 1998.)

The one huge Plus for Wollheim was that Hannes Bok, one of the best and most stylistic artists the field ever produced, was now a member of the Futurians and available as a cover artist. Even though his covers for Wollheim's magazines consisted of black images against "flat" color backgrounds, they were outstanding.

The March 1942 issue of *Stirring Science Stories* was to be the first monthly issue, but, unfortunately, the publisher had made a fatal error. (The United States had just entered World War II; a monthly anything was a bad idea, but the publisher had no control over that.) The March *Stirring* was not a true "pulp"; it was the size of the comic books of the period. Distributors, however, didn't bundle it with comic books but with the pulps. Since *Stirring* had a larger page size than the pulps, the bundling wires cut into the sides of the magazine for an inch or two. Copies of the magazine were effectively DBA—destroyed before arrival. Today, intact copies of the issue are collector's items.

The last major category of magazines in the great boom of the late 1930s and early 1940s were those of "companion" magazines. Rather than come out twice a month or even monthly, it was smarter from a

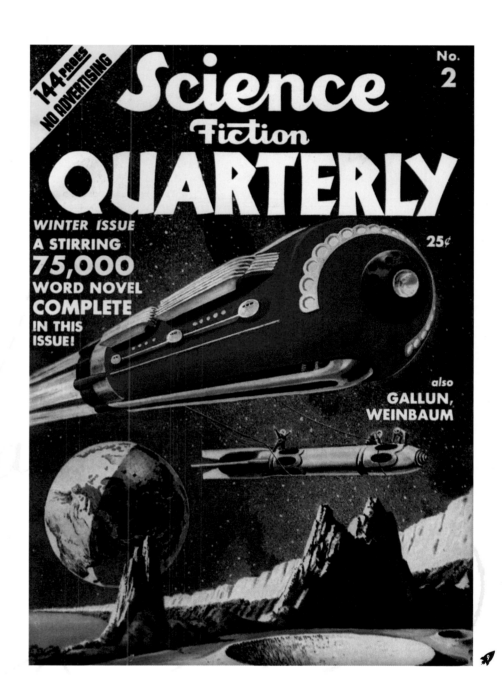

SCIENCE FICTION QUARTERLY
WINTER 1941
FRANK R. PAUL

A companion to *Science Fiction* and *Future Fiction* and a return to the old-time quarterlies, only this time in pulp size. The "Weinbaum" on the cover was Helen Weinbaum, Stanley's sister, with one of the few stories she wrote.

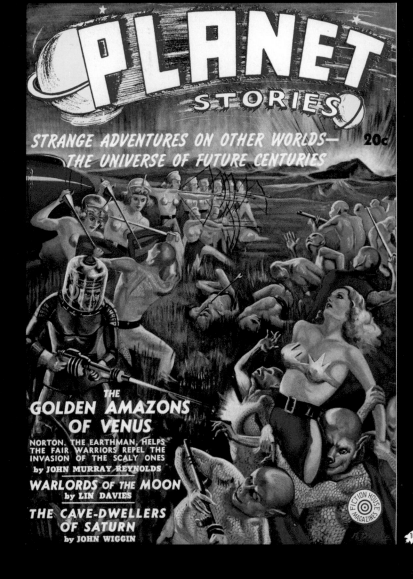

PLANET STORIES
WINTER 1939
M. DRAKE

Another first issue. *Planet Stories* was an unabashed champion of space opera but wasn't above printing stories by Ray Bradbury, which later became *The Martian Chronicles*.

11
PLANET STORIES
FALL 1942
LEYDENFROST

The cover formula remained the same but the execution by Leydenfrost was superb. Featured was a story by fan Bob (later "Wilson") Tucker, who was to make his name writing mystery as well as science-fiction novels.

publisher's point of view to simply issue a companion title. Thus, both magazines would have a longer life on the newsstand.

The first magazine to twin itself was *Thrilling Wonder Stories*. Its companion, *Startling Stories*, printed a "booklength" novel in every issue, along with a scattering of shorts and one "Hall of Fame" reprint from the back files of *Wonder*. The first issue featured *The Black Flame* by Stanley G. Weinbaum; authors in following issues included Edmond Hamilton, Jack Williamson, Leigh Brackett, and Henry Kuttner.

Of particular note were Arthur C. Clarke's *Against the Fall of Night* (expanded in bookform as *The City and the Stars*), Fredric Brown's *What Mad Universe* and John D. MacDonald's *Wine of the Dreamers*. But most notable of all was Philip José Farmer's "The Lovers." It was a frank (for the period) story of love and sex between a human and an alien. Rejected by the editors of *Astounding* and *Galaxy* (the leading digests at the time), it was published in *Startling Stories* in 1952 and won Farmer a Hugo as Best New Author.

Startling Stories was popular enough to go monthly in 1952—but three years later was discontinued as the science-fiction boom in pulp magazines collapsed, along with the rest of the pulps. One issue short of a hundred, *Startling* ended its life as one of the most adult science-fiction magazines on the market.

Startling Stories wasn't the only companion magazine to *Thrilling Wonder*. For a number of years, "hero" pulps such as *The Shadow*, *Doc Savage*, and *The Spider* had thrived. Why not a "hero" pulp in the science-fiction field? *Captain Future* was the answer and featured Captain Curt Newton and his faithful sidekicks Otho, the android; Grag, a seven-foot tall robot; and Simon Wright, the living brain-in-a-box.

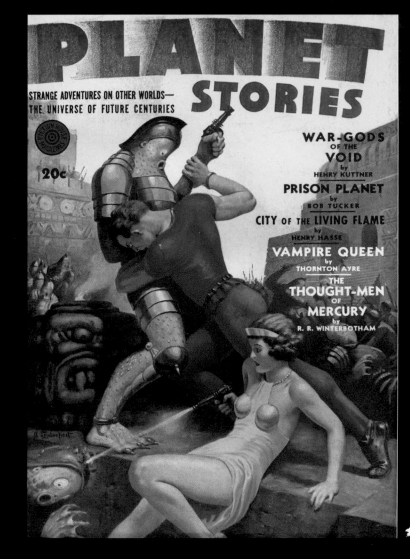

STRANGE ADVENTURES ON OTHER WORLDS—

PLANET
Stories

JAN.

25¢

A. N. C.

A SOUND OF THUNDER by RAY BRADBURY

MARS MINUS BISHA novelet by LEIGH BRACKETT

$5.00 VALUE FOR 25¢

A.N.C.

Two Complete

Science-Adventure
Books

No. 1
WINTER

PEBBLE
in the
SKY
by ISAAC ASIMOV

Published in
book form by
Doubleday &
Co. Inc.
$2.50

The KINGSLAYER
by L. RON HUBBARD
Published in book form by Fantasy Pub. Co. Inc. $3.00

TWO COMPLETE SCIENCE-ADVENTURE BOOKS
WINTER 1950
ANDERSON

The first issue of a reprint
companion to *Planet Stories.*

A miniscule editorial budget but lots of enthusiasm. The magazine was edited by Donald A. Wollheim, later the science-fiction editor of Ace paperbacks.

A companion to *Cosmic* the size of an early comic book. Unfortunately, distributors didn't bundle it with the comics but with the pulps, all of which were smaller. The bundle wires cut into the sides of the magazine, making most of the copies unsaleable—and the issue a collector's item.

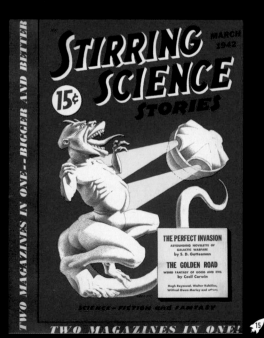

The captain's assignment was to save the Solar System —or perhaps the universe—every three months.

Most of the novels were written by Edmond Hamilton, and the magazine itself lasted seventeen issues. Suspended during the war, an attempt was made to try and revive the hardy Captain afterward but by then "super heroes" had become the province of comic books.

Astounding came out with a companion magazine, *Unknown*, in early 1939 but it published fantasy, not science fiction. The next real "companion" magazine was *Fantastic Adventures*, a large-sized little brother to *Amazing Stories*. (Despite the title, *Fantastic Adventures* was more science fiction than fantasy.)

The first issue was notable for little but the back cover by Frank R. Paul, illustrating "The Man from Mars." But the second issue featured "The Scientists' Revolt" by Edgar Rice Burroughs. The story had been sitting in Burroughs' trunk since 1922 and hadn't seen any takers. Editor Ray Palmer bought it, rewrote it (setting the story in the future), and published it to no great acclaim, though the story undoubtedly boosted circulation.

The magazine went monthly in 1940, then sales sagged and it reverted to a pulp size. It was due for the axe when Palmer asked J. Allen St. John to paint the cover for the October issue featuring *Jongor of Lost Land*, a "Tarzan" type story. St. John and his favorite dinosaurs made their appearance and the magazine promptly doubled in circulation. Palmer ran St. John as the cover artist frequently; the artist was ideal for Burroughs' "Carson of Venus" stories published by the magazine. St. John was also joined by Harold W. McCauley—the "Petty of the pulps" as Palmer called him—who graced the covers with the flair of a pin-up artist.

SUPER SCIENCE STORIES
JULY 1940
UNKNOWN

The editor of both *Super Science Stories* and *Astonishing Stories* was an ex-fan named Frederik Pohl, who was later to edit various other magazines and become one of the field's most popular authors.

ASTONISHING STORIES
APRIL 1941
UNKNOWN

The only ten-cent science-fiction pulp ever published and a companion to *Super Science Stories.*

SUPER SCIENCE STORIES
AUGUST 1942
HUBERT ROGERS

Artist Rogers was a regular for *Astounding Science Fiction* but painted one of his best covers for *Super Science Stories.*

STARTLING STORIES

JANUARY 1939
HOWARD V. BROWN

The first issue of a companion magazine to *Thrilling Wonder Stories*, which eventually eclipsed it—probably because it featured a complete novel in every issue. The lead novel by Weinbaum was published posthumously; he'd died of lung cancer in 1935 after a career that lasted only fifteen months.

STARTLING STORIES

OCTOBER 1953
ALEX SCHOMBURG

The title was now dignified, the girls with the brass bras had disappeared. The magazine had gone upscale with a vengeance, probably because of competition from the better digests.

STARTLING STORIES

SEPTEMBER 1948
EARLE K. BERGEY

What Mad Universe became a classic, but a sign of the times was a short article by R. L. Farnsworth, the president of the U.S. Rocket Society, pointing out that a landing on the moon would happen "sooner than you think!"

the magazine had its moments,
the whimsical tales by Nelson Bond
Mergenthwirker's Lobblies" published
agazine in 1937). Later contributors
lore Sturgeon (*The Dreaming Jewels,*
he Atom), L. Ron Hubbard (with a
uthor's famed *Slaves of Sleep*), Fritz
prague de Camp.
me in 1953, when the circulation
tastic Adventures had started to fade
t of all the other pulps). For a year,
was published in tandem with the
ntastic and then combined with
tastic Adventures" as a title disap-
ely.

n a long-standing outcry against
pulp-fiction field, much of it led by
cations, publishers of *Astonishing*
r Science Stories among others. Some
same way as did many authors. The
a free ride for the publisher, the
o money from them.

rint magazines from the Frank A.
ny were welcomed with open arms.
tic Mysteries and *Fantastic Novels*
ly from the Munsey files of *Argosy*,
Cavalier, and other Munsey publica-
only opportunity to read *The Blind*
in the Golden Atom," *Darkness and*
r Munsey "classics."

itor (Mary Gnaedinger) didn't have
ries, she invested in artwork. Covers
ere by Virgil Finlay and Frank R.
f the best that either one had ever
r, "Lawrence" (Lawrence Sterne
ded.

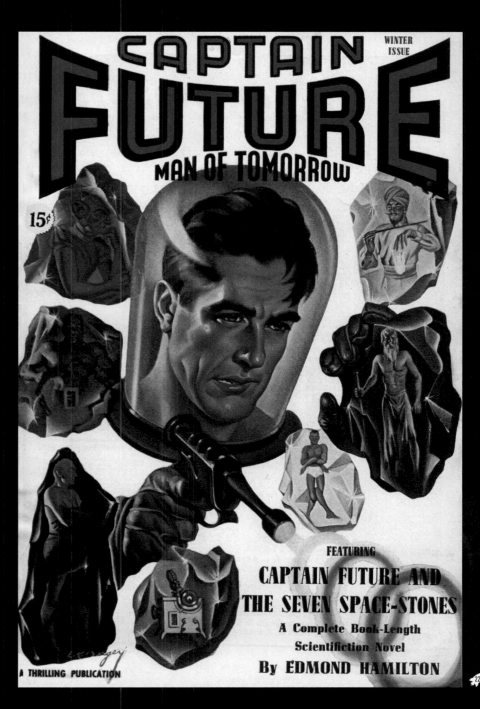

CAPTAIN FUTURE
WINTER 1941
EARLE K. BERGEY

Inspired by the success of *The Shadow* and *Doc Savage, Captain
Future* was launched as a "hero pulp" companion to both *Startling
Stories* and *Thrilling Wonder Stories*.

FANTASTIC ADVENTURES
MARCH 1942
J. ALLEN ST. JOHN

Artist St. John painted all the covers for stories by Edgar Rice Burroughs that ran in *Amazing* and *Fantastic* edited by Ray Palmer.

FANTASTIC ADVENTURES
JUNE 1941
H. W. MCCAULEY

The magazine failed in the large size but prospered as a pulp. A lot of the popularity of the magazine was due to cover artists McCauley and St. John.

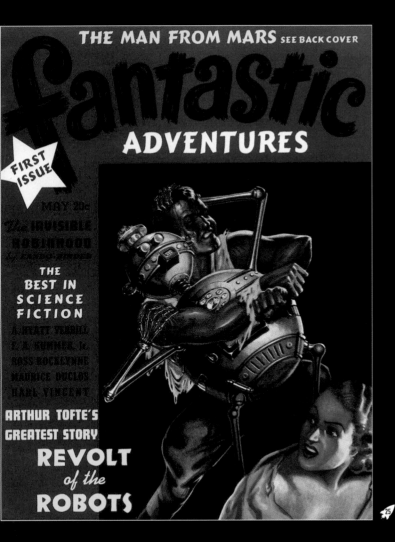

FANTASTIC ADVENTURES
MAY 1939
ROBERT FUQUA

The first issue of a companion magazine to *Amazing* in the old large size. Its cover was by an artist new to the field but its back cover—
"The Man From Mars"—was by old reliable, Frank R. Paul.

DUMMY OF DEATH By LEROY YERXA

fantastic
ADVENTURES

OCTOBER 25¢
IN CANADA 30¢

KING OF THE DINOSAURS
By J. W. PELKIE

PAGANINI-MAN OR DEVIL?
SEE PAGE 130

fantastic
ADVENTURES

GRIM DANGER
IN A LOST WORLD
JONGOR
OF
LOST LAND
By Robert Moore Williams

OCTOBER
20¢

FANTASY – MYSTERY – ADVENTURE
THORNTON AYRE ★ HENRY KUTTNER ★ JAMES NORMAN

FANTASTIC ADVENTURES
OCTOBER 1940
J. ALLEN ST. JOHN

The magazine was about to be cancelled—this was supposed to be the last issue. But cover artist St. John and his dinosaurs doubled the circulation.

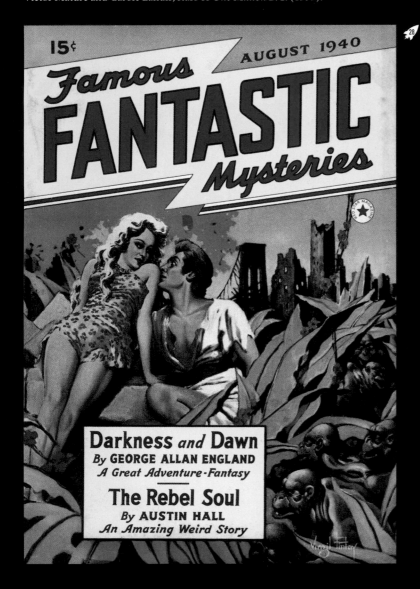

But at the end of 1942, the Munsey pulps were sold to Popular Publications, which had been the leader in the fight against reprints. The editorial policy of *Famous Fantastic Mysteries* abruptly shifted. Magazine reprints were out—but book reprints were okay. From the pulp novels of Abraham Merritt, George Allan England, Ralph Milne Farley, and Austin Hall, readers suddenly were offered Arthur Machen, Algernon Blackwood, Lord Dunsany, William Hope Hodgson, G. K. Chesterton, Jack London, and Ayn Rand.

English teachers who had bewailed those "trashy pulps" for years must have been shocked.

The paper shortage during the war had cut back the number of magazines as well as their size and frequency. But once the war was over, the science-fiction boom resumed and those adjectives that had been neglected before suddenly found popularity. *Marvel* and *Dynamic* were revived, as were *Super Science Stories*, *Fantastic Novels*, and *Science Fiction Quarterly*. New companion magazines were added—*Fantastic Story Magazine* and *Space Stories* to the "Thrilling" line, *Two Complete Science-Adventure Books* to *Planet Stories*. And some titles appeared that were brand new—*Out of This World Adventures* (with a complete 32-page comic book bound in) and *10 Story Fantasy*. Donald A. Wollheim was the editor of both. The first saw two issues, the latter only one.

But that one issue achieved immortality with the publication of "Sentinel of Eternity" by Arthur C. Clarke. The story eventually became the basis of the film and subsequent novel, *2001: A Space Odyssey*.

With paper restrictions lifted, some magazines beefed up from their wartime 112 pages to 176, a number went from quarterly publication to bi-monthly and even monthly.

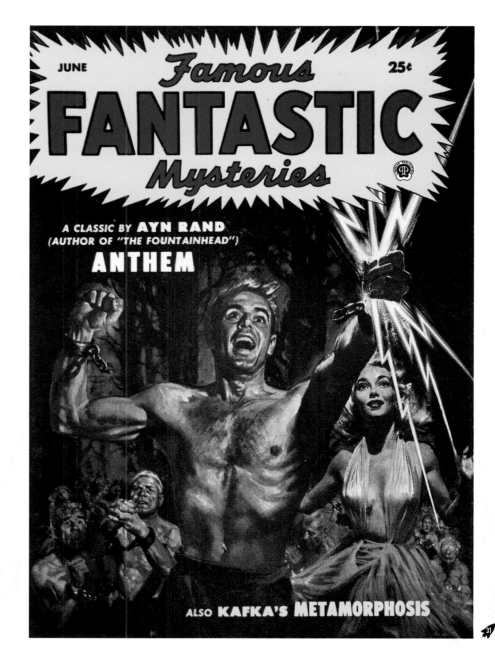

FANTASTIC STORY MAGAZINE
SUMMER 1952
ALEX SCHOMBURG

A primarily reprint magazine and companion to *Startling Stories* and *Thrilling Wonder Stories*.

FANTASTIC NOVELS
JULY 1940
VIRGIL FINLAY

The first issue of a companion magazine to *Famous Fantastic Mysteries*.

FAMOUS FANTASTIC MYSTERIES
JUNE 1953
LAWRENCE

After the magazine was sold to another publisher, it printed only novels that hadn't appeared in the pulps. Readers were startled to find William Hope Hodgson and G.K. Chesterton—and Ayn Rand and Franz Kafka. This was the last issue.

But by 1955, it was all over. The boom was still going for science fiction but it was going for the digest magazines. The pulps had become more adult, had adopted more modern formats, were publishing many of the same authors who were making a name for themselves in the digests. None of it helped.

The pulps as a group were dying. Distributors didn't want to handle them, newsdealers didn't know where to rack them—the only magazines the same size were *Popular Mechanics* and *Popular Science* and they usually enjoyed flat display in the front of the stand. The pulps were given only spine display— if the news dealer bothered with them at all. They didn't sell enough to be displayed flat so potential buyers seldom saw the catchy covers. The "browser" market was gone.

The last science-fiction pulp—and possibly the last pulp, period—was the February 1958 issue of *Science Fiction Quarterly*.

After that, silence.

The noise about science fiction was coming from a different part of the newsstand entirely.

10 STORY FANTASY
SPRING 1951
UNKNOWN

The first and only issue. A companion magazine to *Out of This World Adventures*. You didn't get a comic book with it but you DID get Arthur C. Clarke with a short story titled "Sentinel of Eternity." The story served as the basis for the film *2001: A Space Odyssey*.

OUT OF THIS WORLD ADVENTURES
JULY 1950
UNKNOWN

With science-fiction magazines flooding the newsstands, you had to have a gimmick to attract readers. *Out of this World Adventures* bound a comic book in the middle. It didn't help— the magazine folded after two issues.

SPACE STORIES
OCTOBER 1952
ED EMSH

Still another—if short-lived—companion to *Startling* and *Thrilling Wonder* and *Fantastic Story*. In 1952 there were thirty-seven pulp and digest science-fiction magazines being published and the field was overdue for a shake out.

SCIENCE FICTION QUARTERLY
FEBRUARY 1958
ED EMSH

The last of the pulp science-fiction magazines and very probably the last pulp magazine, period. The end of an era—newsdealers no longer knew where to rack the pulps, nor cared. But the digest magazines were alive and well.

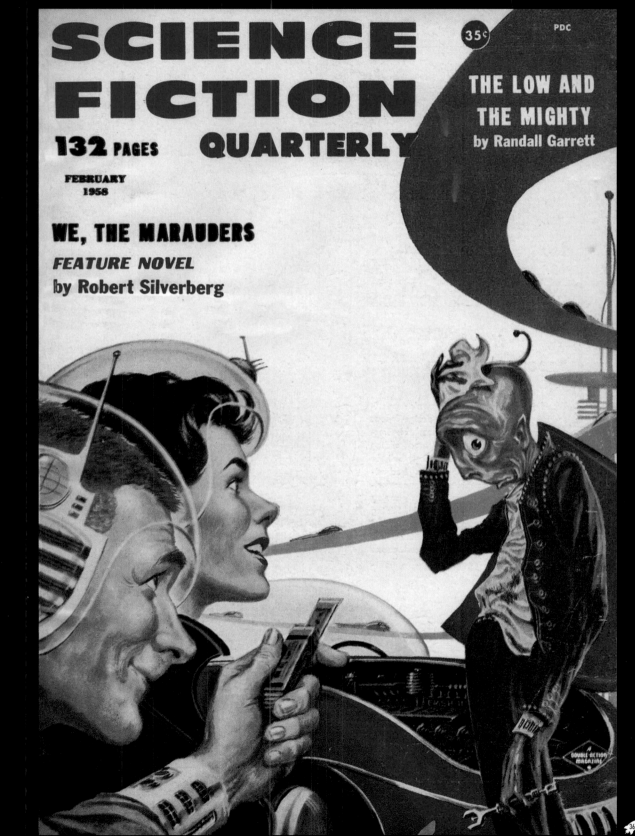

CHAPTER 6
THE MAJOR MOONS
OF JUPITER

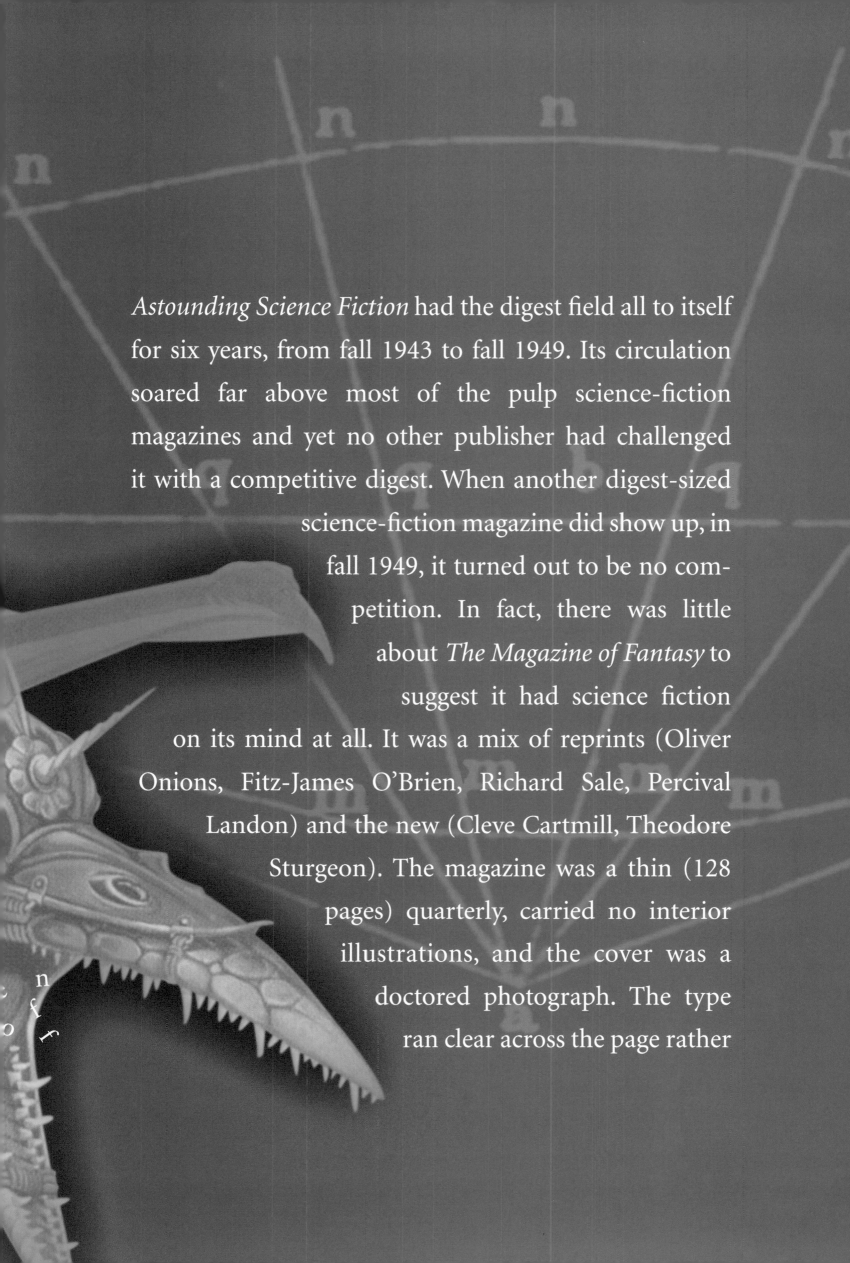

Astounding Science Fiction had the digest field all to itself for six years, from fall 1943 to fall 1949. Its circulation soared far above most of the pulp science-fiction magazines and yet no other publisher had challenged it with a competitive digest. When another digest-sized science-fiction magazine did show up, in fall 1949, it turned out to be no competition. In fact, there was little about *The Magazine of Fantasy* to suggest it had science fiction on its mind at all. It was a mix of reprints (Oliver Onions, Fitz-James O'Brien, Richard Sale, Percival Landon) and the new (Cleve Cartmill, Theodore Sturgeon). The magazine was a thin (128 pages) quarterly, carried no interior illustrations, and the cover was a doctored photograph. The type ran clear across the page rather

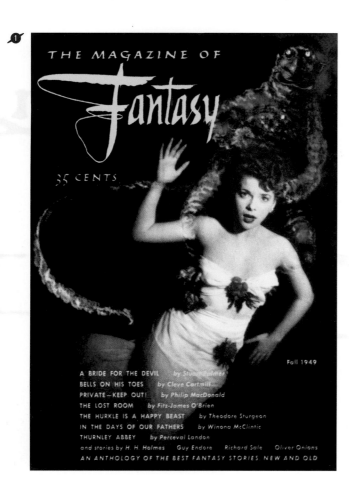

THE MAGAZINE OF FANTASY
FALL 1949
COVER KODACHROME BY BILL STONE

The first issue. The editors were Anthony Boucher, noted mystery reviewer, and J. Francis McComas, co-anthologist of the seminal anthology, *Adventures in Time and Space*. The magazine had a distinct mainstream literary bent.

THE MAGAZINE OF FANTASY AND SCIENCE FICTION
OCTOBER 1952
CHESLEY BONESTELL

With the second issue, the magazine changed its title. A dozen or so issues later renowned astronomical artist Bonestell was painting the occasional cover. Reprint authors included P.G. Wodehouse. P.G. Wodehouse?

than broken into two columns—not the easiest format to read. It carried one badly drawn cartoon but that was hardly innovative, the Palmer *Amazing* had carried cartoons, too. It was an easy magazine to overlook if you were browsing at the newsstand —hardly anything for John W. Campbell to lose sleep over.

The publisher was Lawrence Spivak, who published a gaggle of mystery digests including *Ellery Queen's Mystery Magazine*. Anthony Boucher, one of the editors, was a noted mystery critic and had contributed some science-fiction stories to *Astounding*. His co-editor was J. Francis McComas, editor (along with Raymond J. Healy) of the definitive science-fiction anthology, *Adventures in Time and Space*.

The second issue showed a good deal more promise. It had been retitled *The Magazine of Fantasy and Science Fiction* (eventually known by its acronym of *F&SF*) and had added quite a few recognizable names to the contents page—Ray Bradbury, Damon Knight, L. Sprague de Camp, and Fletcher Pratt among them.

The magazine had a few things going for it that weren't immediately obvious. One, its very thinness meant you could slip it in your pocket without difficulty. Two, the design covers by George Salter meant that nobody on the bus would give you the fish eye if you were a grown man or woman and happened to be reading it. And three, the editors were convinced there was a larger audience for science fiction than teenagers and technicians.

The magazine was edited for adults, dedicated to literacy, and had few taboos. It was an article of faith with John W. Campbell of *Astounding* that when it came to a showdown between humanity and aliens (though Campbell didn't quite believe in aliens),

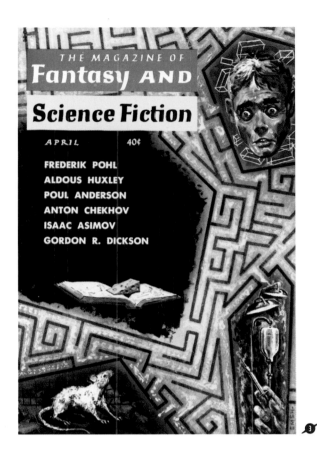

3

THE MAGAZINE OF FANTASY AND SCIENCE FICTION
APRIL 1959
ED EMSH

This issue featured "Flowers for Algernon" by Daniel Keyes, later filmed as *Charly* starring Cliff Robertson who won an Academy Award for his performance.

4

THE MAGAZINE OF FANTASY AND SCIENCE FICTION
JULY 1960
MEL HUNTER

Author Wilson Tucker was a science-fiction fan who published the noted "fanzine" *Le Zombie* and later made his reputation with a series of well-crafted mystery and science-fiction novels.

it would be humanity *uber alles*. Boucher and McComas were willing to entertain the idea that, hey, we might lose!

In addition to all of that, the magazine also had a lighter, more sophisticated tone. Interspersed with the literary nuggets that it reprinted from the past (including some by P.G. Wodehouse, Booth Tarkington, and Robert Louis Stevenson), it ran humorous stories such as the "Gavagan's Bar" series by de Camp and Pratt and the "Papa Schimmelhorn" tales by Reginald Bretnor.

In due time, more stories by Theodore Sturgeon and Ray Bradbury showed up—a lot by both of them—and Fritz Leiber, Cyril Kornbluth, Robert Silverberg, Algis Budrys, Richard Matheson, Alfred Bester, Poul Anderson, Roger Zelazny, and Harlan Ellison followed. The magazine serialized juveniles by Heinlein (*The Door Into Summer*, *Have Spacesuit, Will Travel* and *Starship Soldier*—later published in book form, and filmed, as *Starship Troopers*) on the theory that a juvenile by Heinlein was as entertaining as most other authors' novels intended for adults.

There were other notable stories as well: *Bring the Jubilee* by Ward Moore, a short novel of what the country would be like today if the South had won the Civil War (the novel started an entire sub-genre of alternate history stories). Walter M. Miller's *A Canticle for Leibowitz* (published as three novelettes), Theodore Sturgeon's *The (Widget), The (Wadget) and Boff*, *Venus on the Half Shell* by Philip José Farmer (writing as "Kilgore Trout"), Robert Silverberg's *The Stochastic Man* and *Lord Valentine's Castle*, Thomas Disch's *On Wings of Song*, Algis Budrys' *Michelmas*, Frederik Pohl's *Man Plus*...

The magazine collected Hugos like it was gathering nuts in May. It won eight for the Best Professional Magazine and when that category was discontinued, its editors picked up four more. Robert Bloch won a Hugo for "That Hell-Bound Train," Daniel Keyes for "Flowers for Algernon" (later filmed as *Charly*, which won an Oscar for actor Cliff Robertson), Roger Zelazny a Nebula for "The Doors of His Face, the Lamps of His Mouth," John Varley both a Hugo and a Nebula for "The Persistence of Vision"—the honorees are too numerous to mention.

Isaac Asimov held up the science end of the magazine with a series of articles that ran continuously from November 1958 through February 1992. Other writers contributed science articles as well, including Arthur C. Clarke.

The magazine's book reviews were the best going, especially those by Algis Budrys whose perceptive analytical reviews ran for many years. Nor were the magazine's authors above poking fun at science fiction and themselves. Boucher himself contributed "The Model of a Science Fiction Editor" (think Gilbert and Sullivan) and Isaac Asimov "The Foundation of S.F. Success" (in this case, it's "God Save the Queen").

The magazine ran through a series of editors that reads like Biblical begats. McComas resigned and Boucher edited *F&SF* alone until mid-1954 when he was succeeded by Robert P. Mills, in turn succeeded by Avram Davidson (a talented author as well as editor), then Joseph W. Ferman, his son Edward L., Kristine Kathryn Rusch, and at the turn of the century, Gordon Van Gelder.

Despite the editorial changes, of all the magazines *F&SF* probably showed the least change throughout

5

THE MAGAZINE OF FANTASY
AND SCIENCE FICTION
NOVEMBER 1963
HANNES BOK

A rare cover by noted
artist Bok—and inside
a short story by Ray
Nelson, "Eight O'Clock
in the Morning," later
filmed as *They Live* by
director John Carpenter.

6

THE MAGAZINE OF FANTASY AND SCIENCE FICTION
JULY 1977
KELLY FREAS

The magazine published a series of issues devoted
to specific authors—others honored Ray Bradbury,
Theodore Sturgeon, and Robert Silverberg.

7

THE MAGAZINE OF FANTASY AND SCIENCE FICTION
FEBRUARY 1968
RONALD WALOTSKY

Featured were a stunning wrap-around cover by artist Walotsky,
a reprint story by Booth Tarkington—Booth Tarkington?—and
a regular science column by Isaac Asimov.

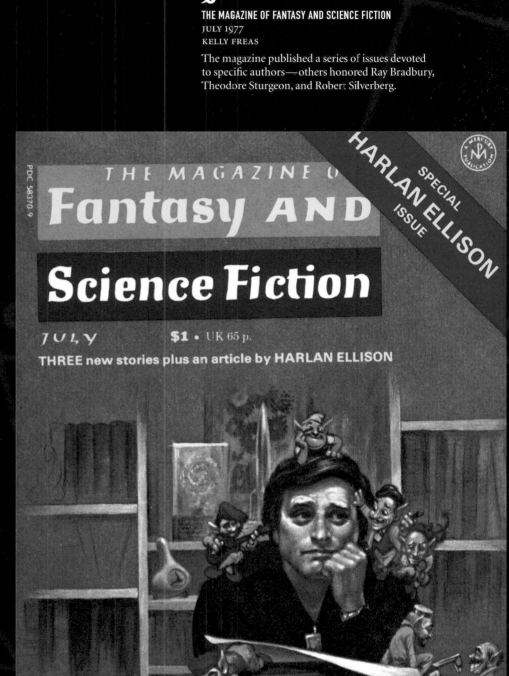

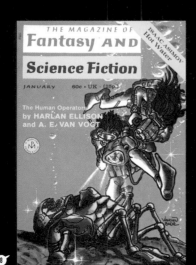

8

THE MAGAZINE OF FANTASY AND SCIENCE FICTION
JANUARY 1971
VAUGHN BODE

A cover by cartoonist Vaughn Bode, science article by Isaac Asimov, book
reviews by James Blish, fiction by Harlan Ellison and A.E. Van Vogt, and a
regular interior cartoon by Gahan Wilson—an all-star issue.

the years (1999 saw its fiftieth anniversary). Editorially, the fiction was consistently well written and possibly more than in any other magazine, the stories were character driven. And in addition to its articles and book reviews, you could expect a cartoon (or even a cover) by Gahan Wilson.

Occasionally the magazine would devote most of an issue to a single author, sometimes featuring him in a front cover painting. Authors so honored included Theodore Sturgeon, Ray Bradbury, Robert Silverberg, Frederik Pohl, and Harlan Ellison.

One of those honored—though not with a cover —was Charles Beaumont, who had published some nineteen stories and articles in the magazine. The story that *F&SF* printed as part of its tribute was "Gentlemen, Be Seated" (a reprint from a *Playboy* clone titled *Rogue*).

The tale was about a very average man named Kinkaid who lived in a world where humor was frowned upon and laughter forbidden. One night Kinkaid's boss—a member of the humor under-ground—takes him to a nightclub in the outskirts of town where Kinkaid is exposed to a vaudeville show and subjected to corny gags and whoopee cushions to see if he's fit for membership in the S.P.O.L.– Society for the Preservation of Laughter.

Sadly, Kinkaid's years of conditioning prevent him from "getting it"—until the next morning. But by then it's too late. His boss denies everything about the night before and Kinkaid is left to wander the no-man's land of the city in search of the club. "…once in a while it almost seemed he could hear the distant laughter. It was a lovely, desperate sound."

Beaumont had been a science-fiction fan at the age of fifteen when he lived in Chicago. He loved King Kong, the Oz books, and old horror movies,

9
THE MAGAZINE OF FANTASY & SCIENCE FICTION
AUGUST 1980
GAHAN WILSON

An issue noted for its cover by Gahan Wilson —and for the charming "The Brave Little Toaster" by critic Thomas M. Disch. The story became extraordinarily successful as an animated cartoon.

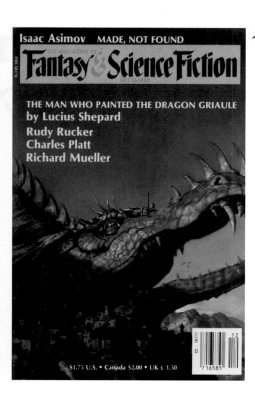

Isaac Asimov   MADE, NOT FOUND

THE MAGAZINE OF
Fantasy & Science Fiction
DECEMBER

THE MAN WHO PAINTED THE DRAGON GRIAULE
by Lucius Shepard
Rudy Rucker
Charles Platt
Richard Mueller

$1.75 U.S. • Canada $2.00 • UK £ 1.50

THE MAGAZINE OF FANTASY & SCIENCE FICTION
DECEMBER 1984
JAMES GURNEY

Cover artist Gurney was to become famous years
later as the author and illustrator of *Dinotopia*,
a book about a father and son shipwrecked in
the 1860s on a lost continent where humans and
dinosaurs live in harmony.

THE MAGAZINE OF FANTASY & SCIENCE FICTION
MARCH 1980
BARCLAY SHAW

A cover which on casual inspection would have
been right at home on the old *Western Story
Magazine*. But on closer scrutiny…

SPECIAL ALL-STAR ISSUE

THE MAGAZINE OF
Fantasy & Science Fiction
MARCH

PDC 583170-9

Manly Wade Wellman
Hilbert Schenck
Charles L. Grant
Robert F. Young
Keith Roberts
Lee Killough
Ron Goulart
Isaac Asimov
Tom Godwin

12

FANTASY & SCIENCE FICTION
MAY 1989
BRYAN LEISTER

The contents were a mix of established authors and newcomers along with an all-star lineup of departments by Orson Scott Card, Algis Budrys, and Harlan Ellison plus the regular science article by Isaac Asimov.

published a fanzine, moved to Los Angeles, and worked in the MGM animation studio, ran a Multilith machine in Universal's music department, and somewhere along the line learned how to write stories. (He was, at one time, a protégé of Ray Bradbury's.)

He eventually hit it big with *Twilight Zone* and especially with *Playboy*, which published a number of his stories. (*Rogue* got those few that *Playboy* for unaccountable reasons rejected. There was no such thing as a Beaumont story that deserved to be rejected by anybody.)

Like Stanley G. Weinbaum, Beaumont died far too early—at the age of 38.

Another author honored by *F&SF* was Harlan Ellison, this time with an outstanding cover portrait by Kelly Freas. Ellison contributed three short stories to the issue, one of which was "Jeffty Is Five." The narrator is a boyhood friend of Jeffty's when they're both five years old. But when the narrator is ten, Jeffty is still five. And when the narrator is a grown man, Jeffty remains a little boy of five.

For Jeffty the world has never changed, and when the narrator is invited into Jeffty's world, he enjoys once again all those things he had enjoyed when he was Jeffty's age. He listens to *Captain Midnight* on Jeffty's radio, though it's a "Captain Midnight" that's been updated to present day. He drinks chocolate milk out of a Little Orphan Annie shakeup mug, goes to the newsstand with Jeffty and buys updated comic books and *current* issues of *Doc Savage* and *The Shadow*, goes to the movies with Jeffty to see *The Demolished Man* starring Franchot Tone, Lionel Barrymore, Evelyn Keyes, and Elisha Cook.

But the magic only works when he's with Jeffty. And then one day Jeffty comes to the television store where the narrator works. He watches a wall of

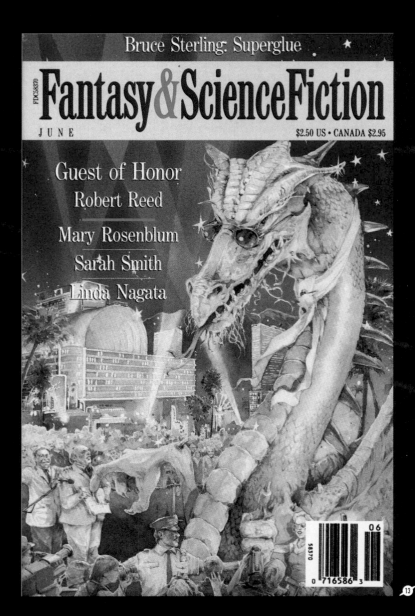

13

FANTASY & SCIENCE FICTION
JUNE 1993
GARY LIPPINCOTT

A stunning cover by new artist Lippincott.

Paolo Bacigalupi: Pocketful of Dharma

CC 58370

Fantasy &ScienceFiction

FEBRUARY

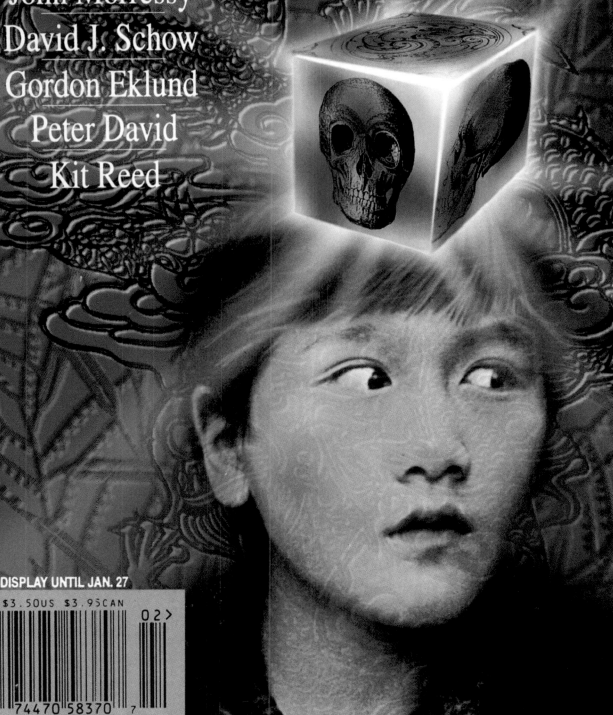

John Morressy

David J. Schow

Gordon Eklund

Peter David

Kit Reed

DISPLAY UNTIL JAN. 27

$3.50US $3.95CAN

02>

0 74470 58370 7

FEBRUARY 1951
25¢
ANC

THE FIREMAN
By Ray Bradbury

Galaxy
SCIENCE FICTION

SEPTEMBER 1951
35¢
ANC

THE PUPPET MASTERS
by Robert A. Heinlein

GALAXY SCIENCE FICTION
SEPTEMBER 1951
DON SIBLEY

Heinlein's novel *The Puppet Masters* was filmed (under the same title) in 1994. Unfortunately, too many other films had used the same central idea, and the movie did poorly at the box office.

GALAXY SCIENCE FICTION
FEBRUARY 1951
CHESLEY BONESTELL

Galaxy Science Fiction was the second magazine to seriously challenge *Astounding*. Ray Bradbury's "The Fireman" was later expanded to a novel (and filmed) as *Fahrenheit 451.*

television sets blaring out their programs—*today's programs*—and nearly loses it. Jeffty escapes the store and on the way home asks to borrow a radio from some bigger kids to hear a snatch of his favorite program. When he hands the radio back, it's locked into Jeffty's world, and the kids can't get the station carrying today's ball game. Naturally, they beat the crap out of Jeffty.

The narrator finally catches up with Jeffty and takes him home to a family that wishes he had never been born. They know he's out of sync, that he'll never grow older, that he'll live forever in the world we all live in when we're five. It's a burden they can't bear, a problem with only one solution.

The story was heartrending, poignant, and won both the Hugo and the Nebula that year.

Ellison had been a science-fiction fan when he was younger, put out a fanzine, moved to New York to try and sell to the professional magazines, finally succeeded, moved to Chicago where he edited *Rogue* and helped found *Regency Books*, then—like Beaumont—moved to Hollywood where he wrote the best episode of the original *Star Trek* series ("The City at the Edge of Forever"), and saw a novel of his made into a movie (*A Boy and His Dog*). In Hollywood he picked up more awards and honors than he had fingers and toes.

More disparate people than Charles Beaumont and Harlan Ellison would be hard to imagine. But their professional careers had much in common and in their stories, at least the later ones, their characters are usually average people with whom the reader can identify because it's so easy to find a part of himself in them.

Both Ellison and Beaumont and writers like them helped science fiction grow up. A great story had not only to pique the imagination, it had to touch the heart. But at the time the stories were written, *F&SF* was probably the only science-fiction magazine that would have printed "Jeffty Is Five" and "Gentlemen Be Seated."

Real competition for *Astounding* showed up in the second major digest magazine to appear. The first issue of *Galaxy* was dated October 1950 and was a 160-page monthly. The editor was H. L. Gold who had been a prominent contributor to *Astounding* under his own and various pen names in the late 1930s and 1940s. (He had also been an assistant editor for *Thrilling Wonder Stories*, *Startling Stories*, and *Captain Future*.)

Gold had been a good writer. For *Galaxy* he turned out to be one hell of an editor. The magazine paid well—three cents a word, half again as much as anybody else—and the editorial standards were far broader than Campbell's. Gold would have loved to see his magazine displayed alongside the major slick magazines like *Collier's* and *Saturday Evening Post*, and he edited accordingly. Which meant he was demanding, cajoling, and sometimes rewrote endings without notice to the author. He had a very good idea of what he wanted, and, for the most part, he got it.

The first issue had stories by Clifford Simak, Theodore Sturgeon, Richard Matheson, Fritz Leiber, Isaac Asimov, and Fredric Brown plus a science article by Willy Ley (science articles by Ley were to become a regular feature) and book reviews by Groff Conklin (another noted anthologist). The second issue added Damon Knight with his classic gag story, "To Serve Man" (the aliens arrive with that stated purpose and then are discovered to be carrying a cookbook in their luggage).

GALAXY SCIENCE FICTION
JANUARY 1952
DON SIBLEY

Bester's *The Demolished Man* was one of the most popular serials *Galaxy* published. Portraying a believable version of conversation between telepaths was a nightmare for the typesetters.

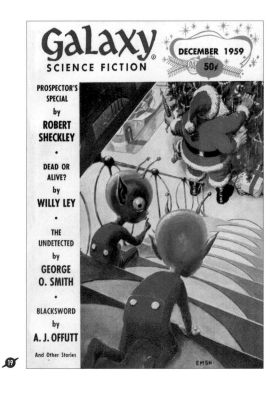

GALAXY SCIENCE FICTION
DECEMBER 1959
ED EMSH

The Christmas cover was an annual tradition. Inside were stories by Robert Sheckley, Philip K. Dick, Frederik Pohl, and Robert Bloch — the editor's Christmas present to his readers.

Nineteen-fifty-one was a stellar year and Campbell finally had something to keep him awake at night. "The Fireman" by Ray Bradbury (Bradbury had sold a lot of stories by this time but had connected with Campbell only once) was a tale about a future in which books are forbidden and a "fireman" is called to burn it when one is discovered. It was a classic story, later expanded to a novel titled *Fahrenheit 451* and filmed by François Truffaut. (In keeping with the story, Truffaut allowed no printed words to appear except "The End.") The cover of the issue was a beautiful painting by Chesley Bonestell illustrating the tying down of a spaceship on Mars in a sandstorm. The reproduction on *Galaxy*'s Kromekote cover stock was spectacularly good.

April saw "The Marching Morons" by C. M. Kornbluth, a satirical story about a world of, well, morons. May had the first cover by Ed Emsh who, along with Kelly Freas, was to become a staple of the science-fiction magazines in the 1950s and 1960s. He shared a Hugo with Hannes Bok in 1953 and won it four more times.

Readers used to associating Robert A. Heinlein's name only with *Astounding* were startled to see his new three-part serial *The Puppet Masters* begin in September. (It was filmed in 1994 under the same title but by then a number of imitations—

"Hollywood haircuts"—had already hit the marquee.) Another three-part serial began a few months later — *The Demolished Man* by Alfred Bester. It was one of the most popular novels *Galaxy* published and won the first Hugo award for Best Novel. A wealthy man commits a murder in a society where murder should be impossible because telepathic policeman can detect the thought before the action. Four years later, Bester was back with *The Stars My Destination*, the sixth most popular science-fiction novel published, according to a poll of the readers of *Locus*.

In one sense, *Galaxy* could be said to have found its niche with the publication of the Bester novels and also with *Gravy Planet* (printed in book form as *The Space Merchants*). A satirical look at the advertising business of the future, it was written by Frederik Pohl and Cyril Kornbluth and set something of a pattern not only for their own collaborations but also for *Galaxy* itself. The magazine was science-fiction light, which didn't mean it lacked action and adventure. But it seldom published "hard science fiction," tending more to the satirical efforts of Pohl and Kornbluth, the "social" novels of Bester and Ted Sturgeon, and the humor of Robert Sheckley.

The old order was changing and the familiar bylines disappearing. Heinlein would still be around, ditto for Asimov and Fritz Leiber, Jr. (In 1958, Leiber would win the Hugo for his novel *The Big Time*). New authors would include Sheckley, Richard Matheson, Cordwainer Smith, Gordon R. Dickson, Algis Budrys, Philip K. Dick, and Larry Niven. And more were to come.

Strangely enough, the Hugo awards for *Galaxy* were relatively few and far between. One of the few short stories that won for *Galaxy* was Harlan Ellison's "'Repent, Harlequin!' Said the Ticktockman," which

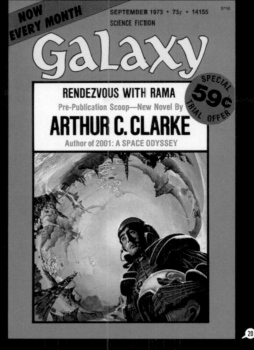

GALAXY SCIENCE FICTION
SEPTEMBER 1973
BRIAN BOYLE

Arthur C. Clarke's *Rendezvous With Rama* was one of his most famous novels and made the *New York Times* best-seller list.

ran away with both the Hugo and the Nebula—an award by the writer's peers in the Science Fiction Writers of America. (Horace Gold was gone by this time—he had been in ill health for some time, and an automobile accident forced his resignation in 1961; Frederik Pohl succeeded him.)

The story takes place in a regimented future where things occur always on time, everything is in its place, and if you're late for work once too often the "Ticktockman" can turn you off. The Harlequin is a man named Everett C. Marm "who had no sense of time." He is, of course, a man intent on sabotaging the society.

The story was well told and admirably suited for *Galaxy*. If it had been submitted to *Analog*, the editor would have wanted the emphasis on the sociology of the society. For *Analog*, sociology was practically a "hard" science (as in the *Foundation* stories by Asimov). If *F&SF* had seen it, they would have preferred to know more about the character of Everett C. Marm and why he rebelled the way he did.

Still, *F&SF* might have taken it. *Analog* definitely would not have (the author's style was too free-wheeling for them). *Galaxy*, which liked satirical, social-science fiction (as opposed to sociological), was the perfect home.

When Frederik Pohl replaced Gold at *Galaxy* (and its companion magazine, *IF*) he resolved to rebuild the magazine (it had lowered its word rates and become a bimonthly). He spent most of his time and energy on *Galaxy*—and was shocked when *IF* earned him three Hugos in a row. It wasn't supposed to happen that way.

Frank Herbert's *Dune Messiah*—the sequel to *Dune*—ran as a four-part serial in the middle of 1969. *Dune* had won both a Hugo and a Nebula but *Dune Messiah* wasn't even nominated.

GALAXY
JULY 1980
LARRY BLAMIRE

Galaxy had a new publisher and was now a companion to that publisher's *Galileo* magazine. This was the one and only issue and a collector's item—it never saw newsstand distribution. Publisher Vincent McCaffrey was (and still is) owner of Boston's popular Avenue Victor Hugo Bookstore.

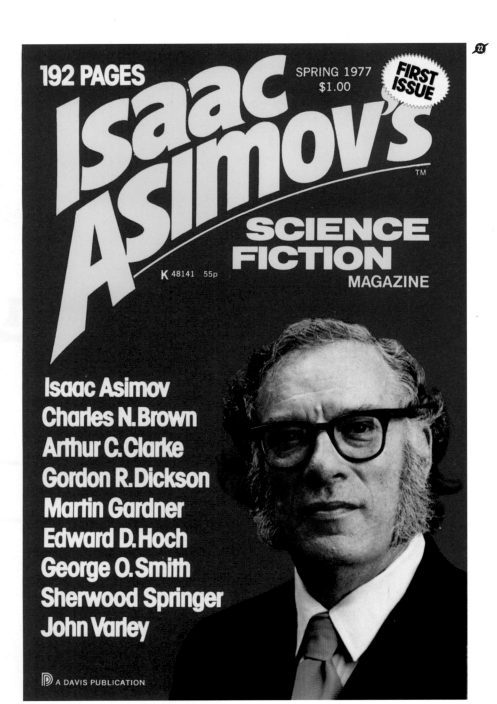

 22

ISAAC ASIMOV'S SCIENCE
FICTION MAGAZINE
SPRING 1977
PHOTOGRAPHER UNKNOWN

The magazine started as a quarterly
with George H. Scithers as the editor,
a photograph of Isaac filling the
cover, and an all-star lineup.

23

ISAAC ASIMOV'S SCIENCE
FICTION MAGAZINE
MAY-JUNE 1978
VINCENT DI FATE

Isaac had retreated to the center of
the "O" and the magazine was now a
bimonthly. Its character wasn't fully
formed yet, but it was obvious the
editor cared a lot about good writing.

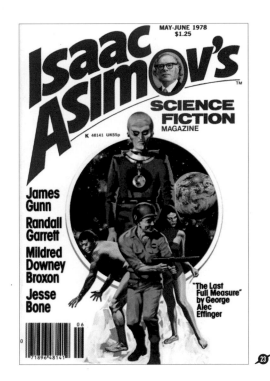

Galaxy and its companion magazines (*IF* and *Worlds of Tomorrow*) were sold in 1969 and Pohl took the opportunity to resign and pursue a career as a freelance editor and full-time writer. The job of editor was taken over by Ejler Jakobsson, an editor for the pulp group Popular Publications in the 1940s and who had succeeded Pohl as editor of *Astonishing* and *Super Science.*

Jakobsson had his triumphs, buying the first stories of a number of new and important authors—George R.R. Martin, Joanna Russ, David Gerrold (later to write "The Trouble With Tribbles" episode for the original *Star Trek* TV series), Joe Haldeman, etc. And the magazine won its share of awards—a Hugo and Nebula for Sturgeon's "Slow Sculpture," a Hugo and Nebula for Isaac Asimov's serial *The Gods Themselves*, a Hugo and Nebula for Arthur C. Clarke's *Rendezvous With Rama*, and a Nebula for Robert Silverberg's *A Time of Changes.*

Despite it all, the magazine's fortunes did not improve. Jakobsson left in 1974, and James Baen, who had been managing editor, took over. The changes were dramatic. *Galaxy* became much more of a "hard science" magazine. Jerry Pournelle, one of the best of the "hard science" writers, had been appointed science writer for *Galaxy* by Jakobsson just before leaving. Pournelle was to become very important to Baen's view of *Galaxy.*

More new authors showed up, including Gene Wolfe, Lisa Tuttle, Fred Saberhagen, and John Varley. Ursula K. Le Guin was nominated for a Hugo and won the Nebula for her short story, "The Day Before the Revolution." And Fred Pohl won both for *Gateway*, the first in his classic series of novels.

Baen left at the end of 1977 for a position with Ace Books (he was eventually to start his own science-

ISAAC ASIMOV'S SCIENCE FICTION MAGAZINE
SEPTEMBER 1979
VINCENT DI FATE
Barry Longyear's novella "Enemy Mine" was later expanded into a novel and filmed—under the same title—starring Dennis Quaid and Louis Gossett, Jr.

fiction publishing company, Baen Books). *Galaxy* went through two more editors, then was sold to the owners of *Galileo* in 1979. Their intention was to revive *Galaxy* as a large-sized bimonthly magazine.

Unfortunately, *Galileo* had its own problems at the time. After having built up a respectable circulation through subscriptions and sales in specialty bookstores, *Galileo* contracted with a distributor to take over its subscriptions and place the magazine on the newsstands.

The experiment had disastrous results, and *Galileo* failed—and along with it *Galaxy*. There was a final issue in 1980 that never saw newsstand distribution and even failed to reach all the subscribers.

The 1950s boom in science-fiction magazines was a fading memory at the launching of still another digest, which would turn out to be one of the most successful and longest lived of all of them.

Isaac Asimov's Science Fiction Magazine (soon to be known simply as *Asimov's*) appeared in the spring 1977. Isaac Asimov was the editorial director, George Scithers the editor, and Gardner Dozois associate editor (Dozois would become the full editor with the January 1986 issue and remains at that post as of this writing—1999). Charles N. Brown, editor and publisher of *Locus*, was the logical choice for the book review column.

The publisher was Davis Publications, headed by Joel Davis, which also published *Ellery Queen's Mystery Magazine* and *Alfred Hitchcock's Mystery Magazine*. To add a science-fiction magazine with an author's name in the title was the obvious way to go. And to use Asimov's name was a no-brainer—he was one of the best-known authors in the field at the time and had also contributed mystery stories to *Ellery Queen.*

(Of historical note is that publisher Joel Davis was the son of Bernard G. Davis, one-time president of the Ziff-Davis Publishing Company which had once published *Amazing Stories* and to which Asimov had sold his first story.)

Asimov contributed his name, a regular editorial, and frequent articles and stories—his name on the magazine apparently did not conflict with his long-running series of science articles for *F&SF*. His editorials were chatty, frequently about the magazine and the various editors he worked with. The bond between Asimov and his readers became a tight one, as tight as the bond had been between Ray Palmer of *Amazing Stories* and *his* readers.

25

**ISAAC ASIMOV'S SCIENCE
FICTION MAGAZINE**
JUNE 1984
WAYNE D. BARLOWE

An outstanding cover to
illustrate an outstanding
story by a new author
—Octavia E. Butler.

Isaac ASIMOV's
SCIENCE FICTION
MAGAZINE

$1.75 JUNE 1984

OCTAVIA E. BUTLER
BLOODCHILD

JAMES PATRICK KELLY

TANITH LEE

VIEWPOINT

ALGIS BUDRYS,
CLARIFYING CLARION

W. Barlowe

0 02648

06

387167

ISAAC ASIMOV'S SCIENCE FICTION MAGAZINE
JANUARY 18, 1982
GEORGE ANGELINI

The magazine now had a more formal appearance, perhaps in keeping with the contents. Asimov's photo had disappeared, but until he died every issue of the magazine carried an editorial with his byline.

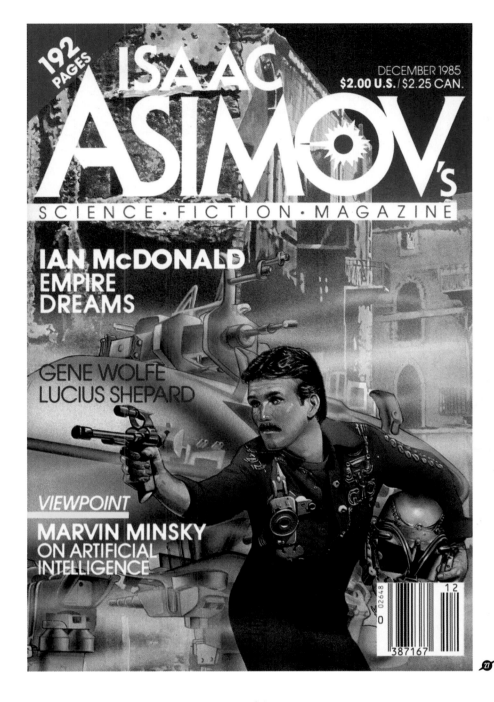

ISAAC ASIMOV'S SCIENCE FICTION
MAY 1989
CHRISTOS ACHILLEOS

A stunning cover by a new artist. A surprise was the editor's willingness to regularly publish poetry—something not seen in a fiction magazine since the days of the old pulp *Argosy*.

ISAAC ASIMOV'S SCIENCE FICTION MAGAZINE
DECEMBER 1985
VAL LAKEY LINDAHN

A new title style and a rare action-adventure cover. The all-star lineup included Gene Wolfe, Lucius Shepard, and Ian McDonald. Marvin Minsky was the world's foremost authority on AI—artificial intelligence.

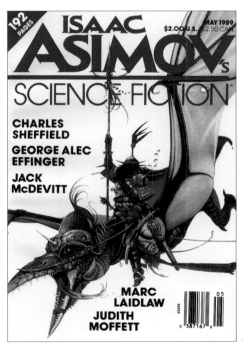

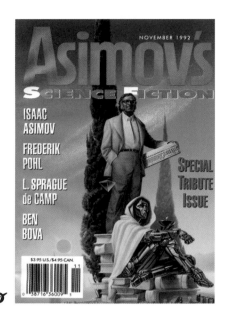

ASIMOV'S SCIENCE FICTION
NOVEMBER 1992
MICHAEL WHELAN

One of the best-loved science-fiction authors in the world had died, and the magazine published a special tribute issue—which included a story by Isaac himself. By now the magazine had acquired a new publisher.

Palmer wrote the same type of chatty editorial, though Asimov was far more self-deprecating than Palmer ever was.

Scithers had been a fan, published a fanzine, was an expert on the fiction of Robert E. Howard, and founded Owlswick Press in 1977. He was to become a science-fiction editorial work horse, editing *Amazing Stories* after leaving *Asimov's* as well as one of the incarnations of *Weird Tales*.

The tone of *Asimov's* was light and optimistic, fantasy was not totally excluded, the "hard science" stories were not all that hard, and it was an inviting market for new writers. In the marketplace, it was welcomed with open arms and became a monthly by 1979. Scithers won the Hugo for Best Professional Editor in 1978 and 1980, and new writer Barry Longyear was to win the John W. Campbell award for Best New Writer. (Longyear's "Enemy Mine" won both a Hugo and a Nebula and was filmed in 1985 to good reviews.)

Scithers—who had been editing the magazine from his home in Pennsylvania—gave up the editorship in 1982, succeeded by Shawna McCarthy for several years and then by Gardner Dozois. McCarthy won the Hugo as Best Professional Editor in 1984 and Dozois (who was Scithers' original associate editor in the beginning) won the Hugo for every year from 1988 through 1998, with the exception of 1994 (Kristine Kathryn Rusch of *F&SF* won for that year).

Writers for *Asimov's* won awards with great regularity: Connie Willis for "Firewatch" and "The Last of the Winnebagos," Greg Bear for "Hardfought," Octavia Butler for "Speech Sounds" and "Bloodchild," and Robert Silverberg for "Sailing to Byzantium" and "Gilgamesh in the Outback." Other award winners included Kate Wilhelm, Lucius Shepard, Orson Scott Card, and Joe Haldeman.

What was significant was that most of the authors winning awards for short fiction in the magazine, were also winning awards for novels that had never appeared in magazines. The old order was changing—a writer's reputation was now made by his books; an award for short fiction was frosting on the cake. It was novels that made an author's reputation; it was novels that paid the bills. And more and more novels were bypassing the magazines altogether to appear first as hardbound books.

Gardner Dozois—as the awards testified—was tops in the field. His editorial policy for *Asimov's* was the least restrictive of all the magazines. As one critic said, for Dozois a story had to be well-written first and science fiction (or fantasy) second—and the definitions for the latter were very broad (especially inviting for new writers, who flocked to *Asimov's*).

Perhaps one of the reasons for Dozois's diversity when it came to picking stories resulted from his other occupation—that of critic and anthologist. He edited a string of anthologies with writer Jack Dann, then took over *The Best Science Fiction Stories of the Year* anthologies from Lester del Rey, and, when that series had run its course, launched another, *The Year's Best Science Fiction*.

Isaac Asimov died in 1992, leaving his magazine in the hands of Gardner Dozois.

Dozois did Asimov proud.

ASIMOV'S SCIENCE FICTION
FEBRUARY 1999
KIM POOR

A new size—slightly—but the same editor (Gardner Dozois), and, as the magazine approached the millennium, the same devotion to story quality that had marked it from the beginning.

FEBRUARY 1999

ASIMOV'S

SCIENCE FICTION

Want to Live Forever?
Are You Willing to
Pay the Price?
Ancient Engines
Michael Swanwick

Tom Purdom
Robert Reed
David Marusek

The Key to Life
or Death Was in
Her Hands...
Living Trust
L. Timmel Duchamp

$2.95 U.S. / $3.75 CAN.

02

0 74820 08621 6

The 1950s were the high point of magazine science fiction. While the pulps slowly withered away, the digests sprouted like weeds. *Galaxy Novel* magazine reprinted classics such as *Sinister Barrier* by Eric Frank Russell, *Odd John* by Olaf Stapledon (probably the most convincing "superman" story ever written), and *Prelude to Space* by Arthur C. Clarke, which was an original novel, not a reprint. *Galaxy Novel* was an obvious attempt to compete with paperbacks but enjoyed only marginal success, eventually becoming a paperback itself. The Galaxy company tried again with *Magabook*—midway between a digest and a paperback and featuring two novels in the same issue, similar to the popular Ace paperback "doubles." It lasted three issues. Probably the most major of the minors was *If Worlds of Science Fiction* (known simply as *IF*). The brain child of twenty-six-year-old Paul Fairman, who had written for the Ziff-Davis pulps, Fairman's only editorial credo was that the magazine be entertaining.

...AND THE MINOR

CHAPTER 7

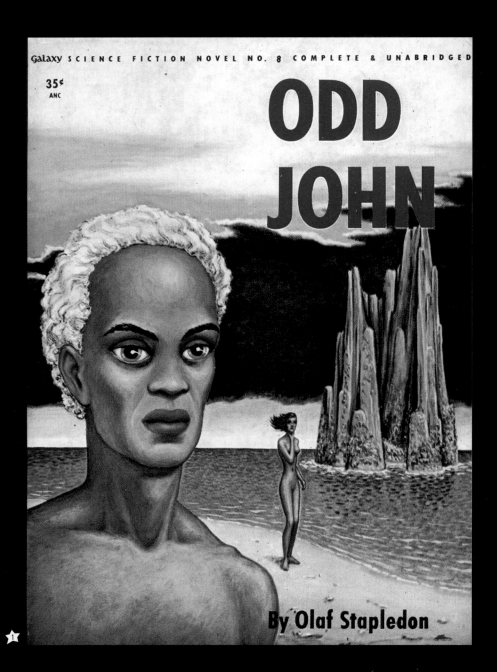

GALAXY SCIENCE FICTION NOVEL NO. 8 COMPLETE & UNABRIDGED

35¢
ANC

ODD JOHN

By Olaf Stapledon

GALAXY NOVEL
NUMBER 8
UNKNOWN

Odd John was the most credible novel of a superman ever written. The first half,
detailing John's "scandalous adolescence"—his observation and manipulation
of the *Homo sapiens* around him—must have repelled readers when the novel
was originally published in 1935.

After four issues (the first was dated March 1952),
Fairman left to become Howard Browne's assistant
at *Amazing*. But for better or for worse, in those
four issues he had shaped the editorial policy of
the magazine.

Publisher James Quinn edited the magazine
himself for a few issues, then hired Larry Shaw, a
well-known fan, as editor. Shaw stayed for a year (his
most memorable editorial selection was "A Case of
Conscience," by James Blish), then left. Quinn did
the editorial chores again for five years, hired
Damon Knight as editor for three issues, then sold
the magazine to Robert Guinn, publisher of *Galaxy*.
Ostensibly, Horace Gold was the new editor but it
was Frederik Pohl who did the serious editorial
heaving and hauling.

IF had always been a neat package with attractive
covers and perfect binding (glue, no staples). It had
also managed to stay afloat during a period when the
number of magazines dropped from a high of forty-
six titles in 1953 to less than a dozen by 1960.

For Fred Pohl, *IF* represented opportunity—
it could serve as a publication for those stories that
weren't quite right for *Galaxy*. Pohl picked up a few
name authors by stringing out the inventory from
Quinn so he could pay a little more for new stories.
He also regarded the magazine as more or less a
"fun" project.

But *Galaxy* was really his baby and was considered
the prestige magazine of the two.

Pohl won three Hugos—1966, 1967, and 1968—
as Best Professional Editor for his work with *IF*.
He was at something of a loss to understand why.
The magazine had managed to go monthly in 1964
(and would remain so until spring 1969) and
somehow—considering Pohl's concentration on
Galaxy—attracted an extraordinary group of authors.

MAGABOOK
1963—NO. 2
ED EMSH

An attempt at innovative publishing—smaller than a digest but larger than a paperback and offering two novels for the price of one.

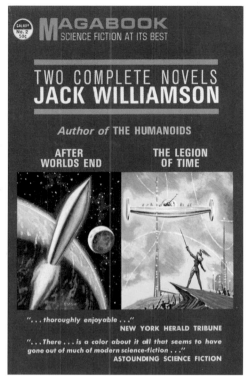

Keith Laumer's "Retief" adventure-oriented stories, ditto Fred Saberhagen's "Berserker" series, Heinlein's *The Moon Is A Harsh Mistress*—one of his best novels, stories by Poul Anderson, Jack Williamson, Arthur C. Clarke, Lester del Rey, Fritz Leiber, Jr., Larry Niven (published first in *IF* with "Neutron Star"), and Kurt Vonnegut, Jr. Pohl even published *Masters of Space* by E. E. "Doc" Smith, the grand old master of space opera.

Pohl was the only one who was surprised when he won three Hugos in a row for editing *IF*. It had been fun, and the fun had showed.

Despite its success, *IF* (along with *Galaxy*) was sold to another publisher in 1969 and Pohl resigned. A few years later the magazine was combined with *Galaxy*. The total run had been 175 issues—one of the longest of all the digests.

Ray Palmer's *Other Worlds* hit the newsstands in late 1949, right after *F&SF*. Palmer had been editing his occult and UFO magazine *Fate* on his lunch hour while still working at Ziff-Davis. He now made the separation complete. For his assistant, Palmer hired a young fan—Bea Mahaffey—who stayed with him until he moved what was left of his magazine operations up to Wisconsin. (When Palmer fell down a flight of basement steps and was seriously injured, Mahaffey took over his duties for a while. She was a more than competent editor in her own right.)

Other Worlds was a thick magazine—160 pages of high-bulk newsprint—and like *IF*, was perfect bound. The lead story in the first issue was "The Fall of Lemuria" by Richard S. Shaver—an in-your-face farewell to Ziff-Davis where he had been forced to soft peddle the "Shaver mystery" during his last years because of the objections of William B. Ziff, chairman of the board.

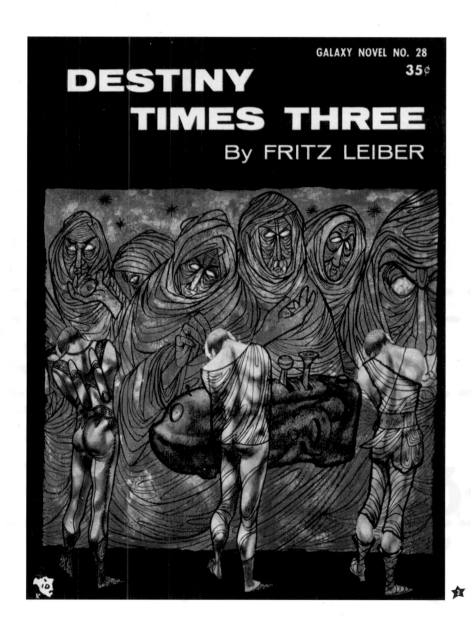

GALAXY NOVEL
NUMBER 28
UNKNOWN

When first published, *Destiny Times Three* was a popular "alternate world" serial in *Astounding* for 1945. This was also one of the last *Galaxy Novels* digests. Effective with No. 32, the magazine became a paperback.

IF
JUNE 1955
KELLY FREAS

Another top-of-its-class digest, soon to become a companion to *Galaxy*.

IF
FEBRUARY 1959
KELLY FREAS

Damon Knight, old-time fan and premiere book critic, was now the editor. The cover by Kelly Freas was one of his zaniest—and best.

IF
NOVEMBER 1968
VAUGHN BODE

A new publisher, a new editor—Frederik Pohl—and a cover by hip cartoonist Vaughn Bode, father of "Cheech Wizard," who won a Yellow Kid Award for his cartooning in 1975.

Palmer's history with *Other Worlds, Universe* and *Science Stories* (at one time or another, all the same magazine) was like that of Eliza clutching her baby to her breast and escaping the snapping creditors by leaping from ice floe to ice floe to cross the river of bankruptcy. Successful at first, his fortunes declined until Palmer had to sell his partnership in *Fate*. His magazines thinned down and payment became erratic if at all (one author recalls writing an entire issue of *Science Stories* for a hundred dollars and a promise to pay more in the sweet by-and-by).

Other Worlds ended as a pulp-sized magazine alternating issues with one titled Flying Saucers. Palmer was reported to own a small printing press in the Wisconsin town of Amherst and operated it himself, doing some work for the University of Wisconsin and putting out *Flying Saucers* and *Other Worlds* when he had the cash.

Palmer had guts, courage, and the single-minded ambition of one who had once been dirt poor. Despite the variable quality of the magazines he published, he loved science fiction. The pity was that he knew good fiction when he read it and had the courage to buck the prevailing trends—but then wasted his courage on the wrong causes.

The type of cause Palmer would have been good at—and conceivably could have made *Other Worlds* a terrific success—was right under his nose. One of the stories he published was a *Harper's* reject by Ray Bradbury. Titled "Way in the Middle of the Air," it related a solution to the race problem in America by African-Americans packing up and migrating to Mars. (Remember, this was the 1950s.) The townspeople who watched them go, suddenly realizing they were going to be without servants and cheap labor, were not lovingly portrayed (a possible reason—aside from it being science fiction—for *Harper's* rejection).

Another story Palmer published was Theodore Sturgeon's "The World Well Lost" in the first issue of *Universe*. It was the first frank treatment of homosexuality in a science-fiction story. Palmer published it because an editor friend had not only rejected the story but had written other editors urging them to reject it as well.

Again, it was "in your face." Since Palmer owned his own publishing company, he could do anything he wanted. He toyed with well-written stories and he toyed with controversy but passed up the chance to make *Other Worlds* the most controversial magazine in the field.

It was the classic "road not taken."

A year after Palmer left Ziff-Davis, one of his editors, William Lawrence Hamling, left to start his own magazine as well. In format, Hamling's *Imagination* mimicked *Other Worlds*. The stories were much like those Hamling had chosen when working for Ziff-Davis.

Imagination soon had its own companion. *Imaginative Tales* was intended to feature Thorne Smith type fantasies by Charles Myers about a "rollicking, ribald" girl named Toffee. Harold McCauley, Chicago's resident pin-up artist, painted the covers in order to provide some visual spice. After two issues, Robert Bloch took over the "rollicking, ribald" chores but by the end of 1955, *Imaginative Tales* had converted to a straight science-fiction magazine.

In 1958—with many of the science-fiction digests falling like flies—the title was changed to *Space Travel*. It didn't help and *Space Travel* died along with *Imagination*. (The slump in the science-fiction titles was partly due to the collapse of the American

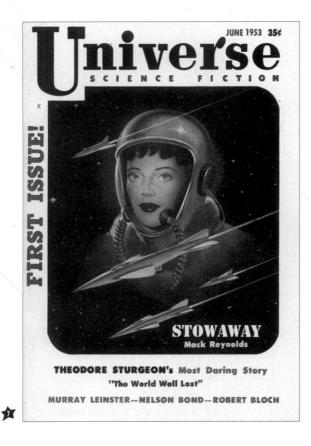

UNIVERSE SCIENCE FICTION
JUNE 1953
MALCOLM H. SMITH
The editor was "George Bell"—a pseudonym for Ray Palmer—and represented a determined effort to break into the first rank of upscale digests, complete with two-color interior illustrations. Sturgeon's story, "The World Well Lost," was one of the first to feature up front gay characters.

News Company, a national distributor that had been bought by speculators for its real estate acquired over half a century.)

Hamling had seen the handwriting on the wall a few years before and entered the "sophisticated men's magazine" market. Hugh Hefner, who had launched *Playboy* in 1953, got Hamling an interview with his distributor. (Hefner and Hamling had once worked together at the same publishing house and even went to each other's parties.) Originally, the plan had been to push a magazine similar to *Stag* or *Male* or any of the other hairy-chested men's magazines. The tentative title was *Caravan*, but when the distributor heard it he asked sarcastically, "What's it going to be about, camels?"

Hamling then suggested *Rogue* and thus was born another clone of *Playboy*—but with some important differences. At one time, Hamling had been a major science-fiction fan with the result that *Rogue* specialized in offbeat fiction, had former science-fiction fans working as editors, and fiction and columns by science-fiction writers Robert Bloch, Alfred Bester, Mack Reynolds, Fred Pohl, Arthur C. Clarke, J.G. Ballard, Fritz Leiber, Robert Silverberg, etc.

By the mid-1950s, almost everybody was putting out a science-fiction magazine. The publishers of *F&SF* took a flyer—twice—with *Venture Science Fiction* before giving up.

Damon Knight edited *Worlds Beyond* with a table of contents for the first issue that included Philip Wylie, Graham Greene, Franz Kafka, and William Seabrook. They were all reprints but an indication of what Knight wanted to buy. The magazine ran three issues but the publisher killed it after the first one; the next two followed only because they were already in the pipeline.

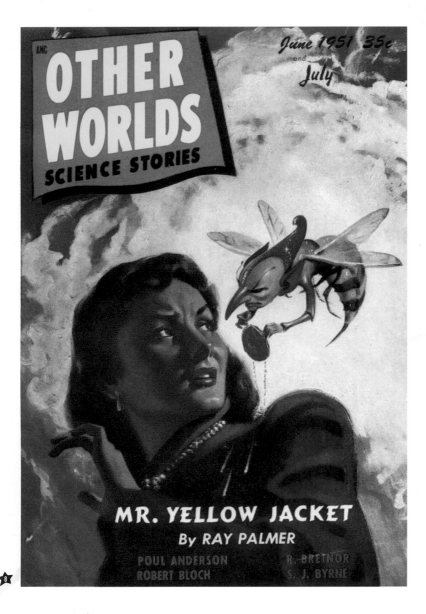

OTHER WORLDS
JUNE & JULY 1951
H. W. MCCAULEY
Raymond A. Palmer, the former editor of *Amazing*, launched *Other Worlds* in late 1949, about the same time as *Fantasy & Science Fiction*. For Palmer, it was an upscale magazine for awhile, publishing stories by Ray Bradbury, Eric Frank Russell, A. E. van Vogt, Friz Leiber, Robert Bloch, etc.

SCIENCE STORIES
OCTOBER 1953
HANNES BOK

The first issue of still another title edited by Ray Palmer (it was probably a retitling of *Other Worlds* which had financial problems with the printers).

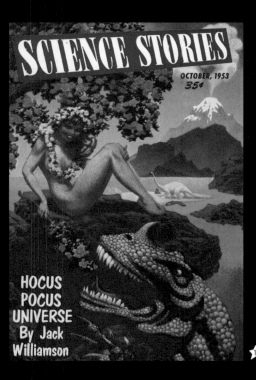

IMAGINATION STORIES OF SCIENCE AND FANTASY
OCTOBER 1950
HANNES BOK

The first issue of a relatively long-lived digest. It looked very much like a Ray Palmer magazine but was actually owned and edited by William L. Hamling, managing editor under Palmer of *Amazing* and *Fantastic Adventures*.

IMAGINATION STORIES OF SCIENCE AND FANTASY
NOVEMBER 1951
PHOTO DYE-TRANSFER PRINT BY MALCOLM SMITH

The magazine had settled into a routine collection of space opera and action stories. This startling cover by Malcolm Smith was one-of-a-kind.

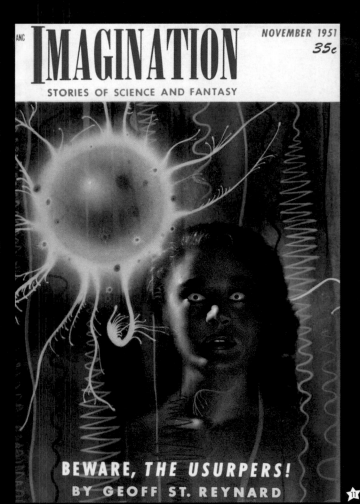

Fantastic Universe, published by Leo Margulies who had been the editorial director of the Thrilling chain of pulp magazines, lasted sixty-nine issues (the last six were pulp size). Name authors occasionally bobbed up in the magazine, including Arthur C. Clarke and Philip K. Dick. But of all the stories it published, perhaps the most famous was "Who?" by Algis Budrys.

Ziff-Davis launched the classiest digest of all, *Fantastic*, in 1952. It had a five-color cover, two-color interiors, and fiction by Bradbury, Asimov, Gold, Walter Miller, Jr., etc. Coming from the publisher of *Amazing Stories* and *Fantastic Adventures*, it was a revelation. The brainchild of editor Howard Browne, it entered a crowded market, and the quality wasn't worth the extra expense. It went through a variety of different editors and was combined with *Amazing* in 1980—after a run of 208 issues.

The publishers of *Galaxy* and *IF* started still another companion magazine, *Worlds of Tomorrow* in spring 1953; it ran until 1971 when it was combined with *IF*. The high point was publication of Philip José Farmer's "Riverworld" series, later rewritten as *To Your Scattered Bodies Go*. The "Riverworld" series had started as a long novel titled *I Owe for the Flesh* which had won first prize in a contest sponsored by Shasta Publishers of Chicago and Pocket Books. Unfortunately, Farmer never saw his prize money. Shasta allegedly spent it on publishing *The Westmore Beauty Book* with plans to pay off the winners of the contest (there were a number of second prizes in addition to the four thousand dollars first prize) once they made a killing on the beauty book. But the book reportedly was printed in two colors and since it was obviously impossible to show the art of makeup with only two colors, the book sold badly.

IMAGINATIVE TALES
SEPTEMBER 1955
H. W. MCCAULEY

A companion magazine that had started as a collection of titillating fantasy stories and ended as a twin of *Imagination.*

14

SPACE TRAVEL
SEPTEMBER 1958
PAUL E. WENZEL

A new title for *Imaginative Tales*, a few two-color illustrations on the inside and an emphasis on space travel didn't help. The magazine died with the next issue.

WORLDS BEYOND
DECEMBER 1950
PAUL CALLE

A mix of reprint and new stories edited by Damon Knight. This first issue carried a tipped-on band plugging "FLYING SAUCER MEN." The magazine lasted three issues, but as far as the publisher was concerned, it was D.O.A.

The year 1953 also saw the publication of *Space Science Fiction*, *Science Fiction Adventures*, and *Rocket Stories* (with a fantasy companion titled *Fantasy Fiction*), all from the same publisher and with the same editor—Lester del Rey. It was the only instance when an entire line of magazines, the lead and all its companions, appeared at roughly the same time. None of them lasted more than eight or nine issues.

After his one-year stint with *IF*, Larry Shaw got another chance to edit science-fiction magazines with *Infinity* and *Science Fiction Adventures* (not to be confused with the earlier magazine of the same name edited by Lester del Rey). Featured on the front cover of the first issue of *Infinity* was Arthur C. Clarke's "The Star," which won the Hugo for Best Short Story. The next issue—February 1956—published Harlan Ellison's first story, "Glow Worm."

Shaw was something of a shy, quiet, and more or less typical science-fiction fan whose first editorial job had been with *Auto Age*. He edited *IF* for a year, then left to resurface as the editor of *Infinity*. The magazine lasted for some twenty issues and was discontinued in 1958 when the boom had definitely started to wind down.

Science Fiction and *Future Fiction* had been reincarnated as pulps in 1950 but converted to digest format in 1953 and 1954. Editor Robert Lowndes did his usual workmanlike job of making bricks from straw, but both magazines were discontinued in 1960, along with the rest of publisher Louis Silberkleit's magazine chain. Silberkleit himself survived with his other enterprise, *Archie Comics*. (Milton Luros, one of the cover artists for the postwar pulp *Science Fiction* and *Future*, had left years before for California, where he founded a major chain of erotic magazines.)

15

FANTASTIC
NOVEMBER 1966
BOB HILBRETH

A new publisher who initially favored
reprints. The Scortia story was new;
the others reprints

FANTASTIC UNIVERSE SCIENCE FICTION
JUNE 1955
KELLY FREAS

A striking cover by Freas for a better-
than-average issue featuring Theodore
Sturgeon, Lester Del Rey, Isaac Asimov,
Robert Sheckley, and Poul Anderson.

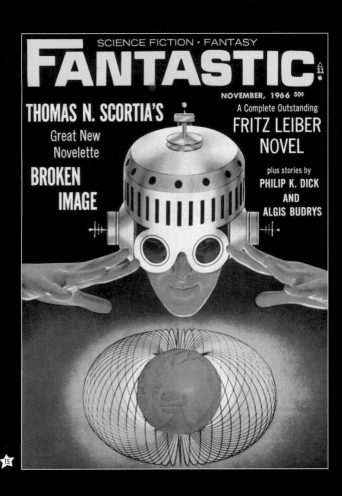

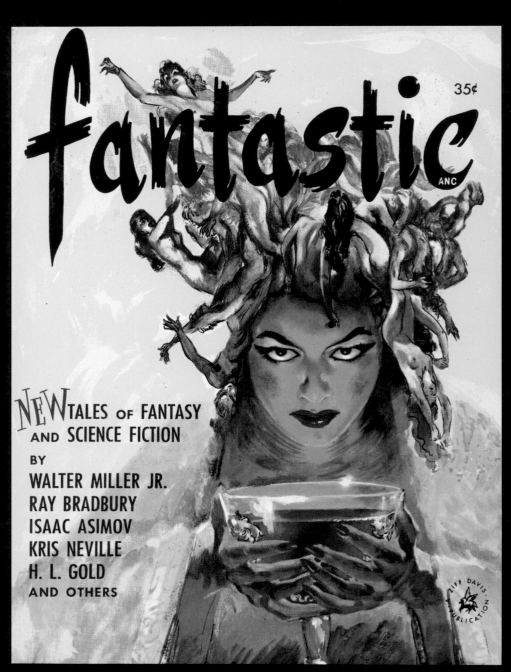

FANTASTIC UNIVERSE SCIENCE FICTION
APRIL 1955
KELLY FREAS

Fantastic Universe lasted for sixty-nine issues,
most of them featuring no interior illustrations.
The cover story for this issue was "Who?" by
Algis Budrys, later expanded into a novel and
nominated for the 1961 Hugo.

FANTASTIC
SUMMER 1952
BARYE W. PHILLIPS AND L.R. SUMMERS

The first issue of a digest magazine for the Ziff-Davis
company. Despite its title, it had little to do with that
company's *Fantastic Adventures*. This was an upscale
digest including a short novel by Raymond Chandler
— *Professor Bingo's Snuff* (a reprint).

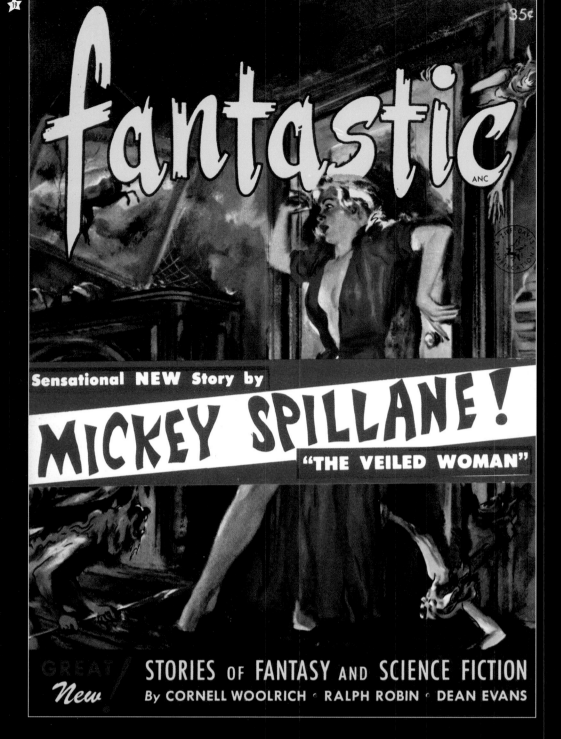

FANTASTIC
NOVEMBER–DECEMBER 1952
BARYE W. PHILLIPS

The third issue probably sold even better than the first two, considering the band around the middle advertising a "sensational new story by Mickey Spillane." At the time, Spillane could have sold millions of copies of the phone book if it had carried his byline.

WORLDS OF TOMORROW
WINTER 1970
JACK GAUGHAN

A new publisher and editor but *Worlds of Tomorrow* wouldn't last many more issues. The cover by Gaughan was one of the most striking ones he painted.

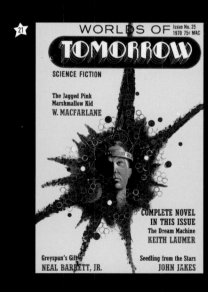

WORLDS OF TOMORROW
APRIL 1963
PEDERSON

The first issue of a companion magazine to *Galaxy* and *IF*. A pricey production job with two-color interior illustrations.

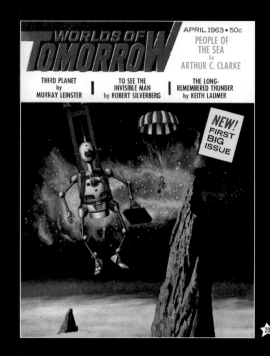

FANTASTIC
MARCH 1974
GLENN MOY

Ted White was now editor and broke his back (and probably heart) trying to breathe life into the magazine while operating on a shoestring. *Frankenstein Unbound* by Brian Aldiss was a major coup.

Leo Margulies, after selling out his share of *Fantastic Universe* to his partner, soon published still another science-fiction digest—*Satellite Science Fiction*. The magazine tried to compete with paperbacks by publishing a long novel plus a few short stories in each issue.

And still the titles came...*Orbit Science Fiction, Saturn Science Fiction* (both edited by Donald Wollheim—Jules Saltman was listed on the masthead of *Orbit* as editor but Wollheim chose the stories), *Cosmos Science Fiction and Fantasy, Star Science Fiction*...The latter was a class magazine published by Ballantine and edited by Fred Pohl to augment its paperback anthology line of *Star Science Fiction Stories* (as a magazine, *Star* lasted only one issue).

Vanguard Science Fiction was another class attempt, edited by James Blish, which also lasted a single issue. *Super-Science Fiction*—definitely *not* a class attempt—lasted for eighteen. Its editor knew little about the field but didn't need to; his chief contributors were Robert Silverberg (thirty-six stories) and Harlan Ellison (ten) with a scattering of other authors. *Super-Science Fiction* was one of the last of the digests of the boom of the 1950s—it started in 1956 when there were approximately twenty-six titles and died in 1959 when (according to an estimate by Fred Pohl) there were perhaps a dozen.

New digest titles continued to appear from time to time—*Gamma* in 1963, *Unearth* in 1977 dedicated to publishing authors who had never been published before and which scored a home run with "Fragments of a Hologram Rose," William Gibson's first published story. Gibson, one of the founders of the "cyberpunk" school, later wrote *Neuromancer*, "Johnny Mnemonic"

(filmed in 1995 with heavy input from digital computer artists Rick Berry and Darrell Anderson), and *Count Zero*.

Science Fiction Digest, a companion to *Asimov's*, was not your usual "digest"—rather than condense books, it presented excerpts. It lasted four issues; readers apparently preferred to buy the complete book.

During this period, Davis Publications—publishers of *Analog* and *Asimov's*—issued a series of anthologies and "one-shots." Probably the most ambitious was *Asimov's Space of Her Own*, an anthology of—and tribute to—women writers of science fiction.

But most of the boom was over by the end of the 1950s. It had largely coincided with the boom in science-fiction movies and that boom had died as well. *2001, Star Wars, Star Trek*, science-fiction television shows, and the special effects extravaganzas of George Lucas and Stephen Spielberg and Ridley Scott and James Cameron were in the future.

As well as an astonishing boom in hardcover science-fiction novels.

In any critical overview—especially of a genre as heavily analyzed as science fiction—there's a distressing tendency to use the word "classic" all too freely. Granted that Shakespeare wrote for the groundlings, that Charles Dickens was immensely popular with the masses, that Edgar Rice Burroughs with "Tarzan" and A. Conan Doyle with "Sherlock Holmes" will outlive Tom Wolfe and Norman Mailer.

But art is frequently the handmaiden of commerce, and none of the aforementioned authors sat down

★
ROCKET STORIES
SEPTEMBER 1953
CIVILETTI

A companion magazine to
*Space Science Fiction. Rocket
Stories* was intended to
specialize in space opera.

with quill pen, typewriter, or computer with the
deliberate intention of writing a "classic." Neither
did the science-fiction writers of the 1950s (or those
who came after, for that matter). They wrote in order
to buy food and pay the rent. Few of them came close
to getting rich.

The digests of the 1950s were a microcosm of the
pulps in the 1930s and 1940s. A hurly-burly of writers
working late into the night, of discussing story ideas
with an editor and then producing the story a week
or perhaps a day later. Word rates ranged from a
penny per word to three cents and for most writers,
how much you made depended on how much you
produced. Writing science fiction in the 1950s meant
scrambling for sales in a market overcrowded with
magazines—but also overcrowded with writers.

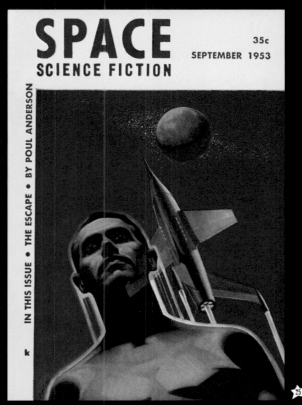

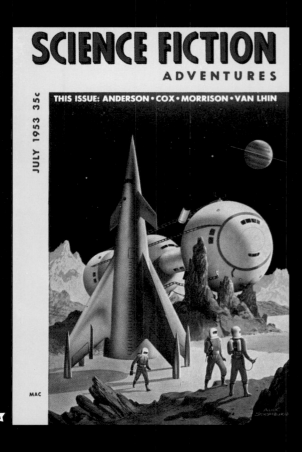

★
SCIENCE FICTION ADVENTURES
JULY 1953
ALEX SCHOMBURG

Another Lester del Rey edited companion to *Space
Science Fiction* and *Rocket Stories*. Though it was intended
for a younger audience, editor Lester del Rey insisted on
upgrading both the writing and the ideas involved.

★
SPACE SCIENCE FICTION
SEPTEMBER 1953
CIVILETTI

The issue contained
Philip K. Dick's novel
The Variable Man,
complete. Dick was
known for his innovative
ideas and skill as a writer
but had yet to achieve
outstanding fame.

INFINITY SCIENCE FICTION
NOVEMBER 1955
ROBERT ENGLE

The first issue of another science-fiction title during the boom of the 1950s. Arthur C. Clarke won a Hugo for his story "The Star" and Damon Knight won one for his role as book critic. Old-time fan Larry Shaw was the editor (he'd also briefly been the editor of *IF*).

INFINITY SCIENCE FICTION
FEBRUARY 1956
ED EMSH

The second issue was remarkable—stories by Charles Beaumont (who was to become a *Twilight Zone* regular), L. Sprague de Camp, Damon Knight, Frederik Pohl & C. M. Kornbluth, and a newcomer—Harlan Ellison—with his first published story, "Glow Worm."

Perhaps the best one to summarize what it was like back then was Harlan Ellison, at the end of the century A Man for All Seasons when it came to writing but back in the 1950s a young author working for the rent. In Harlan's own words:

NAKED DERANGED PSYCHO THRILL—DEMON or.
BITCH—SLUT GUN—CRAZY HOMICIDAL RAT
by Harlan Ellison

I loved W. W. Scott. He was the editor of a trio of digest-sized, determinably lowbrow, detective story and science fiction magazines during the mid-Fifties. They were called Guilty *and* Trapped *and* Super-Science Fiction, *and they invariably sported covers on which desperate men were menacing women with their skirts hiked to their thighs, their blouses ripped to expose milky cleavage, and a look of utter terror at the gun, rope or blowtorch held by the desperate men...*

Or...

Covers on which exquisite but desperate women with their skirts hiked to their thighs and their blouses ripped to expose milky cleavage, menace men who looked with utter terror at the gun, knife, rope or blowtorch held by the desperate women.

The incomparably fascinating thing about Bill Scott was his naked lust for publishing even the most ordinary stories under titles so violent and demented that Kafka or Sacher-Masoch would have given him a standing ovation for sensationalism.

I was only a year or three into my professional career as a writer. It was a swell time to be living in New York; what I'm told was the last really wonderful period for the city.

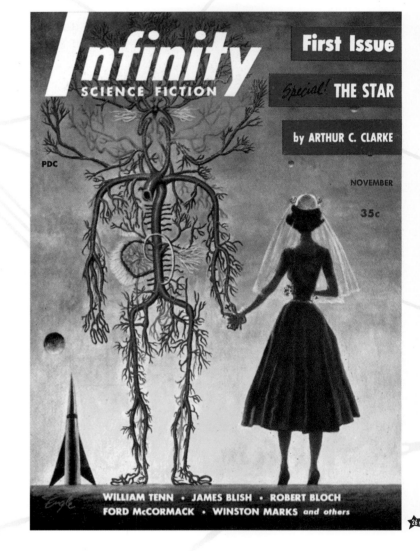

SCIENCE FICTION ADVENTURES
JUNE 1957
ED EMSH

A companion magazine for *Infinity*, not to be confused for the magazine of the same name that was a companion magazine to *Space Science Fiction*. It featured two or three short adventure novels per issue.

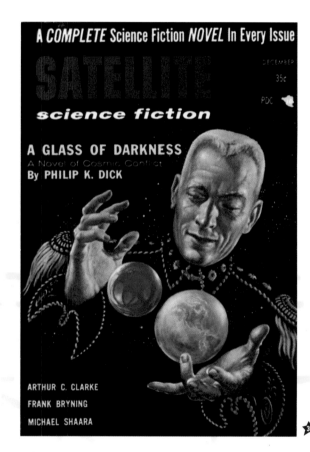

FUTURE SCIENCE FICTION
OCTOBER 1954
KELLY FREAS

The digest version of the old pulp *Future Fiction*. Robert A. W. Lowndes, the editor, was an expert at putting out low-cost magazines with a veneer of quality.

SATELLITE SCIENCE FICTION
DECEMBER 1956
KELLY FREAS

Satellite's "book-length" novels really were book length —an attempt to compete with paperbacks at the time. *Satellite* lasted eighteen issues, the last four large size. Its more successful mystery companion, *Mike Shayne Mystery Magazine*, lasted for 300.

AUG.
25¢

Marvel
SCIENCE
FICTION

SEED
NEW NOVEL BY
RAYMOND F. JONES

VAN VOGT NEVILLE LEINSTER PHILLIPS LATHAM MERRIL TENN LEY

MARVEL SCIENCE FICTION
AUGUST 1951
HANNES BOK

A short-lived digest version of the old pulp *Marvel Science Stories*. It was generally unmemorable except for this knock-out cover by Hannes Bok.

It was the last days of the pulp magazines. Most of them had long-since given way to the slicks, the paperback originals, and the digest-sized magazines. But if you wrote hard, and you wrote fast, you could eke out a decent living at a penny-a-word. That meant writing detective stories this week, science fiction next week, a western for Doc Lowndes at 1/2 cent a word on publication and an "exposé" for one of the imitations of Confidential *the week after that. It was always hand-to-mouth, but the subway was 15 cents a token; a big spaghetti dinner at the Ronzoni near Times Square was a buck; paperback books were just testing the waters at 35 cents, up from a quarter; you could get a good seat for the matinée performance of* My Fair Lady *or Leonard Bernstein's* Candide *for about five dollars; and every night for the price of a couple of glasses of seltzer water, you could hang out in one of the jazz clubs and listen to Dizzy, Count Basie, the MJQ or*

THE ORIGINAL SCIENCE FICTION STORIES
NOVEMBER 1958
ED EMSH

The digest incarnation of an older pulp science-fiction magazine. A companion to *Future* and also edited by Robert A. W. Lowndes.

ORBIT SCIENCE FICTION
NOVEMBER–DECEMBER 1954
ALEX SCHOMBURG

Still another short-lived magazine but better than average, probably because Donald A. Wollheim—then working for Ace paperbacks—actually chose the stories. August Derleth was a regular contributor as was Charles Beaumont before Beaumont moved on to the decidedly greener pastures of *Playboy*.

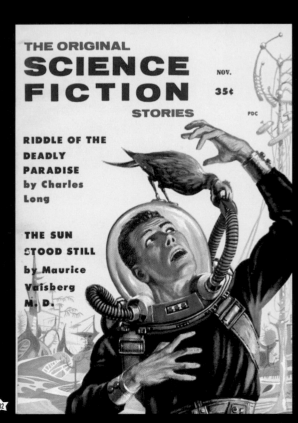

THE ORIGINAL
SCIENCE
FICTION
STORIES

NOV.
35¢

RIDDLE OF THE
DEADLY
PARADISE
by Charles
Long

THE SUN
STOOD STILL
by Maurice
Vaisberg
M. D.

ORBIT
Science Fiction

THE LAST OF
THE MASTERS
by Philip K. Dick

James Causey, August Derleth,
Gordon R. Dickson, Chad Oliver

No. 5 • 35¢

even Bird (who was working with this interesting sideman, Miles Davis).

We didn't realize what a ducky time it was.

Probably because all of us were hustling as fast as we could just to make ends meet. And when you found a new market, you kept it to yourself till you'd become a part of the stable that produced the bulk of fiction they needed. And then you told your buddies.

That was the situation with Crestwood Publishing, the prototypical schlock New York publishing company. There were many little shops like Crestwood during the Fifties. Some of them got the entire contents of their magazines in a package from Scott Meredith's agency, essentially a closed market unless you happened to be represented by Meredith. Others bought "over the transom" and didn't much care about quality. And then there were the hole-in-the-wall companies like Crestwood, uptown at 1790 Broadway, just before you hit the park.

How I found out they were starting up a string of digest-sized fiction magazines, I don't remember. But I went down from west 82nd (between Amsterdam & Columbus) one afternoon, and I met W.W. Scott, and overnight I wrote a fast hardboiled story for him, and Scott liked it…and I was home free.

I contributed three, maybe four or five, stories a month to the mystery magazines. Scott took 'em all. Ran 'em under a plethora of bylines—Jay Charby, Landon Ellis, Cordwainer Bird, Ellis Hart, Jay Solo— and between Robert Silverberg and myself, we could glut the entire table of contents. (Not to mention the other stories I was writing for the sf magazine and the semi-slick men's adventure magazine Crestwood published.)

It was a bonanza. Bill Scott paid two cents a word, often three cents; and the check was instant. I could stay up all night writing a 7000 word crime novelette,

take it in the next morning, Scotty would read it while I waited, and if it was a go he'd get the bookkeeper to cut me a check for a hundred and forty on the spot. And I'd rush home and pay the rent.

The stories for Guilty and Trapped were straight out of the Manhunt school (For those born too late to remember Manhunt, it was to hardboiled crime fiction of the Fifties what EQMM has been to the more literary aspects of mystery fiction since its inception. It was a tough, utterly unsentimental magazine in digest-size, and it paid terrific wages for that time. Everybody wanted to hit Manhunt. Not only because it was a saucy payday, but because they commanded all the headliners—Craig Rice, Mickey Spillane, Evan Hunter, Richard Prather, Hal Ellson. To be found in that company meant you had arrived.) They were usually one-punch stories, gritty and streetwise, very much of the period and loaded with stereotypes. But the Crestwood books were identifiable from all the others, particularly Manhunt, by the derangement of W. W. Scott's penchant for blood-drenched titles.

"I'll See You in Hell!"	*"The Cheap Tramp"*
"Die Now, My Love"	*"Kill Them One by One"*
"This Is Your Death"	*"Make Me a Widow"*
"Kooch Dancer"	*"Naked on the Highway"*

These were the least of Bill Scott's inventions. Silverberg and I would make our trips regularly to the Crestwood offices; and because we lived near each other, we would schlep each other's stories in. If I was working, and Bob was going down to see Scott about something, he'd take my latest novelette. If I had a check to pick up, I'd stop by and grab Bob's latest offering, and deliver it. And we'd always pick up copies of the latest issues of Guilty and Trapped or Super-Science Fiction in which the yarns we'd written just six weeks earlier were already in print.

And we would marvel at how Scotty had retitled us.

SATURN SCIENCE FICTION AND FANTASY
MARCH 1958
UNKNOWN

Short-lived as a science-fiction magazine (it enjoyed another reincarnation as a detective magazine and then a horror magazine), *Saturn* was edited by Donald A. Wollheim. In its five issues it published a surprising number of good authors including John Brunner, Robert Heinlein, and Harlan Ellison.

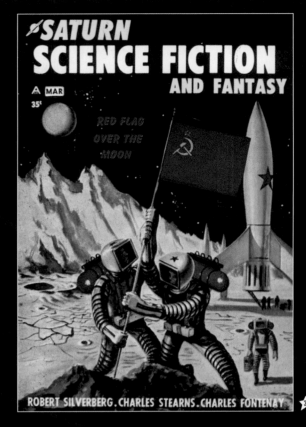

COSMOS SCIENCE FICTION AND FANTASY MAGAZINE
SEPTEMBER 1953
UNKNOWN

The first issue of another short-lived magazine. It boasted a remarkable line-up for a minor magazine.

STAR SCIENCE FICTION
JANUARY 1958
RICHARD POWERS

Star Science Fiction Stories originally appeared as a Ballantine paperback anthology in the early 1950s to promote Ballantine authors. As a magazine, *Star Science Fiction* was a one-shot but reappeared some months later—again as a paperback. Frederik Pohl edited both the magazine and the paperback anthologies and paid a nickel a word—a small fortune then.

SUPER-SCIENCE FICTION
DECEMBER 1957
KELLY FREAS

In its lifetime, *Super-Science Fiction* published 120 stories, thirty-six of them by Robert Silverberg and ten by Harlan Ellison under their own and various pen names. (Robert Bloch's name is misspelled on the cover and the front cover painting, credited to Kelly Freas, was probably by Ed Emsh.)

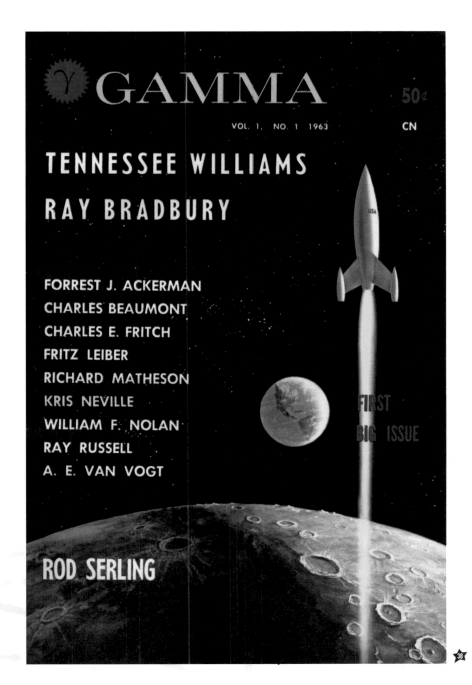

GAMMA
1963
MORRIS SCOTT DOLLENS

A short-lived digest out of Los Angeles. It featured media-oriented writers such as Charles Beaumont, Ray Bradbury, Rod Serling (in an interview), George Clayton Johnson, Richard Matheson, and Forrest J Ackerman (no period after "J"). The editor was William F. Nolan, co-author of *Logan's Run*. The Tennessee Williams story—"The Vengeance of Nitocris," originally published when the author was seventeen—was a reprint from a 1928 *Weird Tales*.

VANGUARD SCIENCE FICTION
JUNE 1958
ED EMSH

Vanguard was edited by writer James Blish who had high hopes for it as an upscale digest. Unfortunately, the boom in digest magazines was nearly over, and the magazine saw only one issue.

Since we had written so many stories, and since we didn't know in what order Scott was using them, we would try to figure out which story titled "Psycho Killer" was the one we'd titled "Last Dream Before Morning."

But "Horror in the Night" and "Blackmail Girl" were pale offerings. When Bill Scott was at full flower he could warp the English language so demonically, we were left in awe.

It got be a matter of pride with us, to see if we could anticipate his thinking, cobble up a title so redolent of decay and corruption that Scotty wouldn't change it. He would sit there and read one of these monstrous fables, a small pear-shaped man who affected a green celluloid eyeshade, like a faro dealer, and when he had finished it, he would titter briefly, look up sweetly from under the eyeshade and say, "That's a nice little story." Rape, pillage, murder, arson, corruption, disfigurement, loathsomeness…they were "sweet little stories" to the amazing Bill Scott. But no matter how good the title was, he would line it out with his red pencil and scribble in something as deranged as a fruit-bat.

I thought I'd finally hit the mother lode of this titling lunacy, when I wrote a story called "Thrill Kill!" Now, tell me, can you think of anything more perfect than that? I was in heaven. Silverberg gave me a high-five. I'd finally beaten W.W. Scott at his own caper. I submitted the story, and he bought it on the spot. "Sweet little story," he said.

And he published it as "Homicidal Maniac."

I gave up. There are Masters; and there are those who will always be Salieri.

For the curious, representative titles from *Super-Science Fiction* include "Psycho at Mid-Point" (by Harlan), "The Aliens Were Haters" (by Silverberg), "Monsters That Once Were Men," "Creatures of Green Slime," "Vampires From Outer Space," "Planet of Parasites," and "Pariah Girl."

The titles got worse as the magazine went on. After eighteen issues, *Super-Science Fiction* wasn't discontinued; it drowned in a sea of its own gore.

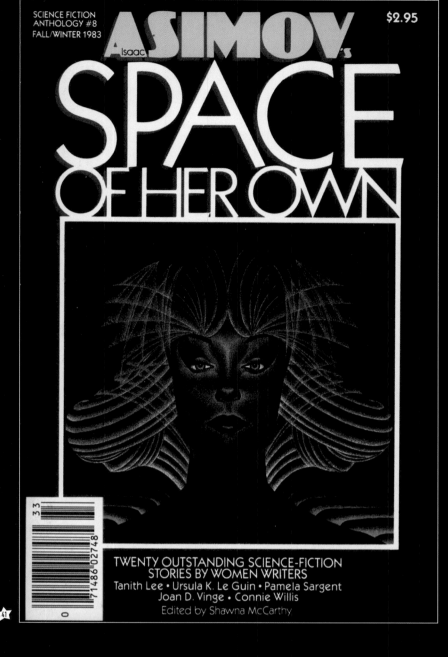

SCIENCE FICTION
ANTHOLOGY #8
FALL/WINTER 1983

$2.95

Isaac ASIMOV's
SPACE OF HER OWN

TWENTY OUTSTANDING SCIENCE-FICTION
STORIES BY WOMEN WRITERS
Tanith Lee • Ursula K. Le Guin • Pamela Sargent
Joan D. Vinge • Connie Willis
Edited by Shawna McCarthy

JANUARY/FEBRUARY 1982 $1.95 CC

SCIENCE
FICTION DIGEST

Featuring excerpts—in the author's own words—of the
best in current fantasy, horror, occult, speculative and science fiction.

THE SILVER   THE KEEP   LITTLE, BIG
METAL LOVER   F. PAUL   JOHN
TANITH LEE   WILSON   CROWLEY

CUJO
STEPHEN KING
#1 BEST SELLER

DAVIS

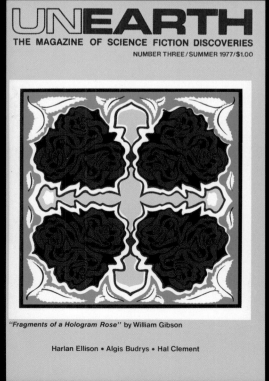

UNEARTH
THE MAGAZINE OF SCIENCE FICTION DISCOVERIES
NUMBER THREE/SUMMER 1977/$1.00

"Fragments of a Hologram Rose" by William Gibson

Harlan Ellison • Algis Budrys • Hal Clement

41

ASIMOV'S SPACE OF HER OWN
FALL/WINTER 1983
UNKNOWN

At one time, women science-fiction writers were a rarity. This anthology included stories by twenty women authors ranging from Ursula K. Le Guin and Tanith Lee to Pamela Sargent and Connie Willis. The big explosion of digest science-fiction magazines in the 1950s was now a fading memory; by the 1980s there were less than ten.

42

SCIENCE FICTION DIGEST
JANUARY/FEBRUARY 1982
PHOTO: JILL KREMENTZ

Science Fiction Digest specialized in "stand-alone" excerpts. It lasted four issues, then died when readers decided it was foolish to buy excerpts when they were probably going to buy the full novel anyway.

43

UNEARTH
SUMMER 1977
MARTHA FLOOD

Subtitled "The Magazine of Science Fiction Discoveries," *Unearth* specialized in unpublished authors. The magazine discovered a number of talented new writers and hit the jackpot with "Fragments of a Hologram Rose" by William Gibson, who would later write the classic cyberpunk novel *Neuromancer*.

THE BIG
AND THE BRITISH

CHAPTER 8

Bigger Is Not Always Better Ever since the first issue of *Amazing* in 1926, there had been something of a mystique about magazines published in the large size. Gernsback kept going back to it and from time to time, new publishers (and sometimes established ones) have tried new titles and old in the large format. The reason had always been two-fold—greater exposure on the newsstand and the increased opportunity for advertising. *Analog* tried the large size several times. The first, under the title of *Astounding*, in 1942-43 and again—as *Analog*—in 1963-65. The paper shortage killed the experiment the first time, the lack of interest on the part of advertisers the second. (There was very little chance of new publishers adopting the old pulp size—W.F. Hall and Cuneo Press, the largest printers of the old pulps, had long ago junked their letterpress equipment designed for printing pulps.)

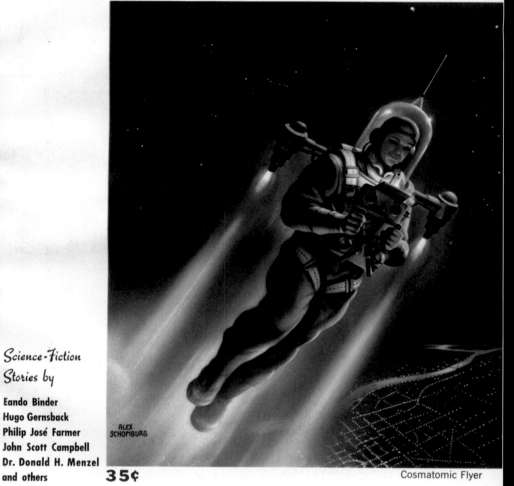

MARCH 1953

HUGO GERNSBACK, *Editor*

Science-Fiction PLUS

preview of the future

Science-Fiction
Stories by

Eando Binder
Hugo Gernsback
Philip José Farmer
John Scott Campbell
Dr. Donald H. Menzel
and others

35¢

Cosmatomic Flyer

THE MAGAZINE OF SCIENCE FICTION

MIND CONTROL DEVICES · HEINLEIN ON SCIENCE FICTION·THE FUTURE OF ORGAN TRANSPLANTS · THEORY AND PRACTICE OF TIME TRAVEL·

Ray Bradbury
Robert Silverberg
Larry Holden
Harry Harrison
Larry Niven
Herman Wrede

Gregory Benford
Ed Bryant
Terry Carr
Harlan Ellison
William Rotsler
Forry Ackerman

VOLUME ONE/NUMBER ONE/ $1.50 PM#51

❶ SCIENCE-FICTION PLUS
MARCH 1953
ALEX SCHOMBURG

A slick paper, large-size magazine with Gernsback as publisher and old-time fan Sam Moskowitz as the editor. But *Science-Fiction Plus* looked like a 1950s version of Gernsback's old *Science and Invention* and lasted only seven issues.

❷ VERTEX
APRIL 1973
VINCENT DI FATE

Vertex was the first true slick science-fiction magazine aimed at a general audience. William Rotsler, a writer and fan artist, was the "visual coordinator." The magazine was upscale in both appearance and content.

❸ VERTEX
JUNE 1975

A paper shortage that had become acute by 1975 forced the publisher to try a tabloid format. The tabloid *Vertex* failed after three issues, though the magazine lasted for sixteen overall. During its short life it had showcased Larry Niven, Jerry Pournelle, Spider Robinson, George R. R. Martin, and John Varley among others.

But that still didn't kill the interest of other publishers, though for most of them the possibility of major advertising was remote.

The first large-size magazine to appear after *Astounding* was published by, of all people, Hugo Gernsback. Word was that Gernsback, backstage at the 1952 World Science Fiction Convention in Chicago where he was guest of honor, counted the audience out front and when he got to a thousand decided the time was ripe for another shot of the Good Old Stuff.

The title was *Science-Fiction Plus*, a monthly, sixty-four-page slick paper magazine. The covers were by Alex Schomburg and Frank R. Paul (both dating back to Gernsback's long ago *Science and Invention*). Hugo wrote the editorial and contributed a long novelette and a "story behind the cover" by "Greno Gashbuck." As usual, his name was also on the cover as editor (though fan and genre historian Sam Moskowitz did the story picking).

The appearance of the magazine, and many of the stories, could best be described as "back to the future." It was a strange, retro magazine for the period. Sales were a crushing disappointment to Gernsback who must have thought his return to the field would be greeted with open arms. The magazine saw seven issues and then was interred without honors.

Vertex was a different story. A conscious attempt at an adult, slick-paper science-fiction magazine the first issue featured a cover by Vincent Di Fate and articles and/or fiction by Bradbury, Silverberg, Niven, Gregory Benford, Ellison, and others. It was a first-class job of layout and design, with writer/artist and long-time fan Bill Rotsler as "visual coordinator."

The first issue in 1973 was a hundred-page bi-monthly magazine from Mankind Publishing Co.,

also responsible for a competitor—*Mankind*—to *The American Heritage*. The company, in turn, was a subsidiary of Holloway House which published *Adam, Knight, Cad* and a gaggle of other girly magazines. But never mind, their heart was in the right place. (As of the late 1990s the company was a well-respected publisher of African-American fiction, primarily in paperback format.)

Unlike many science-fiction magazines toward the end of the century, which enjoyed substantial subscription lists but sold poorly on the newsstands, for *Vertex* it was the opposite. The magazine reportedly sold as high as eighty percent of its print run on the newsstands but had difficulty maintaining strong subscription sales.

Content wise, the magazine printed John Varley, Spider Robinson, George R.R. Martin, and a number of other new writers in addition to Heinlein and Ellison and Silverberg. But no good deed shall go unpunished, and the slick-paper *Vertex* died in 1975 issue because of another paper shortage. The paper was needed for *Adam* and *Knight* and other magazines in the company that made a good deal more money than *Vertex* did. Three newsprint tabloid issues appeared and then the magazine was gone for good. (The tabloid issues, fragile to begin with and prone to browning when exposed to sunlight, are now collector's items.)

Galileo was another magazine that should have made it but didn't. A hundred page pulp paper quarterly, it had none of the glitz and slickness of *Vertex* but was a solid, enjoyable magazine with a mix of new and established writers. Published by Vincent McCaffrey (owner of Boston's Avenue Victor Hugo Bookstore) with Charles C. Ryan as editor, it started

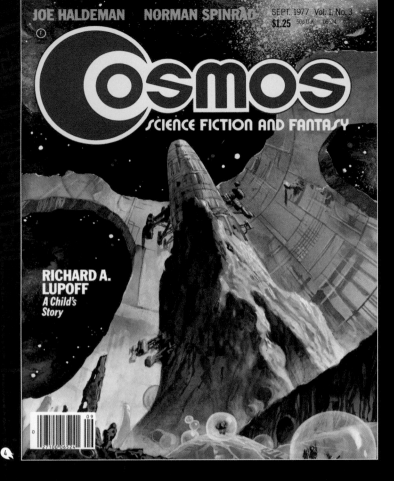

with a national distributor for newsstand distribution. Sadly, newsstand sales of *Galileo*, predicted at forty percent of the press run, failed even to come close. The last issue was never fully distributed, the newly purchased *Galaxy* never got off the ground. The total run for *Galileo* was fifteen issues. A few issues before the end, when optimism was still the order of the day, the magazine announced an increase in word rates and began the serialization of Larry Niven's *The Ringworld Engineers*, the sequel to Niven's popular *Ringworld*. Fortunately for readers, the last issue managed to include the final installment.

About the same time as *Galileo*, *Cosmos Science Fiction and Fantasy* joined the galaxy of science-fiction magazines. *Cosmos* had fewer pages than *Galileo*—only seventy-two—but they included eight full-color pages. Edited by David Hartwell, one of the more accomplished book editors in the field, it conceivably could have gone places. Authors included Fritz Leiber, Brian Aldiss, Larry Niven, Joe Haldeman, and Richard Lupoff.

It failed after four issues—a companion magazine in a different field had gone down the tubes, and *Cosmos* wasn't capable of supporting the entire company by itself.

Asimov's SF Adventure Magazine had good bloodlines but it, too, failed after four issues. Intended as an "adventure" companion to the digest *Asimov's*, not even Isaac's name could help. The first issue of fall 1978 was 120 pages—the most of any of the large-size magazines—including a bound-in four-color "poster." The layout was attractive, the usual editorial by Asimov was present, and the roster of authors included Poul Anderson, Harry Harrison, L. Sprague de Camp, John Brunner, David Gerrold, and Barry Longyear.

slowly. The first issue printed eight thousand copies and sold primarily through specialty bookstores and small distributors.

The next year the magazine went bimonthly, and by 1978 *Galileo* had a circulation of 56,000. Not bad for a new kid on the block. The bulk of the circulation was in direct subscriptions, a difficult chore for a bookstore owner to handle. A professional subscription agency was hired, and trouble began immediately. The agency was inept, its new computer system failed miserably, and subscriptions suffered a dramatic decline. To make up for the loss, McCaffrey signed

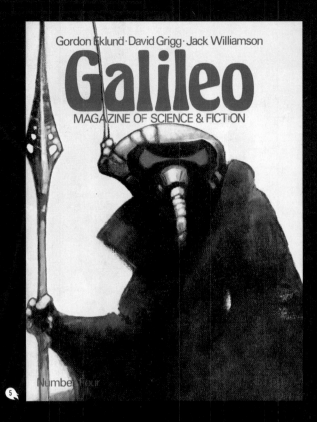

GALILEO MAGAZINE OF SCIENCE & FICTION
JULY 1977
TOM BARBER

A magazine that should have made it—but didn't. At the start, publisher Vincent McCaffrey restricted distribution to subscriptions and specialty bookstores. When he hit 56,000 subscriptions, he hired a computerized agency to handle them. The experiment was a disaster, as was his decision to try newsstand sales. The magazine failed after fifteen issues.

⑥

ASIMOV'S SF ADVENTURE MAGAZINE
FALL 1979
STEPHEN E. FABIAN

Intended as an action/adventure companion to the more literate *Asimov's*, the magazine had a run of four issues. Asimov's editorial in this last issue was unfortunately titled: "The Boom in Science Fiction."

⑦

ODYSSEY
SPRING 1976
KELLY FREAS

The first issue of another large-sized magazine, this time printed on pulp paper. Anthologist Roger Elwood was editor. Poor production values and inadequate distribution contributed to *Odyssey's* death after two issues.

SCIENCE FICTION AGE
SEPTEMBER 1998
JOHN BERKEY

Six years after the first issue *Science Fiction Age* showed no decline in quality. If anything, its ties to media (films, TV, gaming) had increased and healthy advertising revenue continued to make the magazine profitable.

TOMORROW SPECULATIVE FICTION
FEBRUARY 1994
RON AND VAL LAKEY LINDAHN

The editor was Algis Budrys, an acclaimed author and later editorial director of Writers of the Future. *Tomorrow* encouraged new writers but never expanded beyond its base of subscriptions and sales through specialty bookstores. It finally became an Internet magazine.

ABORIGINAL SCIENCE FICTION
1988 ANNUAL ANTHOLOGY
CARL LUNDGREN

Aboriginal, edited by Charles C. Ryan who had once edited *Galileo*, relied more on subscriptions and specialty bookstore sales than on newsstand distribution. Despite a limited budget it presented authors such as David Brin, George Zebrowski, Connie Willis, Frederik Pohl, and Mike Resnick.

And yet, and yet…Perhaps it depended too much on a nonexistent nostalgia for adventure science fiction, maybe it struck the potential reader as merely more science-fiction "product," perhaps it was an implied condescension on the part of the publisher that if you didn't care for the high-brow *Asimov's*, you might like the low-brow "adventure" version.

In a sense, it was blue collar versus white collar and blue collar lost.

The most merciful death was meted out to *Odyssey*, a large-size magazine with two-color interiors. Edited by Roger Elwood, a book anthologist of some experience, the magazine was unattractive, despite some name authors for the fiction and departments. The first issue was eighty pages of pulp paper with a cover by Kelly Freas. The second sported a two-color cover (by Jack Gaughan), which didn't help sales at all. There was no third issue.

Charles C. Ryan, who had edited *Galileo*, came back to the field with *Aboriginal Science Fiction*, a tabloid-sized magazine printed on a hard-surface newsprint with four-color full-page illustrations scattered throughout. Effective with the fourth issue, the magazine became the standard large size printed on either slick stock or newsprint. *Aboriginal* depended primarily on new authors, with a scattering of seasoned professionals. The magazine was variable in production quality but, at its best, was a handsome magazine.

Author Algis Budrys entered the fray with a late entry in 1993. The January issue of *Tomorrow* was an attractive sixty-four page large-size magazine (the page count was to vary between sixty-four and one hundred twenty-eight). Budrys relied heavily on new writers with a scattering of "name" authors. Budrys himself was a well-respected science-fiction

writer, was known as an incisive book reviewer, and for many years had managed the "Writers of the Future" contest and program, started by L. Ron Hubbard and now sponsored by his Hollywood literary agency, Author Services, Inc.

Like *Galileo* in its early issues and *Aboriginal Science Fiction*, *Tomorrow* sold primarily through specialty stores and by subscription. It was an uphill battle for Budrys, and the magazine went "online" after issue Number 24. A few months after that, the online venture was cut back.

Probably the most spectacular debut of the large-sized magazines was that of *Science Fiction Age*. The magazine began as eighty pages of slick stock with four color throughout, allowing for pages of full-color advertising from book publishers, book clubs, computer games, collectible cards, etc. Well-financed and produced, the magazine sold well on the newsstand and had a respectable subscription list.

Scott Edelman, the editor, shrewdly covered all the science-fiction oriented media as well as printing fiction by name authors and unknowns. The magazine relied heavily on a tie to television shows and films. Best-selling issues reliably were those with covers featuring *Star Trek* (in any of its incarnations) and *Babylon 5*.

The magazines most successful in the new millennium may be those, like *Science Fiction Age* and *Amazing Stories*, that expand the print medium to include the visual (film and TV).

SCOOPS
FEBRUARY 10, 1934
SERGE DRIGIN

The first issue of the first
British science-fiction
magazine. A boys' story
paper, it was published
as a semi-tabloid weekly
for twenty issues.

The British are Coming!

Science fiction has never been strictly an American phenomenon. Mary Shelley wrote *Frankenstein*, H. Rider Haggard was famous for *She* and *King Solomon's Mines*, and H. G. Wells, according to some critics, practically founded the genre. It should come as no surprise that the British had their share of magazines and that several of them played important roles in modern science fiction.

The first magazine of note was *Scoops*, a boys' story paper of which the British aren't particularly proud. But to give credit where credit was due, it was the first—and only—weekly science-fiction magazine ever printed. It was published by the firm of C. Arthur Pearson, noted for its *Pearson's Magazine* earlier in the century that carried stories by H.G. Wells and A. Conan Doyle.

Scoops, a semi-tabloid printed on rough newsprint with a two-color cover, ran for twenty issues during 1934. There's little that can be said about the fiction except it was written for boys. Young boys.

A far more substantial effort was *Tales of Wonder*, which began as a one-shot in 1937 and soon became a quarterly. It was pulp magazine size with 128 pages, trimmed edges, and attractive covers. Then the war came, the magazine grew thinner and thinner, finally adopting an all-type cover, and then disappeared completely in 1942 after sixteen issues. (Like many of his American counterparts, editor Walter Gillings came from the ranks of fandom and had published a fan magazine in 1937-1938. After the war, he resurfaced as the editor of *Science Fantasy*.)

Contributors to *Tales of Wonder* were primarily British, with the occasional story by American authors like Edmond Hamilton and Lloyd A. Eshbach (known later primarily for his specialty publishing company,

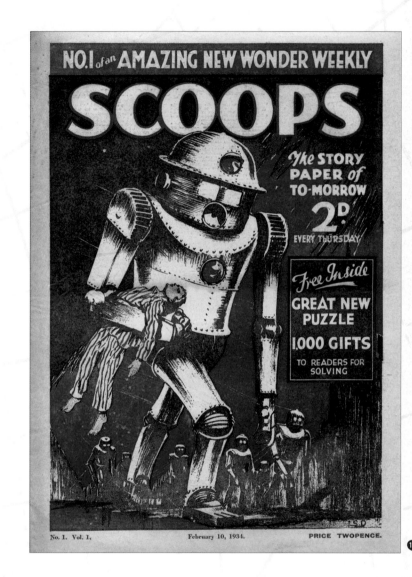

No. 1. Vol. I.   February 10, 1934.   PRICE TWOPENCE.

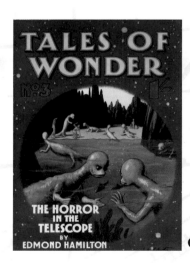

TALES OF WONDER
SUMMER 1938
L. J. ROBERTS

An unfortunate time to publish a
magazine. Editor Walter Gillings
was drafted early in World War II,
and the paper shortage killed the
magazine, but not before it had
published Arthur C. Clarke's first
two professional pieces—including
one titled "We Can Rocket to the
Moon—Now!" (Summer 1939).

Fantasy Press). But the most important contributor of all was Arthur C. Clarke, another British fan, with articles titled "Man's Empire of Tomorrow" and "We Can Rocket to the Moon—Now!"

A forecast of things to come: Clarke used a fictional technique to open and close his article about rocketing to the moon. These fictional portions were vintage Clarke. Of further interest: Clarke was not yet important enough to warrant a mention in the "Authors' Corner" column.

The British *Fantasy* was one of a series of pulps issued by George Newnes Ltd. of London. It had been discussed as early as 1935 but nothing substantial was done until *Tales of Wonder* had appeared and was a success. *Fantasy* ran for three issues—the first in 1938—and was later discontinued for two reasons. One was the impending paper shortage because of the war, and two was that editor Stanhope Sprigg had enlisted in the RAF.

Not noted for much outstanding fiction, *Fantasy* did offer one surprise in its cover artist, S. Drigen— the same S. Drigen who had done the sketchy scrawls for the covers of *Scoops*. His work for *Fantasy*, by comparison, was quite accomplished.

After the war, *New Worlds*, the first and most important of all British science-fiction magazines, hit the ground running in 1946. The editor was long-time science-fiction fan John Carnell. The magazine was thin—sixty-four pages—and midway in size between a pulp and a large-size magazine. The front cover was a shambles, and, all in all, it wasn't a very prepossessing magazine and didn't sell well. For the publishing company, it was either kill it or get behind it, and they chose the latter. The second issue sold out.

(Prior to his professional editorship, Carnell had been an associate editor, along with fellow fans

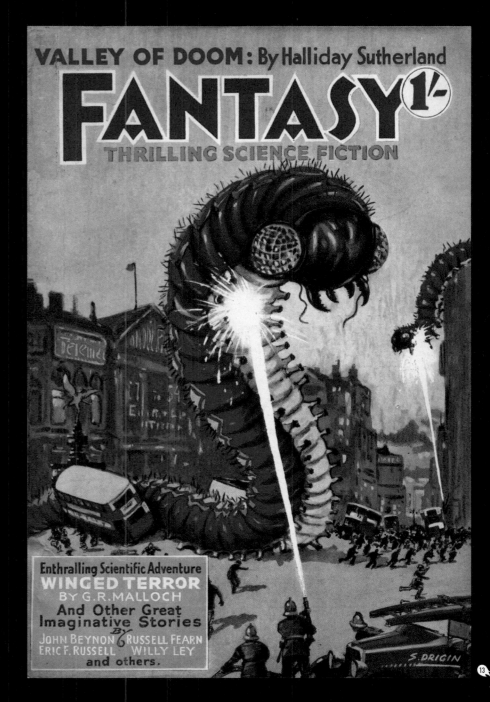

FANTASY
#2—1939
SERGE DRIGIN

Fantasy saw three issues, then the editor enlisted in the RAF, and the magazine fell victim to the wartime paper shortage.

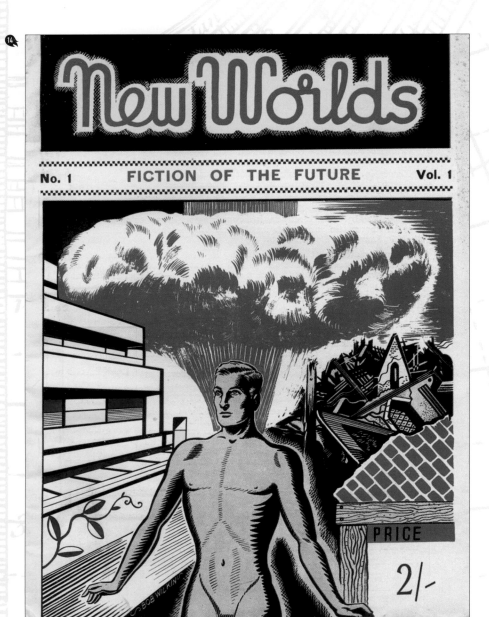

Arthur C. Clarke and William F. Temple, of a fan magazine called *New Worlds*, a retitling of *Novae Terrae*. We all know what became of Arthur C. Clarke. But Temple also became quite a good professional writer, turning out—among other fiction—the *Four Sided Triangle*, published in both magazine and book form and filmed in 1953.)

After the third issue of *New Worlds* came out, the publisher collapsed. British fans and writers then decided to form their own company and publish the magazine. The fourth issue appeared in 1949 as a digest, and by 1950 the magazine had become a quarterly—popular enough that a companion magazine, *Science Fantasy*, was issued the same year. By 1954, *New Worlds* was a monthly, and by 1959 it had added another companion magazine, *Science Fiction Adventures* (not to be confused with the two American magazines of the same name).

The contributors were primarily British, among them Arthur C. Clarke, John Beynon Harris, Brian Aldiss, John Brunner, J. G. Ballard, and Colin Kapp. American writers began showing up as well—Cyril Kornbluth (*Take-Off*); Philip K. Dick (*Time Out of Joint*); Wilson Tucker (*Wild Talent, The Time Masters*); Theodore Sturgeon (*Venus Plus X*), etc.

Science Fiction Adventures folded in 1963, and there was talk of folding *New Worlds* and *Science Fantasy* as well. Instead, they were sold to another publisher, and Michael Moorcock (recommended by outgoing editor Carnell) became the new editor.

As editor, Moorcock was a different cup of tea entirely. He was twenty-five years old, had written for fan magazines, wrote some heroic fantasy (he was to become famous for his "Elric of Melnibone" series), and had been a blues singer in a nightclub… perhaps exactly the right resume for somebody who wanted to shake up the science-fiction field.

The first change in *New Worlds* was one of format—it became a magazine in paperback form (as did *Science Fantasy*, which morphed into *sf impulse*, another paperback magazine but not edited by Moorcock). The type of fiction that *New Worlds* published also suffered a sea change. At heart something of a polemicist, Moorcock wanted more social commentary, more relevancy. Characters not only had romances, they also had sex. What happened to real people in the outside world should be reflected in what happened to fictional ones. British writers Brunner and Aldiss became regular contributors, as did Charles Platt and Moorcock himself. (Moorcock's novella "Behold, the Man" won a Nebula and his "Jerry Cornelius" tales became a regular feature.) American writers such as Roger Zelazny and Thomas M. Disch, noting the wide-open editorial policy, also began to contribute.

What the British were publishing became known as the "New Wave" of science fiction. It was concerned with the psychological and sociological impact of technology on society and was specifically connected to the social upheaval of the 1960s—explicit sexuality, gender identity, the anti-Vietnam war movement—and totally dedicated to various forms of artistic expression. Two anthologies that included stories incorporating the tenets of the New Wave were *Dangerous Visions* (1967—edited by Harlan Ellison) and *England Swings SF* (1968—edited by Judith Merril).

Some authors who had been around a while ran with the concept. Moorcock himself was famous for his barbarian adventure stories—but his "Behold, the Man" was about a time traveler who seeks out the historical Jesus and, finding him to be a helpless mental defective, takes his place. J. G. Ballard, formerly a traditionalist when it came to writing science

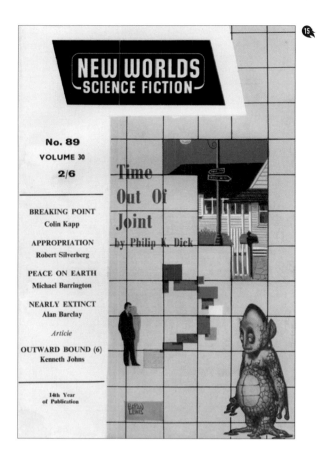

15

NEW WORLDS
DECEMBER 1959
BRIAN LEWIS

The magazine was printing the best of British authors such as J. G. Ballard and Brian Aldiss, as well as Americans Philip K. Dick and Robert Silverberg.

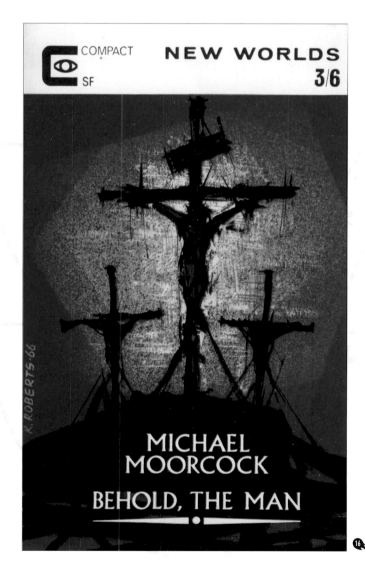

16

NEW WORLDS
#166—1966
K. ROBERTS

A new publisher, a new format, and a new editor—Michael Moorcock. It later became a slick-paper magazine supported in part by a grant from the British government. Historically, *New Worlds* was largely responsible for "new wave" science fiction.

SCIENCE FANTASY
#29—1958
LEWIS

Walter Gillings, who had edited *Tales of Wonder* before the war, was the first editor, succeeded by John Carnell. True to its title, the magazine included more fantasy than did *New Worlds*. It became a paper-back anthology and later changed its title to *Impulse*.

fiction, turned out books such as *The Crystal World* with its apocalyptic visions while John Brunner wrote *Stand on Zanzibar* about the frightening overpopulation of the future.

(Not all stories that could be described as New Wave appeared in *New Worlds*. Richard A. Lupoff's story "Stroka Prospekt" dealt with the use of forbidden sexualities as a form of political control; it appeared simultaneously as a chapbook in a series edited by Thomas M. Disch and in the American *Asimov's*.)

All of this was a drastic departure from the safe and familiar turf of rayguns and rocketships and wasn't welcomed by everybody. The publishing company started to go belly up, and, in what was presumed to be the last few issues, Moorcock published Brian Aldiss's *Report on Probability A* and reprinted "The Assassination of John Fitzgerald Kennedy Considered as a Downhill Motor Race" by J. G. Ballard. (Ballard wrote more than just science fiction—*Empire of the Sun*, an autobiographical novel, was filmed by Stephen Spielberg in 1987.)

In addition to the more or less "experimental fiction" being published by *New Worlds* went an increasingly reluctant attitude on the part of some of its contributors to have their wares shopped as "science fiction." Charles Platt even stated in the magazine that "*New Worlds* is not a science-fiction magazine." The label had become too restrictive, too predictive. The reluctance would surface later in the publication of novels whose authors strenuously tried to avoid being "ghetto-ized" and publishing companies labeled an occasional science-fiction novel as something else or simply avoided the label altogether.

In 1966 *New Worlds* got a grant from the Arts Council of Great Britain for a partial subsidy for the

★ EARTH IS BUT A STAR by JOHN BRUNNER ★

magazine. It now blossomed as a slick-paper magazine from July 1967 on. The lead novel in the issue was *Camp Concentration* by Thomas M. Disch, in which a mutated syphilis virus is used in a secret government program to enhance human intelligence. Along the way, his main character used words seldom seen in science fiction. Succeeding issues printed Norman Spinrad's *Bug Jack Barron* (another poster boy for the Free Speech movement), Samuel R. Delany's "Time Considered as a Helix of Semi-Precious Stones," and Harlan Ellison's "A Boy and His Dog" (the latter two were both award winners, while the Spinrad novel was nominated for both a Hugo and a Nebula). Spinrad's novel caused members of the House of Commons to question just why the Arts Council was sponsoring such filth. (Similar questions were raised years later in the U.S. Congress when members wondered why the National

Endowment for the Arts was sponsoring some of its projects.)

The experimental fiction and the complaints in the House of Commons had their effect. Some distributors refused to handle the magazine and the flow of revenue began to shrink. The 200th issue was published in 1970. By then the Arts Council had withdrawn its support, distribution had turned sour and Moorcock found himself £3,000 in debt. There was a 201st issue—a "Special Good Taste" issue—that went out to subscribers but was otherwise never distributed.

The "New Wave" had its detractors and supporters in the United States. But with time its hallmarks of

free speech and "innerspace" as opposed to outer became part and parcel of the field, especially in novels. Space opera and novels about musclebound barbarians came back—they had never really gone away—but the influence of the New Wave still echoed in many stories and books. More than any other magazine, *New Worlds* had demanded that science fiction grow up, that it assume its position in mainstream fiction, that since real people led real lives, the characters in science-fiction stories should at least try to mirror them.

New Worlds was the most important British science-fiction magazine—though it may be more accurate to say it was the most important English one. *Nebula Science Fiction* was published in Scotland, the brainchild of eighteen-year-old Peter Hamilton. His family owned a printing firm which frequently had "down time" on its presses, periods when the presses were idle. Hamilton was quick to take advantage of it. A young science-fiction fan, his first plan was to publish novels, then abandoned that in favor of a regular magazine.

The first issue of *Nebula* was dated autumn 1952 and featured British writers. Its list of contributors (both original and reprint) eventually included Eric Frank Russell and Robert Heinlein. It was Peter Hamilton who bought the first story by Robert Silverberg and the first by Brian Aldiss.

Nebula's publishing schedule was irregular—it went on press when the family business had nothing else to print. Hamilton eventually found himself another printer and switched to a regular schedule, including monthly publication.

Young Hamilton had everything figured out except distribution. A third of his sales were in America, a

SF IMPULSE
#6—1966
UNKNOWN

The old *Science Fantasy* under a new name and in a different format. *Make Room! Make Room!* was subsequently filmed in the U.S. as *Soylent Green*, starring Charlton Heston and Edward G. Robinson.

SCIENCE FICTION ADVENTURES
#31 — 1963
GERALD QUINN

A companion to *New Worlds* and *Science Fantasy* during a period when all three were edited by John Carnell. Originally a reprint of the American magazine of the same name (1956-1958). When that magazine died, the British version soldiered on with new stories by primarily British authors.

quarter in Australia, and ten percent in South Africa. Import restrictions by the different countries cut Hamilton off at the pockets and after forty-one issues he was forced to call it quits.

(There were very few magazine editors who could claim to be their own publishers. Ray Palmer and Bill Hamling in the States and Peter Hamilton in Scotland, and that was about it.)

At the end of the century, the most prominent British science-fiction magazine was *Interzone* which had logged 138 issues by the close of 1998. Like the last issues of *New Worlds*, *Interzone* was funded, at least in part, by the Arts Council of Great Britain. A sixty-four page large-size monthly, it could also lay claim to having the same experimental approach to science fiction that *New Worlds* did, though in a much more attractive package.

The magazine started as the product of an editorial collective that rapidly thinned out. By 1988, David Pringle was the first among equals as both editor and publisher. The magazine was almost evenly divided between fiction and features, including a letter column, author interview, a film review column, a television review column, drama reviews, commentary about science fiction on the Internet, and book reviews. It could also boast of having published Brian Aldiss, J. G. Ballard, Gregory Benford, Michael Bishop, David Brin, Bruce Sterling, Lisa Tuttle, Gene Wolfe, Bob Shaw, Thomas M. Disch, William Gibson, William Cowper, etc.

Because of *Interzone*, at the end of the century some of the most challenging science fiction was being published in the country where—according to most critics—it was born.

NEBULA
SCIENCE FICTION
MONTHLY
2/-
NUMBER 36

FOR READING THAT'S DIFFERENT

NEBULA SCIENCE FICTION
NOVEMBER 1958
EDDIE JONES

The first—and only—science-fiction magazine to be based in Scotland. Eighteen-year-old editor Peter Hamilton published Robert Silverberg's first story, "Gorgon Planet," and also bought Brian Aldiss's first story.

INTERZONE
JUNE 1998
JIM BURNS

Started in 1982 as a quarterly, *Interzone* was still going strong at the end of the century as a monthly. A large-size slick-paper magazine, it was credited with revitalizing science fiction in the United Kingdom.

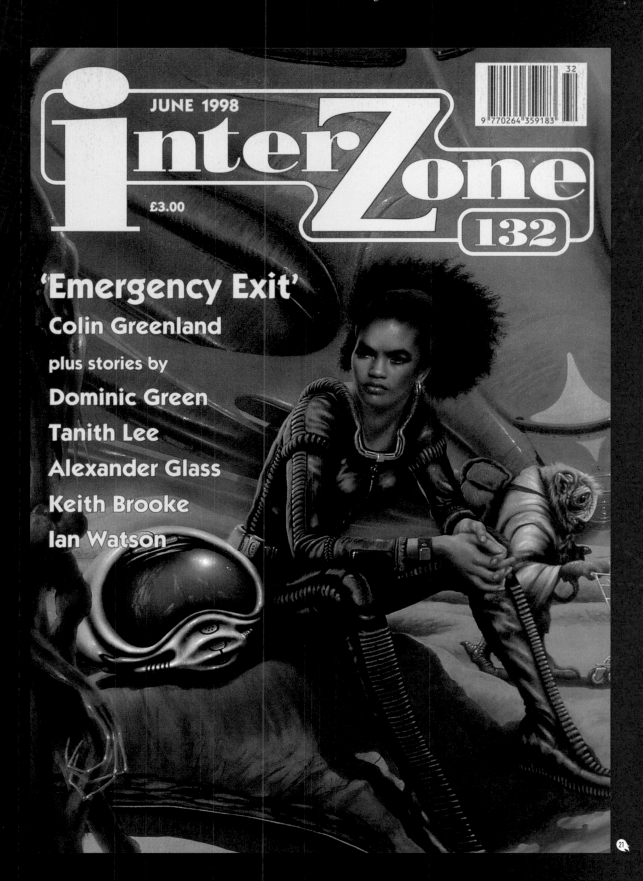

JUNE 1998

interZone
132

£3.00

'Emergency Exit'
Colin Greenland
plus stories by
Dominic Green
Tanith Lee
Alexander Glass
Keith Brooke
Ian Watson

Paperbacks used to be the "afterburner" market for hard-cover books, much as tapes and DVDs and cable are the "afterburner" market for films. All those who don't want to spend seven or eight dollars to see the film in its first run can rent it for a few dollars per night or watch it on cable in the comfort of their home. And all those who didn't want to spend twenty dollars or more for a hard-cover book could buy the paperback for six or seven. Back in the 1940s, of course, the price differential was that between a few dollars and a quarter—which exactly equalled the new Federal minimum wage. You would sell a lot more copies of the paperback than the hardcover, so even at the lower price, the author could make money. (At the end of the century, the cost of a paperback was still roughly equal to the minimum wage.)

GOOD THINGS
IN SMALL PACKAGES
CHAPTER 9

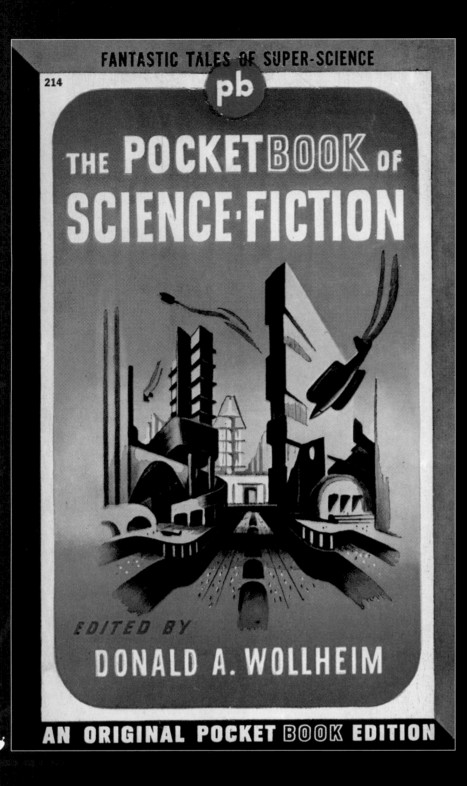

FANTASTIC TALES OF SUPER-SCIENCE

214

pb

THE POCKETBOOK OF SCIENCE·FICTION

EDITED BY

DONALD A. WOLLHEIM

AN ORIGINAL POCKET BOOK EDITION

THE POCKETBOOK OF SCIENCE FICTION
EDITED BY DONALD A. WOLLHEIM
1943
UNKNOWN

The very first paperback devoted completely to science fiction. Editor Donald A. Wollheim eventually founded his own publishing company, DAW Books.

The usual procedure for an author was to sell his novel first for magazine serialization, then as a hardcover for the prestige and the reviews (few newspapers reviewed paperbacks), then come out with a mass market paperback edition. Hardbacks sold a few thousand copies, mass market paperbacks sold in the tens of thousands. If you were really lucky, you might even be selected by the Science Fiction Book Club.

Pocket Book, New American Library, Dell, and Signet published the occasional paperback reprint of a hardcover science-fiction novel. But it wasn't until 1952, with the founding of Ballantine Books, and 1953 when Ace Books was established, that you had paperback houses with major science-fiction lines, not only reprinting material but also publishing "paperback originals."

Ballantine Books was founded by Ian and Betty Ballantine as a general paperback publishing house. Ian Ballantine had helped found Bantam Books, then left to start his own publishing company. A general publishing house (the mainstream novel *Executive Suite* was its first selection), Ballantine also had a prestigious science-fiction line in which they published titles simultaneously in both paperback and hardback formats. (They frequently used the same plates for both, which meant most Ballantine hardbacks were smaller than the standard hardback of the period. Print runs for the hardbacks were also lower than usual, which meant Ballantine hardbacks quickly became collector's items.)

As a paperback, a Ballantine book was well produced, slightly taller than the average paperback, and—if science fiction—usually had a cover by Richard M. Powers that was surrealistic and immediately gave a more modern and adult "look" to the book. The much imitated Powers was something of

EARTH ABIDES
GEORGE R. STEWART
1949
ROBERT ABBETT

One of the earliest "post-holocaust" novels—in this case, most of America has been depopulated by a plague—*Earth Abides* concerns the attempts to rebuild civilization.

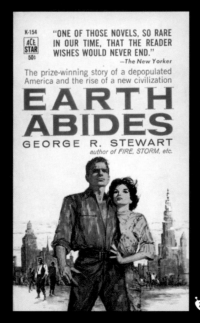

K-154
ACE STAR
50¢
"ONE OF THOSE NOVELS, SO RARE IN OUR TIME, THAT THE READER WISHES WOULD NEVER END."
—The New Yorker

The prize-winning story of a depopulated America and the rise of a new civilization

EARTH ABIDES
GEORGE R. STEWART
author of FIRE, STORM, etc.

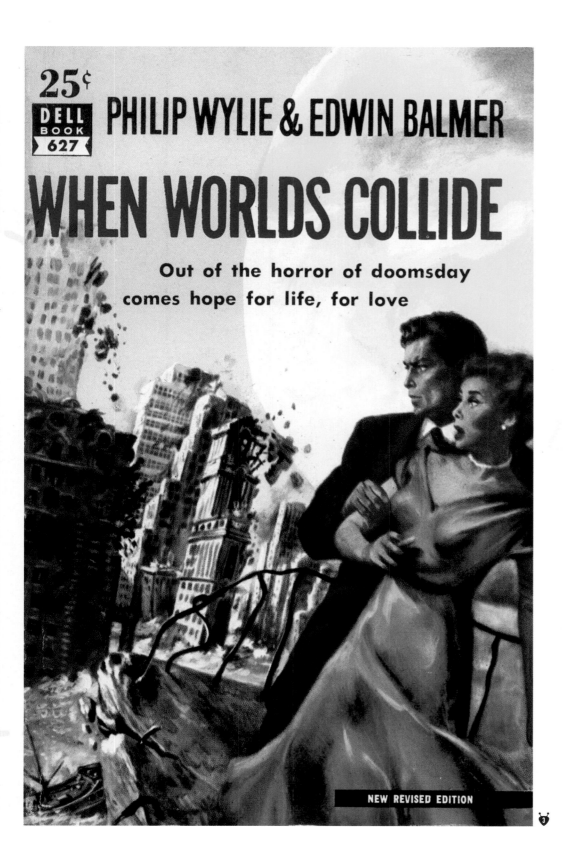

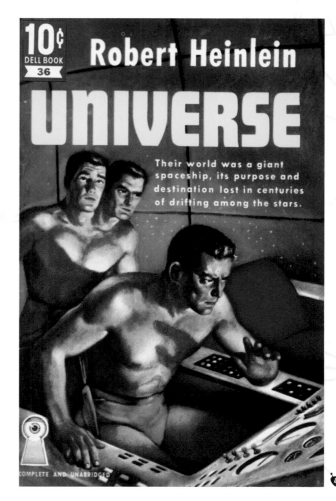

WHEN WORLDS COLLIDE

PHILIP WYLIE AND EDWIN BALMER
1951
ROBERT STANLEY

First serialized in *Blue Book* in the early 1930s (and filmed in 1951 by George Pal), *When Worlds Collide* was an immensely popular science-fiction novel.

UNIVERSE

ROBERT HEINLEIN
1951
ROBERT STANLEY

One of the very few ten cent paperbacks published. The story, originally published in *Astounding*, was a pioneer generation-ship tale.

MORE THAN HUMAN

THEODORE STURGEON
1953
RICHARD M. POWERS

Theodore Sturgeon was probably the most compassionate writer the genre has known. "Baby Is Three"—the middle of the three connected stories in this collection— originally appeared in *Galaxy* and is an acknowledged classic.

CHILDHOOD'S END
ARTHUR C. CLARKE
1953
RICHARD M. POWERS

Even though Clarke is known as a "hard science" author —and the inventor of the communication satellite—some of his most famous novels (among them *Childhood's End*) have a heavy streak of mysticism.

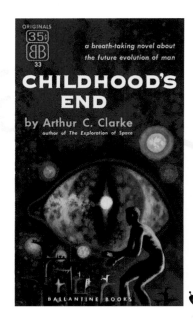

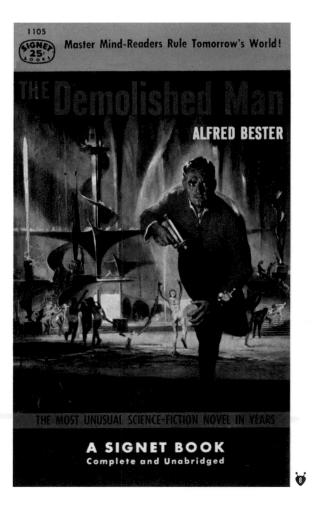

THE DEMOLISHED MAN
ALFRED BESTER
1954
STANLEY MELTZOFF

The wealthiest man in the world has killed a man— and is pitted against a detective who can read minds. *The Demolished Man* was one of the most popular science-fiction novels of the 1950s. Through stylized printing techniques, the conversations between telepaths is convincingly presented.

THE SPACE MERCHANTS
FREDERIK POHL AND C. M. KORNBLUTH
1953
RICHARD M. POWERS

The Space Merchants, the first and most successful of the Pohl-Kornbluth novel-length collaborations, was a devastating satire of the world a hundred years from now when the advertising agencies have taken over.

WHO?
ALGIS BUDRYS
1958
ROBERT ENGLE

An American scientist is exchanged during the Cold War—and returns with a metal arm and a metallic dome for a head. Who is he? Really? Probably the most popular novel by author Budrys.

a New Wave in commercial art all by himself. More than a hundred of the early Ballantine covers were by Powers, who became a trademark of their science-fiction line.

Ballantine's first science-fiction paperback novel was *The Space Merchants* by Frederik Pohl and C.M. Kornbluth, soon followed with books by Clarke and Sturgeon and others. When the company issued its *Star Science Fiction* anthologies, Fred Pohl became the editor.

Ballantine was sold to Random House in 1973 and after Ian and Betty left, Judy-Lynn Del Rey—who had been an associate editor at *Galaxy*—became the science-fiction editor. She was soon joined by husband Lester and a few years later, the Del Reys had their own imprint of "Del Rey Books" at Random House, publishing both mass market paperbacks and hardback books. An acknowledged marketing genius, Judy-Lynn was expert at editing and packaging hardcover fantasy and science-fiction books for a mainstream audience and, as a result, frequently hitting the best-seller lists.

Donald A. Wollheim was the science-fiction editor at Ace Books when it began in 1953. There were few editors who knew the field better than he did. He had been a longtime science-fiction fan, sold his first story to Gernsback's *Wonder Stories* when he was twenty, helped found the Futurians in the late 1930s, edited *Cosmic Stories* and *Stirring Science Stories* in the early 1940s for no money and little glory, and turned out the occasional story or juvenile novel himself.

He eased into the anthology field with two ground breaking books—*The Pocketbook of Science Fiction* (1943) and the *Viking Portable Novels of Science* (1945). He also edited the *Avon Fantasy Readers*

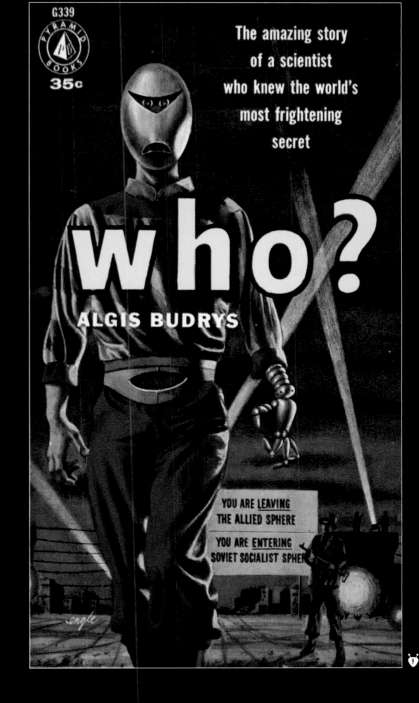

G339
PYRAMID BOOKS
35c

The amazing story of a scientist who knew the world's most frightening secret

who?
ALGIS BUDRYS

YOU ARE LEAVING
THE ALLIED SPHERE

YOU ARE ENTERING
SOVIET SOCIALIST SPHER

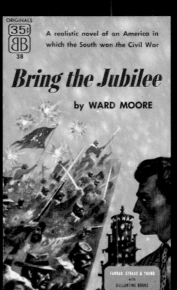

ORIGINALS
35¢
BB
38

A realistic novel of an America in which the South won the Civil War

Bring the Jubilee
by WARD MOORE

BRING THE JUBILEE
WARD MOORE
1953
RICHARD M. POWERS

What if the North had lost the Battle of Gettysburg in the Civil War? And would that war now be known as the War of Southern Independence? *Bring the Jubilee* was one of the first of the popular alternative-history novels.

THE LINCOLN HUNTERS
WILSON TUCKER
1958
LEO AND DIANE DILLON

Tucker was a long-time science fiction fan who sold his first novel—a mystery (*The Chinese Doll*)—in the late 1940s. He was one of the few writers to achieve popularity in both the mystery and science-fiction genres.

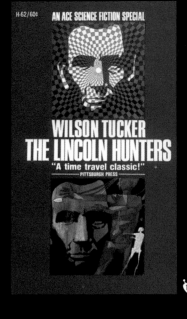

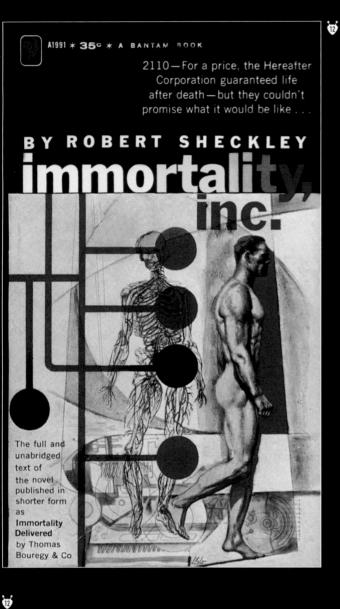

IMMORTALITY, INC.
ROBERT SHECKLEY
1959
UNKNOWN

Sheckley earned an early reputation as a writer of urbane and witty short stories. His novel, *The Seventh Victim*, was filmed as *The Tenth Victim* (starring Ursula Andress with a "loaded" bra). *Immortality, Inc.* was filmed as *Freejack* with Mick Jagger.

THE SEEDLING STARS
JAMES BLISH
1959
PAUL LEHR

The Seedling Stars was a collection of stories based on early genetic engineering. The author's *A Case of Conscience*, which won the 1959 Hugo, was an early science-fiction novel dealing with religion.

S1752

SIGNET 35¢ BOOKS

They were Earthmen blessed
with extraordinary
life-spans — compelled to
wander the distant stars

ROBERT A. HEINLEIN
Methuselah's CHILDREN

A SIGNET BOOK COMPLETE AND UNABRIDGED

METHUSELAH'S CHILDREN
ROBERT A. HEINLEIN
1960
PAUL LEHR

One of Heinlein's most popular early novels dealt with families genetically blessed with long lifespans who are persecuted by normal short-lived humans. The novel introduced Lazarus Long, Heinlein's favorite character.

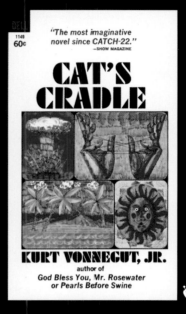

"The most imaginative novel since CATCH-22."
—SHOW MAGAZINE

1149 60¢

CAT'S CRADLE

KURT VONNEGUT, JR.
author of
God Bless You, Mr. Rosewater
or Pearls Before Swine

CAT'S CRADLE
KURT VONNEGUT, JR.
1965
MURRAY TINKLEMAN

Vonnegut avoided being stereotyped as a science-fiction writer and crossed over to the literary mainstream with *Cat's Cradle* and *Player Piano*. One of his fictional characters was a science-fiction writer named "Kilgore Trout" (probably in homage to Theodore Sturgeon). Phil Farmer used the name as a pseudonym for his novel *Venus on the Half-Shell*.

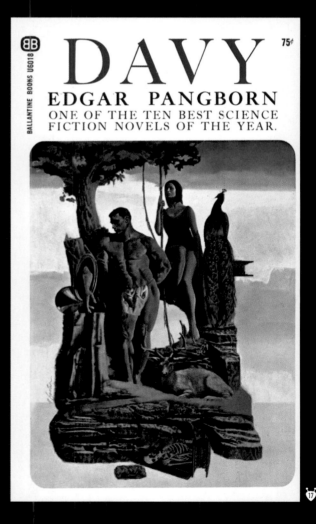

75¢

BALLANTINE BOOKS U6018

DAVY
EDGAR PANGBORN
ONE OF THE TEN BEST SCIENCE
FICTION NOVELS OF THE YEAR.

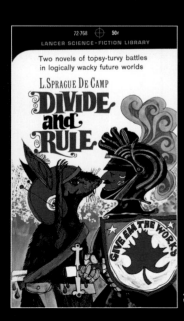

72-768 50¢
LANCER SCIENCE-FICTION LIBRARY

Two novels of topsy-turvy battles
in logically wacky future worlds

L. SPRAGUE DE CAMP
DIVIDE and RULE

GIVE 'EM THE WORKS

DIVIDE AND RULE
L. SPRAGUE DE CAMP
1964
UNKNOWN

The volume contains both *Divide and Rule* and *The Stolen Dormouse.* A prolific author, de Camp wrote both fantasy and science fiction, as well as numerous nonfiction books. Most of his genre fiction was marked by a wacky sense of humor.

DAVY
EDGAR PANGBORN
1964
ROBERT FOSTER

Nominated for a 1965 Hugo, *Davy* takes place in a post-holocaust future. Critics have called it the *Tom Jones* of science fiction.

I HAVE NO MOUTH & I MUST SCREAM
HARLAN ELLISON
1967
LEO AND DIANE DILLON

Ellison has been a notable anthologist, television and movie screenwriter, toastmaster at conventions, and definitely has a way with book titles. The title story in "I Have No Mouth and I Must Scream" won the 1968 Hugo.

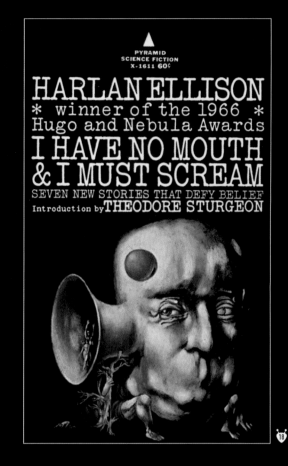

STAR TREK
ADAPTED BY JAMES BLISH
1967
JAMES E. BAMA

Movie tie-ins and adaptations are among the best-selling science-fiction books. In this case, author Blish adapted a number of scripts from the original television series to short stories.

and the *Avon Science Fiction Readers*, as well as (uncredited) the first original paperback science-fiction anthology, *The Girl With the Hungry Eyes*.

At Ace he edited an enormous amount of science fiction in the popular "Ace Doubles" series—two novels bound back to back. It was two for the price of one, though readers usually found a "name" author coupled with an unknown. But the name authors alone were worth the price of admission. They included Philip K. Dick (the most famous of all the Ace Double authors), Thomas M. Disch, Robert Silverberg, and Samuel R. Delany.

In 1964, Terry Carr—another science-fiction fan —joined the company and became the editor of the "Ace Specials." Carr wrote some science fiction but was best known as a brilliant editor, editing Ursula K. Le Guin's famous *The Left Hand of Darkness* as an Ace Special. He co-edited (with Wollheim) a number of the "World's Best" science-fiction anthologies and after leaving Ace in 1971 edited the *Universe* original anthologies.

Carr also edited a best-of-the-year anthology series on his own, then returned to Ace in the 1980s to edit another series of Specials. This time around he edited the original publication of William Gibson's first novel, *Neuromancer* (which eventually sported the first computer-painted cover by Rick Berry); Kim Stanley Robinson's first novel, *The Wild Shore*; Lucius Shepard's first novel, *Green Eyes*; and Michael Swanwick's first novel, *In the Drift*.

Carr had the most valuable characteristic any editor can have—a nose for talent. In 1985 and 1986 he won the Hugo for Best Professional Editor. Quoting Malcolm J. Edwards and John Clute of *The Encyclopedia of Science Fiction*, Carr's authors "seemed to speak to the heart of their times."

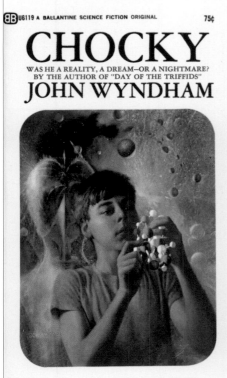

CHOCKY

JOHN WYNDHAM
1968
ROBERT SCHULZ

UK writer John Wyndham Parkes Lucas
Beynon Harris started writing for *Wonder
Stories* in 1931 as simply "John Beynon
Harris." Probably his most successful novels
were *The Day of the Triffids* (filmed in 1963)
and *The Midwich Cuckoos*, filmed as *Village
of the Damned* in 1960 and remade in 1995.

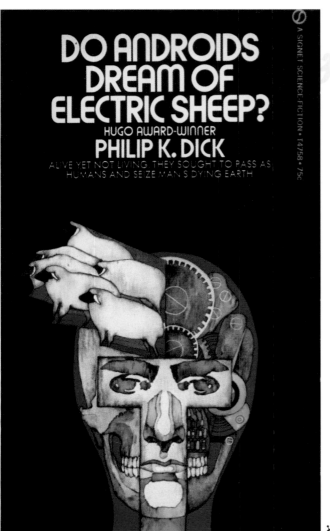

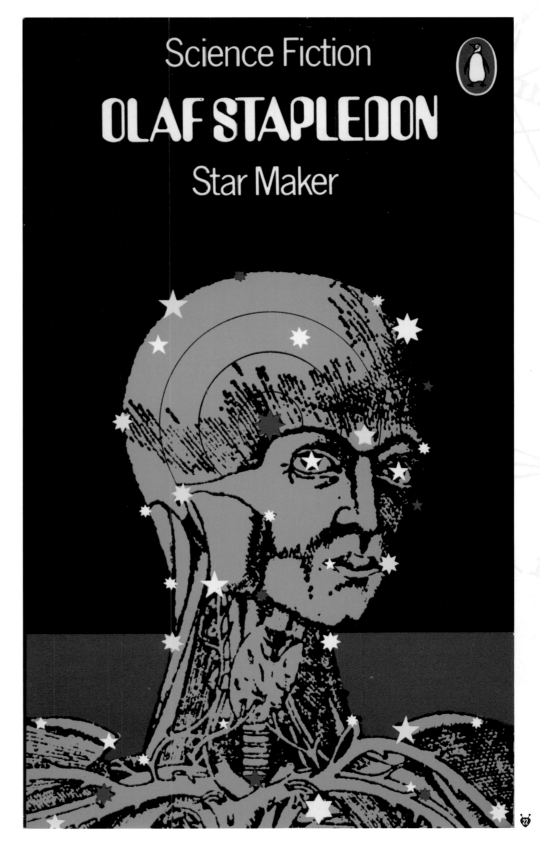

DO ANDROIDS DREAM OF ELECTRIC SHEEP?

PHILIP K. DICK
1969
UNKNOWN

Filmed by Ridley Scott in 1982, the
novel is best known by its movie title
of *Blade Runner*. The film has since
become a cult classic.

STAR MAKER

OLAF STAPLEDON
1972
(FIRST PUBLISHED 1937)
DAVID PELHAM

In *Star Maker* Stapledon envisions a future that extends
for a hundred billion years—a time scale employed by
few other science-fiction writers.

EARTHWRECK
THOMAS N. SCORTIA
1974
JOHN BERKEY

Scortia wrote innovative short stories and his novels *Artery of Fire* and *Earthwreck* were well-received. In the 1970s, he collaborated with Frank M. Robinson on a series of "techno-thrillers." *The Glass Inferno* (along with Richard Martin Stern's *The Tower*) was filmed as *The Towering Inferno*.

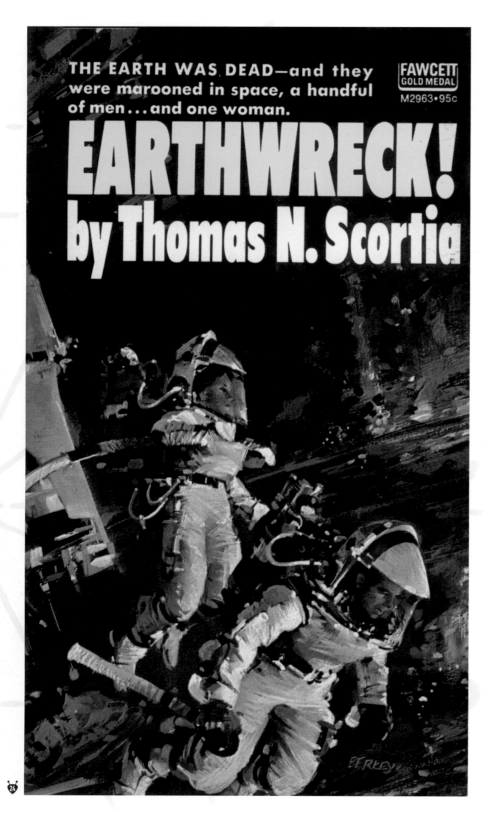

WHEN H.A.R.L.I.E. WAS ONE
DAVID GERROLD
1988 (FIRST PUBLISHED 1972)
UNKNOWN

Gerrold sold "The Trouble With Tribbles"—one of the best loved of the original *Star Trek* episodes — while still in college. His novels include *The Man Who Folded Himself* and *When H.A.R.L.I.E. Was One*. He won both the Hugo and the Nebula for his story "The Martian Child."

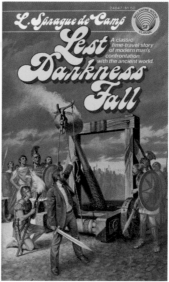

LEST DARKNESS FALL
L. SPRAGUE DE CAMP
1974
DARRELL K. SWEET

A story about an archeologist who travels back in time to just before the fall of the Roman Empire— and spends 80,000 delightful words trying to prevent the Dark Ages.

Ace Books made its biggest coup when Wollheim discovered that a number of the magazine versions of Edgar Rice Burroughs' books were in the public domain. Actually, Canaveral Press had discovered it first and started to reprint Burroughs in hardback editions. Wollheim, who had tried to buy the reprint rights from Edgar Rice Burroughs, Inc., and whose letters of inquiry were never answered, immediately investigated.

Edgar Rice Burroughs had died in 1950 and by the 1960s the management of his company was primarily interested in negotiating film rights to "Tarzan" and selling parcels of California real estate that Burroughs had bought decades before. Management had little interest in his novels and had neglected to renew the copyrights. In the 1960s, Ace started a reprint campaign to return the majority of the stories by the creator of Tarzan to print.

At the same time, Ballantine launched a similar campaign. Hulbert Burroughs, a son of Edgar R., now stepped in, installed new management at Edgar Rice Burroughs, Inc., and arranged amicable settlements with both Ace and Ballantine. Ace got the Pellucidar and Venus series plus most of the "independent" titles; Ballantine got the Tarzan and Martian series.

Both companies went all out to package the titles as attractively as possible. Ace brought in Frank Frazetta and Roy Krenkel, who painted a series of sensational covers for the books. Ballantine did almost as well with Michael Whelan and Boris Vallejo.

Both Ace and Ballantine had broken the usual process in reprinting books. If an author who had sold the hardback rights to a book subsequently sold the paperback rights, he had to split the money with the original hardback book publisher. But by selling

A FREDERIK POHL SELECTION
STRANGER IN A STRANGE LAND,
THEN **DUNE** AND NOW,
THE MAJOR NOVEL OF LOVE
AND TERROR AT THE END OF TIME

DHALGREN
BY SAMUEL R. DELANY
FOUR-TIME NEBULA AWARD-WINNER

DHALGREN
SAMUEL R. DELANY
1975
DEAN ELLIS

Delany has been acclaimed by some critics as "the best science-fiction writer in the world" (Algis Budrys). *Dhalgren* became a best seller. Delany's novels *Babel-17* and *The Einstein Intersection* both won Nebulas.

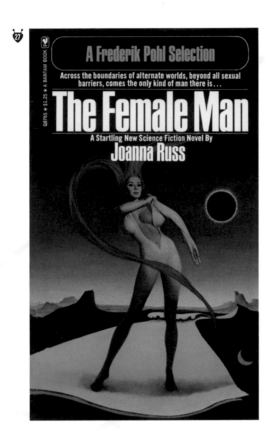

THE HERITAGE OF HASTUR
MARION ZIMMER BRADLEY
1975
JACK GAUGHAN

The "Darkover" series of books is one of the longest running in literature. Written over some thirty years, it relates the history and adventures of human colonists on the planet Darkover.

THE FEMALE MAN
JOANNA RUSS
1975
ARTIST: UNKNOWN

A pioneer of feminist science fiction, Joanna Russ writes about protagonists who are tough, capable, and female. Her writing has been described as both inventive and savage, but she never betrays her heroines—or her readers.

his book as a paperback "original," the author didn't have to share his royalties. He might lose out on the prestige and reviews, but, on the other hand, he might conceivably make more money. (And there was always the possibility of later hardback editions, as was the case with William Gibson's *Neuromancer* and Ursula K. Le Guin's *The Left Hand of Darkness*.)

Ace and Ballantine were hardly the only early paperback houses either specializing in or with a science-fiction imprint. There was Lancer Books (edited by Larry Shaw), Monarch, Tower, Belmont, Regency, etc. (At the end of the century there was DAW—founded by Wollheim in 1972 after leaving Ace, Ace, Baen Books, Del Rey, Warner Aspect, HarperPrism, Avon Eos, Bantam Spectra, White Wolf, Roc, Tor, and a number of others.)

On the surface, authors should have been in seventh heaven. Some of them were. Many of them weren't. At one time, it had been possible for the science-fiction enthusiast to buy everything that came out during the year without either going broke or running out of time to read what he bought. Soon after World War II that became impossible. There was a glut of product…and there was a glut of writers.

Many science-fiction fans had always wanted to be writers, and now there was help. There was the "Writers of the Future" contest, which encouraged new writers, and there were the various writing workshops that sprang up on college campuses offering to teach would-be authors just how it was done.

The great granddaddy of them all was the Milford Science Fiction Writers Conference, co-founded by Damon Knight along with James Blish and Judith Merril and which Knight more or less ran in succeeding years with wife Kate Wilhelm. Knight was the ideal man for the project. A seasoned editor, writer,

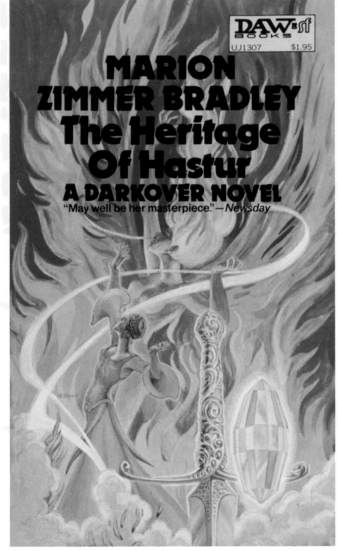

25597/$1.50

BALLANTINE BOOKS SF CLASSIC

FROM THE AWARD-WINNING AUTHOR OF DUNE,
"A NOVEL THAT RANKS WITH THE BEST OF SCIENCE FICTION."
—The New York Times

FRANK HERBERT
UNDER PRESSURE

(Originally: The Dragon in the Sea)

UNDER PRESSURE
FRANK HERBERT
1976
RICK STERNBACH

Under Pressure was written years before Herbert's "Dune" series. Critics called it an accurate portrayal of future warfare beneath the sea. (Variant book titles were *The Dragon in the Sea* and *21st Century Sub.*)

A DIFFERENT LIGHT
ELIZABETH A. LYNN
1978
UNKNOWN

Lynn is proficient in both science fiction and fantasy (winning the World Fantasy Best Novel Award for *Watchtower*). Her first science-fiction novel was *A Different Light*, followed by the highly acclaimed *The Sardonyx Net*.

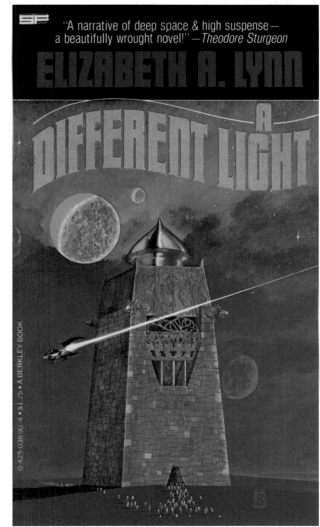

"A narrative of deep space & high suspense—a beautifully wrought novel!" —*Theodore Sturgeon*

ELIZABETH A. LYNN

A DIFFERENT LIGHT

THE OPHIUCHI HOTLINE
JOHN VARLEY
1977
BORIS VALLEJO

The Ophiuchi Hotline has been called Varley's best novel. An award-winning author, Varley's novel *Millennium* was filmed in 1989.

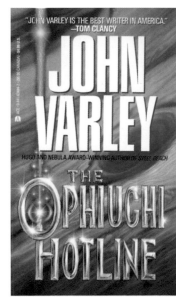

"JOHN VARLEY IS THE BEST WRITER IN AMERICA."
—TOM CLANCY

JOHN VARLEY

HUGO AND NEBULA AWARD-WINNING AUTHOR OF *STEEL BEACH*

THE OPHIUCHI HOTLINE

THE GENTLE GIANTS OF GANYMEDE
JAMES P. HOGAN
1978
H. R. VAN DONGEN

A systems-design engineer, Hogan
turned to writing and became a highly
popular "hard science" fiction writer.

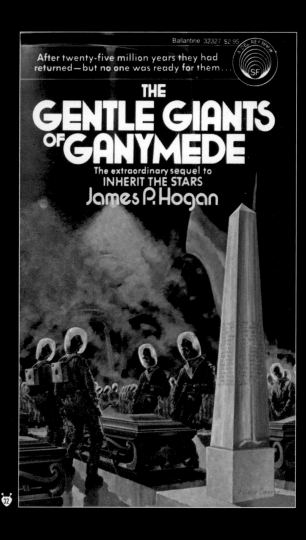

Ballantine 32327 $2.95

After twenty-five million years they had
returned—but no one was ready for them...

THE
GENTLE GIANTS
OF GANYMEDE
The extraordinary sequel to
INHERIT THE STARS
James P. Hogan

KEVIN O'DONNELL, JR.

MAYFLIES

THE STORY OF
THE MAN WHO BECAME
A UNIVERSE

A
BERKLEY
SHOWCASE
SF
ORIGINAL

Tom and Pat were identical
telepathic twins—and though one would
age and one wouldn't, they both
had to be kept alive at all costs

Ballantine
26073
$1.75

ROBERT A.
HEINLEIN
TIME FOR THE STARS

writers of juvenile
ndré Norton and
r juveniles by
rman Jones and
l Travel.

MAYFLIES
KEVIN O'DONNELL, JR.
1979
VINCENT DI FATE

A generation ship story, *Mayflies*' hero is a
human brain linked to the ship's computer.
He's entrusted with keeping the humans on
board—the "mayflies"—alive even though
they can be very annoying.

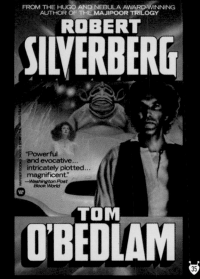

ROBERT SILVERBERG

"Powerful
and evocative...
intricately plotted...
magnificent."
—*Washington Post
Book World*

TOM O'BEDLAM

35

TOM O'BEDLAM
ROBERT SILVERBERG
1986
UNKNOWN

One of the most prolific of all
science-fiction writers, Silverberg
is best known for the "Majipoor"
fantasy trilogy and a number of
intense science-fiction novels—
Dying Inside, *The Book of Skulls*,
and *Up the Line* among others.

17749 • 3.95

THE SNOW QUEEN

Dell SF

JOAN D. VINGE

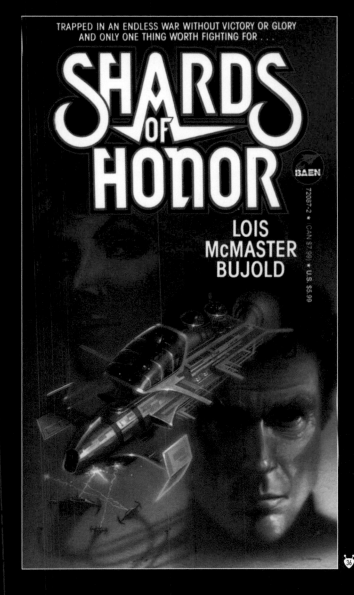

SHARDS OF HONOR

BAEN

72087-2

CAN $7.99 • U.S. $5.99

LOIS McMASTER BUJOLD

36

36

SHARDS OF HONOR
LOIS MCMASTER BUJOLD
1986
ALAN GUTIERREZ

Bujold has won her share of Hugos and
Nebulas writing stories and novels that
are both humorous and character-based.

37

THE SNOW QUEEN
JOAN D. VINGE
1981
LEO AND DIANE DILLON

Vinge's second novel, *The Snow Queen*, won a 1981
Hugo. Besides being a prolific short-story writer,
Vinge has written a number of movie tie-in novels.

SONGMASTER
ORSON SCOTT CARD
1987
DENNIS NOLAN

Originally published in book form in 1980,
Songmaster is one of Card's most popular
novels. Card handled a basically delicate
theme with great insight and humanity.

and especially critic, he had also been co-founder
and first president of the Science Fiction Writers
of America.

The Milford Writers Conference led to the estab-
lishment of the Clarion Science Fiction Writers'
Workshop, which in turn produced such notable
alumni as Octavia Butler, Vonda McIntyre, Kim
Stanley Robinson, and Lucius Shepard—and a
small army of others.

The digests had slumped by the end of the 1950s
and one of the reasons was the success of the original
paperbacks. They were even smaller and more
convenient, they featured—in the main—novels,
though collections of short stories were by no means
infrequent. (The number of hardback books had also
multiplied but if you didn't want to pay the hardback price, there was always the paperback reprint or
the Doubleday Science Fiction Book Club.)

For the author, it brought mixed blessings. The
paperback original novels and the original anthologies filled the commercial gap that had opened
because of the decline in the number of magazines.
But where there had once been a glut of magazines
on the newsstands, there was now a glut of paperbacks. At one time a writer could depend on a first
printing in paperback of a 100,000 copies or more.
With more and more paperbacks offered, print runs
fell until by the end of the century 20,000 copies was
the average.

Some publishers cut back on the number of paperbacks published, turning to "trade paperbacks"
instead. The size and shape of a hardbound book but
bound in heavy paper instead of boards, trade paperbacks averaged 4,000 copies. The big advantage was
that distribution was through book stores where the
shelf life was considerably longer than that of a mass

market paperback for sale at the airport or the local
supermarket, which in turn meant that the ruinous
rate of returns was considerably less.

Despite the century-end popularity of science
fiction, low advances and low sales per title made it
difficult for a writer to earn a living. There was a
name for it—supply and demand. And the truth
was that as enormously popular as the field had
become, supply had swamped demand.

Science fiction had become too much of a
good thing.

FINAL BLACKOUT
L. RON HUBBARD
1991
FRANK FRAZETTA

Hubbard's *Final Blackout* was one of the most popular novels to appear in *Astounding* during that magazine's Golden Age—Robert Heinlein called it "…as perfect a piece of science fiction as has ever been written." Face of main figure is a self-portrait of artist.

A FUTURISTIC WAR NOVEL

If you want justice on tomorrow's mean streets, it's going to cost you. Particularly if you're guilty.

GLASS HOUSES
LAURA J. MIXON
1991
TOM CANTY

The first novel b[...]
Mixon launched
the better genre
the 1990s. *Glass*
combined scienc[...]
with a first-rate [...]
thriller, creating [...]
genre—*future m[...]*

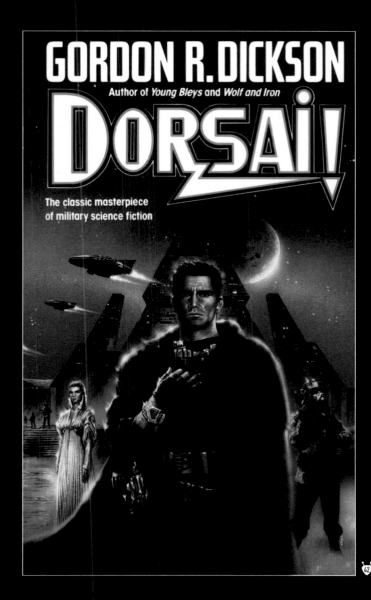

GORDON R. DICKSON
Author of *Young Bleys* and *Wolf and Iron*
DORSAI!
The classic masterpiece
of military science fiction

ALIEN STAR SWARM
ROBERT SHECKLEY
1991
DAVID M. DAVIS

The smallest paperback ever published, roughly half the size of a standard paperback.

SCIENCE FICTION   only $1.99
ALIEN STARSWARM

THERE ARE NO BOUNDARIES
ROBERT SHECKLEY

DORSAI!
GORDON R. DICKSON
1993
ROYO

Dickson started writing in 1950 and later won acclaim for *Dorsai!*, first published in book form in 1976. *Dorsai!* is rated along with Heinlein's *Starship Troopers* as one of the finest examples of military science fiction.

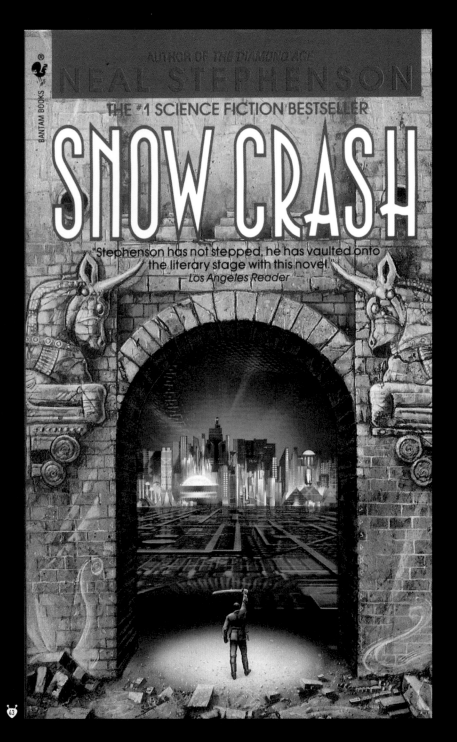

44

A FIRE UPON THE DEEP
VERNOR VINGE
1993
BORIS VALLEJO

A Fire Upon the Deep won the 1993 Hugo for Best Novel (tying with *Doomsday Book* by Connie Willis). The *New York Times* called it "Thoughtful space opera at its best…"

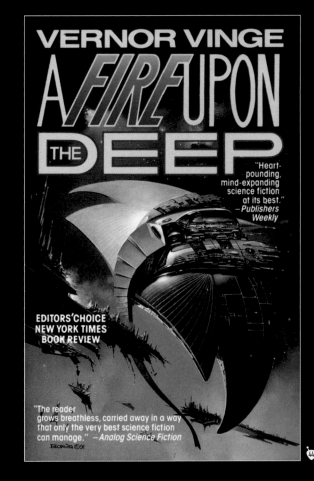

SNOW CRASH
NEAL STEPHENSON
1993
BRUCE JENSEN

A relative new writer to the field, Stephenson has won critical kudos from the *New York Times* and *Newsweek*. *Snow Crash* is his first novel.

EMPIRE'S END
ALLAN COLE AND CHRIS BUNCH
1993
BRUCE JENSEN

Cole and Bunch, disillusioned television scriptwriters, left Hollywood and turned to science fiction. They've written a number of novels in the action-adventure "Sten" series.

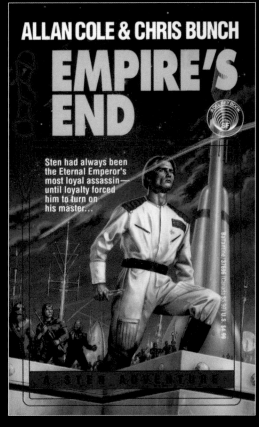

TROUBLE AND HER FRIENDS

MELISSA SCOTT
1995
NICHOLAS JAINSCHIGG

Scott won the 1986 John W. Campbell Award for Best New Writer. Known for well-crafted space operas, Scott stuck much closer to home with *Trouble and Her Friends*. Character driven, the novel is *cyberpunk noir* and takes place less than a hundred years in the future.

L. RON HUBBARD PRESENTS WRITERS OF THE FUTURE

EDITED BY DAVE WOLVERTON
1998
PAUL LEHR

A volume dedicated to new writers and illustrators, this is the fourteenth in a series that grew out of the "Writers of the Future" contest. For many years, writer Algis Budrys oversaw the contests and annual paperbacks.

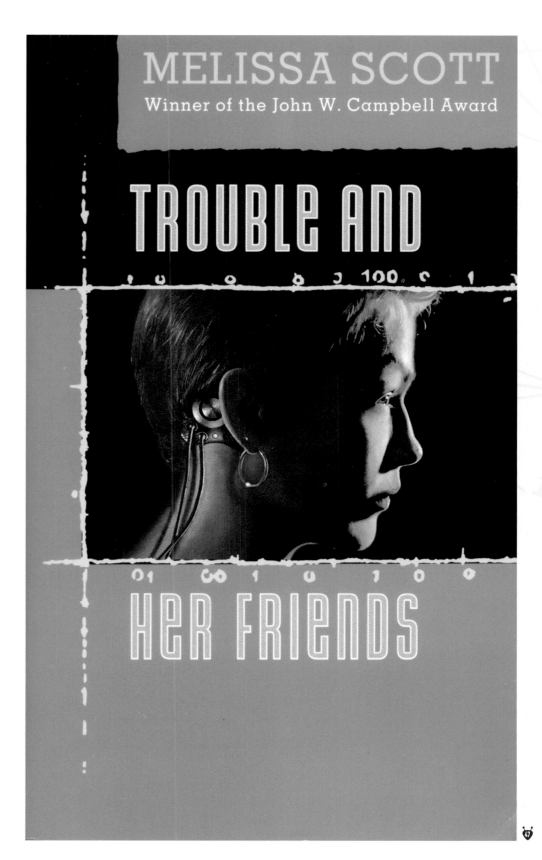

Before Hugo Gernsback coined the word "scientifiction" (which never really caught on) and "science fiction" (which did), before there were science-fiction magazines devoted to the subject, there was the occasional story that appeared in general magazines—and there were books. They weren't called science-fiction books—if they were called anything at the turn of the century, they were called "scientific romances." According to *Webster's*, a romance was "...a prose narrative treating imaginary characters involved in events remote in time or place and usually heroic, adventurous, or mysterious." To preface it with "scientific" was simply to help the book buyer know what he or she was getting into. Some experts date science fiction back to Plato's *Atlantis* and Lucian of Samosata's *Icaro-Menippus*, about a trip to the moon made with the aid of a wing from a vulture and another from an eagle.

CHAPTER 10
BOUND TO BE READ

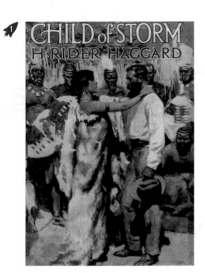

CHILD OF STORM
H. RIDER HAGGARD
1913
UNKNOWN

Haggard was a hugely popular writer of "lost race" stories —one who wrote anthropological science fiction, usually set in Darkest Africa. *Child of Storm* is part of the Quatermain series that began with *King Solomon's Mines*.

AT THE EARTH'S CORE
EDGAR RICE BURROUGHS
1922
J. ALLEN ST. JOHN

Burroughs wrote many stories about "Tarzan" and set other tales on Mars or Venus or in a land at the earth's core—"Pellucidar." A failure at many businesses, he found the gold at the rainbow's end when he tried writing.

THE DAY OF THE BROWN HORDE
RICHARD TOOKER
1929
UNKNOWN

The Day of the Brown Horde is a story of cavemen, "the saga of Kaa, the Unnamed," who—oddly enough—live around the Gulf of California. Quaint by modern standards, the book was popular in its day.

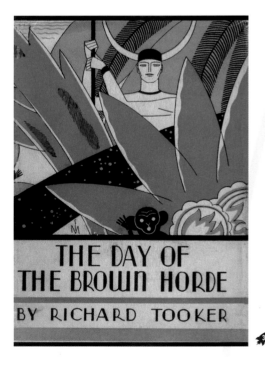

The tale was intended as satire, but one wonders if young Greeks might have read it for the imagination and the adventure and skipped the satirical aspects.

Science-fiction stories had been written since then up through the 1800s. Mary Shelley's *Frankenstein* was available in cheap editions, as were most of the stories by Poe and Verne. For books dating before then, some readers checked out the special reserve rooms at the local public or college library. But many science-fiction readers were also collectors, and the collecting bug really didn't hit until Edgar Rice Burroughs came on the scene.

Curling up with a copy of Wells or Verne or Poe from the library was fine, but Edgar Rice Burroughs hit science-fiction fans where they lived and with the fantastic and evocative dust jackets by J. Allen St. John and others, fans wanted to do more than read them. They wanted to *own* them, just like they owned the magazines they had saved.

The next step after starting a collection of novels by Burroughs was to collect hardbound books by other authors in the field. But if by other authors, you meant Heinlein and Asimov and Bradbury, forget it—there weren't any.

Some enterprising science-fiction fans recognized the desire and started their own small publishing companies specializing in nothing but science fiction or fantasy or horror. The first—Fantasy Publications —was founded by William L. Crawford whose initial effort was a small book, *Mars Mountain*, by Eugene George Key, hardly a household name.

The book was amateurish, but it was the very first book by a specialty science-fiction press.

Crawford's next endeavor was Visionary Press, which published H.P. Lovecraft's *The Shadow Over Innsmouth*. Four hundred copies were printed but

KING KONG
DELOS W. LOVELACE
1933
UNKNOWN

A novelization of the movie's screenplay (James A. Creelman and Ruth Rose—with some uncredited input by Edgar Wallace). The movie was a huge success, and the novelization a collector's item.

TARRANO THE CONQUEROR
RAY CUMMINGS
1930
UNKNOWN

'Ray Cummings wrote a number of serials for *Argosy* and Hugo Gernsback's *Science and Invention* (in which "Tarrano" ran as a fourteen-part serial).

ADVENTURES IN TIME AND SPACE

EDITED BY RAYMOND J. HEALY AND J. FRANCIS MCCOMAS

1946

GEORGE SALTER

Adventures in Time and Space was the seminal science-fiction anthology published shortly after World War II—and the first anthology to draw heavily on the science-fiction pulps, primarily *Astounding*.

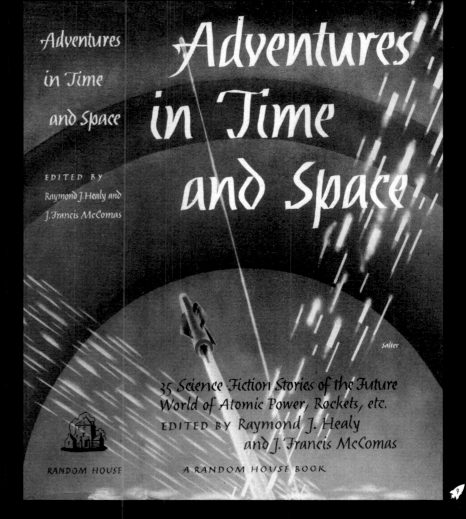

only two hundred bound; the rest were destroyed in a fire. Lovecraft was a considerably better known writer —a mainstay of *Weird Tales* at the time—and a fine copy at this writing will cost you around $5,500.

A more professional small press—Arkham House, founded by August Derleth and Donald Wandrei (both writers for *Weird Tales* and other magazines) —published another Lovecraft volume, *The Outsider and Others* in 1939. It was followed at more or less regular intervals with other horror and fantasy collections, including some by Ray Bradbury and Robert Bloch. In 1946 Arkham published A.E. van Vogt's science-fiction novel *Slan* in hardcover. It was one of the first science-fiction novels to be reprinted from the golden age of *Astounding*.

Adventures in Time and Space, the seminal science fiction anthology of short stories, appeared in 1946 as well. The publisher, Random House, later included the book in their Modern Library series. Editors Raymond J. Healy and J. Francis McComas also chose almost all their stories from *Astounding*, the first time a science-fiction magazine had been recognized to that extent by a mainstream publisher. The book sold amazingly well.

Perhaps most important of all, it showed there was a hardcover book market for modern science fiction. The specialty presses grew up like dandelions. Probably the biggest in number of titles published was Fantasy Press, founded by old-time fan and writer Lloyd Eshbach. It reprinted novels by John W. Campbell, L. Sprague de Camp, Williamson, and Weinbaum but its bread and butter were the space operas by E.E. "Doc" Smith.

Other specialty presses followed in short order. Prime Press, which published the seminal Sturgeon

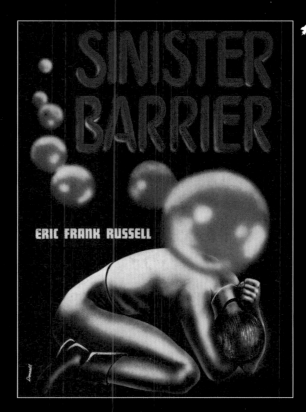

SINISTER BARRIER

ERIC FRANK RUSSELL

1948

A. J. DONNELL

Sinister Barrier, based on the idea that the human race is "property," launched *Unknown* magazine in 1939 It was published in book form in the U.S. by Fantasy Press, one of the more popular specialty presses.

THE HOMUNCULUS
DAVID H. KELLER, M.D.
1949
L. ROBERT TSCHIRKY

A contributor to the early *Amazing Stories* ("The Revolt of the Pedestrians"), Keller wrote a number of science-fiction and horror stories. The book was published by still another specialty press, Prime Press.

THE KINGSLAYER
L. RON HUBBARD
1949
WILLIAM BENULIS

Hubbard was famous for his fantasies that ran in *Unknown* and for his science-fiction novels *Final Blackout* and *To the Stars*, published in *Astounding*. *The Kingslayer* was published by FPCI, an early specialty press.

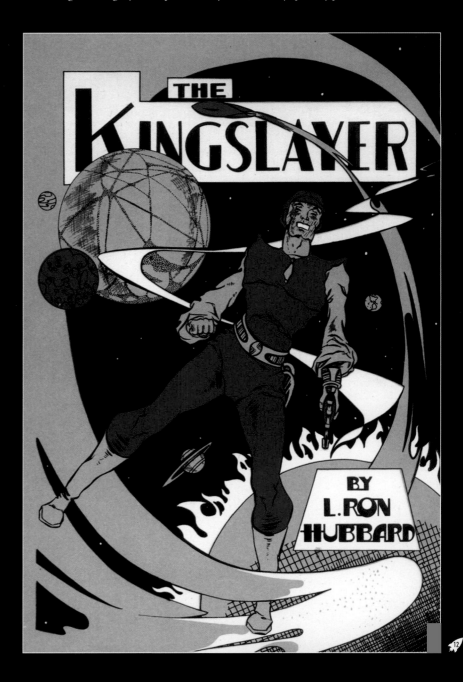

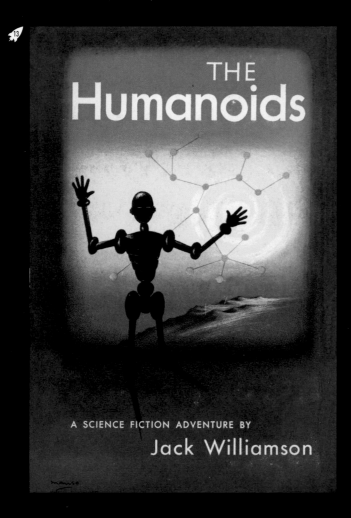

THE HUMANOIDS
JACK WILLIAMSON
1949
LEO MANSO

Williamson started writing science fiction in 1928 and is still writing as this book goes to press. Williamson's longevity is due to his ability to reinvent himself—from early space opera to later philosophical novels.

SIDEWISE IN TIME
MURRAY LEINSTER
1950
HANNES BOK

Leinster's career stretched from "The Runaway Skyscraper" (*Argosy*, 1919) until 1970. Like Williamson, he was adept at reinventing his writing to fit the changing times. This book, from Shasta—a specialty press—features a spectacular Hannes Bok wraparound dust jacket, presented here both front and back.

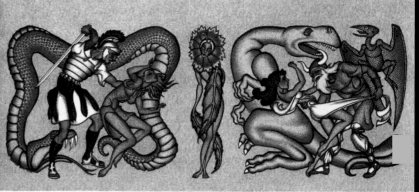

FOUNDATION AND EMPIRE
ISAAC ASIMOV
1952
EDD CARTIER

The model for the "Foundation" series was the fall of the Roman Empire—updated to thousands of years in the future. The stories took place in an entirely human universe—at editor Campbell's request, there were no aliens.

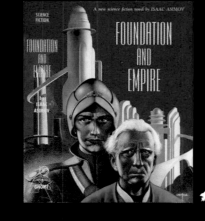

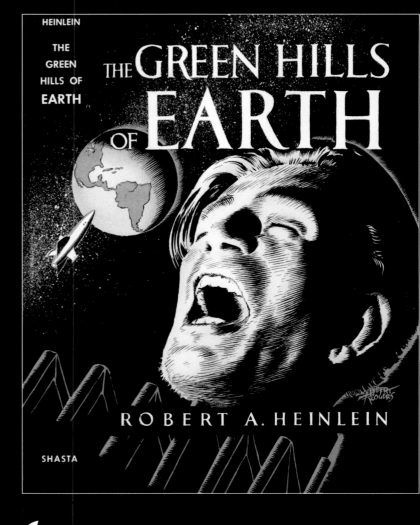

THE GREEN HILLS OF EARTH
ROBERT HEINLEIN
1951
HUBERT ROGERS

Another volume from Shasta with an evocative jacket by Hubert Rogers showing "Rhysling, the blind singer of the spaceways." One of the best of the Heinlein collections of short stories.

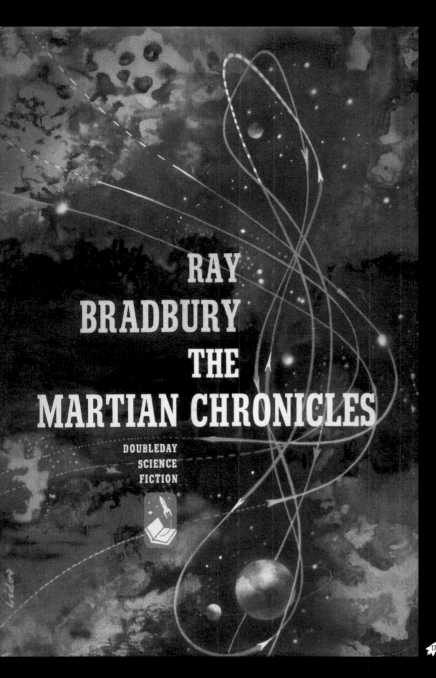

THE MARTIAN CHRONICLES
RAY BRADBURY
1950
LIDOV

This collection of short stories made Bradbury's reputation and promoted him from the pulps to the slicks. A craftsman in mood and character, Bradbury made Mars a curiously down-home and familiar place. A 1979 TV mini-series.

MISSION OF GRAVITY
HAL CLEMENT
1954
JOE MUGNAINI

A "hard science" author, Clement writes of a high-gravity world where humans would be crushed by their own weight—and the native Mesklinites must recover a lost rocket under the direction of the humans circling above.

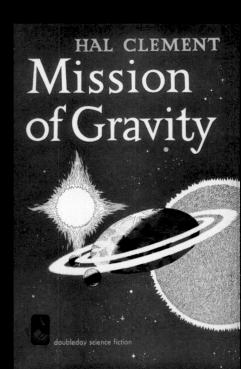

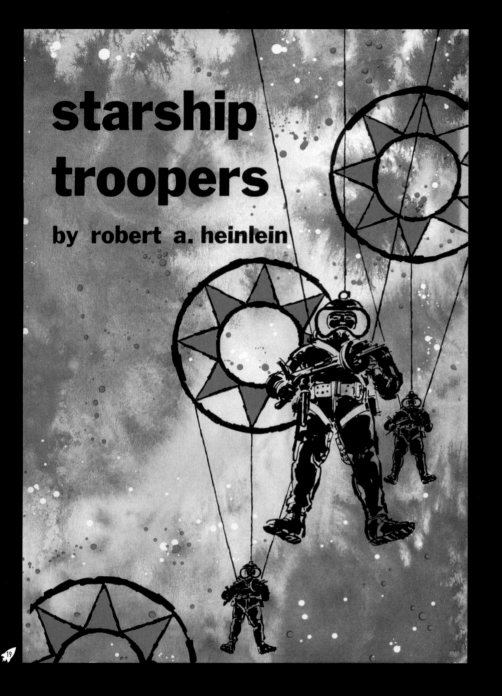

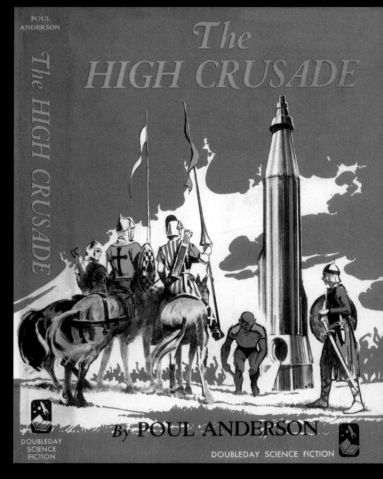

STARSHIP TROOPERS
ROBERT HEINLEIN
1959
JERRY ROBINSON

Intended as a juvenile, *Starship Troopers* was initially rejected because of its violence. The book revealed Heinlein's strong political and social opinions. The book still won the Hugo.

A CANTICLE FOR LEIBOWITZ
WALTER M. MILLER, JR.
1960
MILTON GLASER

The Catholic Order of Leibowitz has the task of preserving scientific knowledge during the Dark Ages that follow a nuclear holocaust 600 years before. A 1961 Hugo winner.

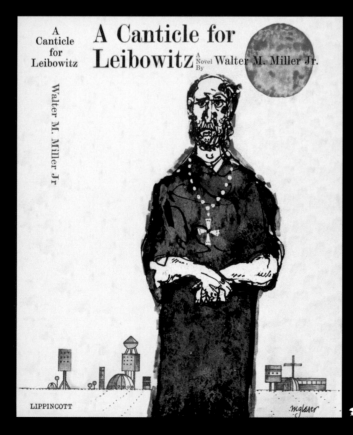

THE HIGH CRUSADE
POUL ANDERSON
1960
HARRY SCHAARE

Poul Anderson wrote every type of science fiction from "hard science" to humor. *The High Crusade* concerns a medieval baron who takes over an alien spaceship when it lands in the back-forty and sets out to found a galactic feudal empire.

STRANGER IN A STRANGE LAND
ROBERT HEINLEIN
1961
BEN FEDER, INC.

Heinlein's most famous novel and a distinct departure from his previous books. Far more philosophical in tone, it championed free love and became a cult favorite of both hippies and students in the 1960s.

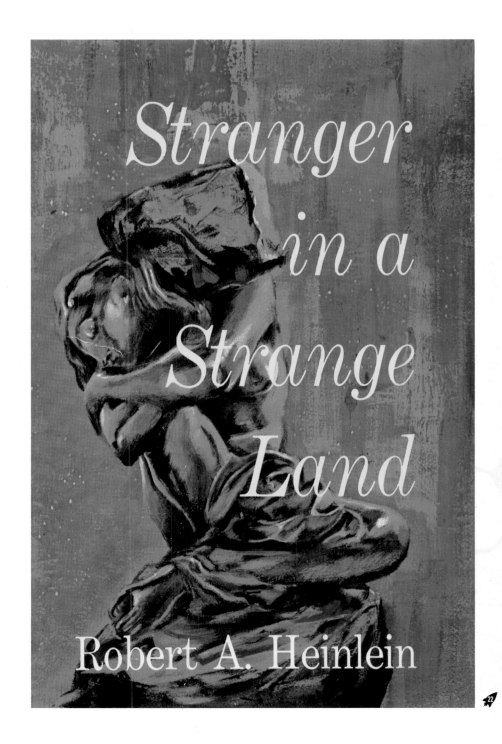

Sorcery. Gnome Press, founded in 1948 by Martin Greenberg and David A. Kyle, which published some fifty books and lasted into the 1960s. Among their authors were Robert E. Howard with his *Conan* series, Isaac Asimov, Arthur C. Clarke, and Robert A. Heinlein.

Shasta Publishers of Chicago made a name for itself with the publication of E.F. Bleiler's *The Checklist of Fantastic Literature* in 1948, initially regarded as helpful to collectors but vastly more important than that. It established science fiction as a literary field with a long history and tradition and gained the genre a foothold in libraries and universities.

Shasta went on to publish novels and collections by Robert A. Heinlein, John W. Campbell, L. Ron Hubbard, and L. Sprague de Camp. It was noted for its spectacular dust jackets by Hannes Bok and notorious for its sponsorship of a science-fiction novel competition along with Pocket Books. Philip José Farmer's *I Owe for the Flesh* won the contest. But Farmer never saw the prize money, and the publishing company died shortly thereafter.

Specialty houses still thriving at the end of the millennium included Donald M. Grant, Publishers, known for its collections and special "first editions" of Stephen King. Grant's 1997 hardback edition of King's *Dark Tower IV: Wizard and Glass* sold 40,000 copies and made the New York Times best-seller list—the first time a specialty house had done so.

Advent: Publishers, Inc., which had published Damon Knight's collection of critical essays *In Search of Wonder* early on, published Howard Devore's updated compendium of Hugo and Nebula winners in 1998. Dark Harvest came out with a boxed collection of stories by Charles Beaumont; Tachyon Publications of San Francisco with a collection of stories by Clifford

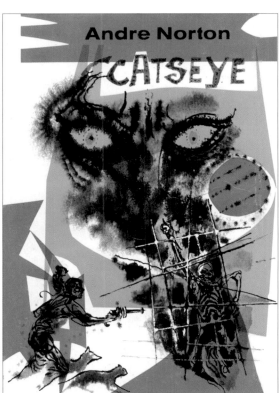

CATSEYE
ANDRÉ NORTON
1961
RICHARD M. POWERS

André Norton, a librarian for years before writing her "children's" books, has had two writing careers: science-fiction novels taking place against a galactic civilization background, followed by a series of fantasy books.

A CLOCKWORK ORANGE
ANTHONY BURGESS
1963
LARRY TURIN

A composer as well as a writer, as a novelist Burgess is best known for *A Clockwork Orange*, told in the fascinating first person argot of Alex, a juvenile delinquent in the near future. Filmed under the same title.

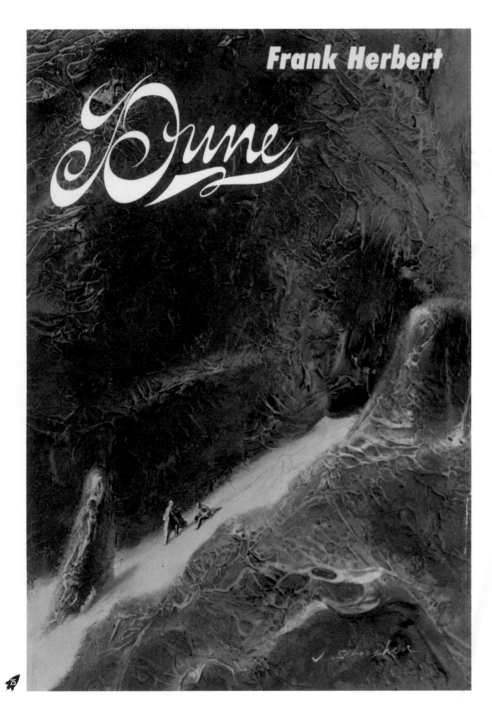

DUNE
FRANK HERBERT
1965
JOHN SCHOENHERR

Dune won the 1965 Nebula and shared the 1966 Hugo. One of the most popular science-fiction novels written, it was a complex novel of adventure and galactic politics set on the desert planet of Arrakis. It spawned five sequels and was later filmed by director David Lynch.

Simak, Underwood Books (formerly Underwood-Miller) with a spectacular boxed edition of Harlan Ellison's "'Repent, Harlequin!' Said the Ticktockman" with a jacket by Rick Berry; Fedogan & Bremer with books by Donald and Howard Wandrei as well as Richard A. Lupoff's collection, *Before…12:01… and After*. NESFA Press continued with its collections of Cordwainer Smith, James Schmitz, and Murray Leinster…

The specialty presses did books of high quality for the collector or researcher. Print runs were small, prices were high. Many of them splurged on quality book jackets famous for their style and art, a trend that mainstream publishers followed. By the end of the '90s, science-fiction jackets were spectacularly eye-catching in art and design, making the books some of the most attractive in the store.

It was the success of the early specialty houses that encouraged major publishers to look into the salability of Isaac Asimov and Robert Heinlein and others. The flood of 1900-plus genre books for 1998 actually started as a very small trickle in the early 1950s…

Certain authors stand out like beacons in the hardcover book field. The first is Edgar Rice Burroughs, one of the most collected authors of the 20th century. Never really successful at various business ventures, Burroughs' first sale was *Under the Moons of Mars* to *All-Story Magazine* in 1912. His second was *Tarzan of the Apes*, published complete in *All-Story* for October of that year. The first won high praise; the second created a sensation. Both novels did very well later on in hardback (and reprint) versions by A.C. McClurg and Grosset and Dunlap.

But the term "science fiction" hadn't been invented yet and "scientific romance" didn't seem appropriate to *Tarzan*. The novels were simply novels by Edgar

LORD OF LIGHT

ROGER ZELAZNY
1967
HOWARD BERNSTEIN

Winner of a 1968 Hugo and a 1968
Nebula nominee, Zelazny was a
prominent member of the "new
wave" in science fiction. A later
book, *Damnation Alley* (1969),
was filmed with all of the action
but none of the poetry.

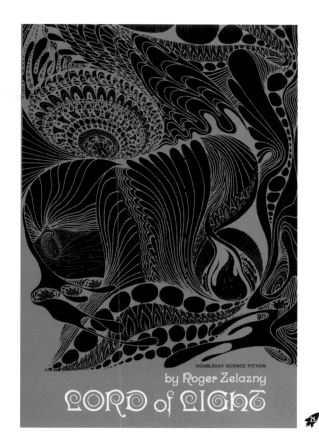

Rice Burroughs. This distinction became important
to later writers in the field.

The first two major authors to hit the best-seller
lists who sprang directly from the science-fiction
field were Ray Bradbury and Robert Heinlein.
Bradbury was your typical science-fiction fan—he
discovered fandom when he was seventeen and even
published his own fan magazine. He served his
apprenticeship in the magazines of the 1940s for
which he wrote a series of "linked" stories about
Mars. Later collected in a book, *The Martian
Chronicles*, they made Bradbury's reputation—and
not just among science-fiction readers per se. From
then on, Bradbury's short stories appeared primarily
in the *Saturday Evening Post*, *Esquire*, *McCall's* and
Collier's—all major slick magazines of the period.
Bradbury's smooth, dream-like style and his ability
to evoke images of childhood and life in small-town
America endeared him to mainstream readers.

Bradbury wasn't turned on to technology to the
same degree that other science-fiction writers were.
But he was optimistic about the future, and whenever
a television show or a publisher needed a sound bite
or a quote about life in the next millennium, the first
author they thought of was Ray Bradbury.

Bradbury soon became involved in film as well as
books. His movies included *Fahrenheit 451*, *Something
Wicked This Way Comes*, *The Illustrated Man*, and

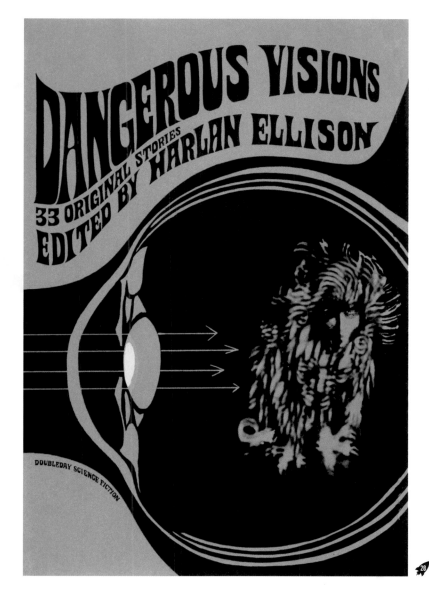

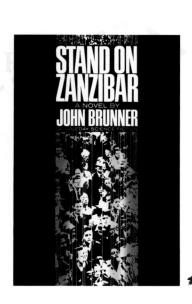

STAND ON ZANZIBAR

JOHN BRUNNER
1968
S.A. SUMMIT, INC.

A 1968 Nebula nominee and 1969
Hugo winner, Brunner's classic
novel also won the 1970 British
Science Fiction Award and the
French translation won the 1973
Prix Apollo.

DANGEROUS VISIONS

HARLAN ELLISON
1967
DIANE AND LEO DILLON

A seminal science-fiction anthology emphasizing the unique
and the new. Edited by one of the most honored writers in
the field, Ellison has written everything from short stories to
film scripts to the best single episode of the original *Star Trek*.

CAMP CONCENTRATION
THOMAS M. DISCH
1969
SAUL LAMBERT

An author whose stories and novels showed up regularly on early Hugo and Nebula lists, Disch is also a poet and theater critic—and a somewhat acerbic analyst of science fiction and its attendant culture.

BUG JACK BARRON
NORMAN SPINRAD
1969
JACK GAUGHAN

A stunning example of "new wave" science fiction, *Bug Jack Barron* was nominated for both a Hugo and a Nebula but lost out to a more traditional science-fiction novel, *The Left Hand of Darkness*, by Ursula K. Le Guin.

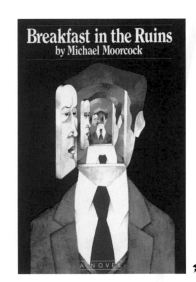

BREAKFAST IN THE RUINS
MICHAEL MOORCOCK
1971
UNKNOWN

Moorcock is a protean British talent, the author of dozens of fantasy and science-fiction novels, one-time editor of *New Worlds*, which pioneered the "new wave," and—early in life—a blues singer in nightclubs.

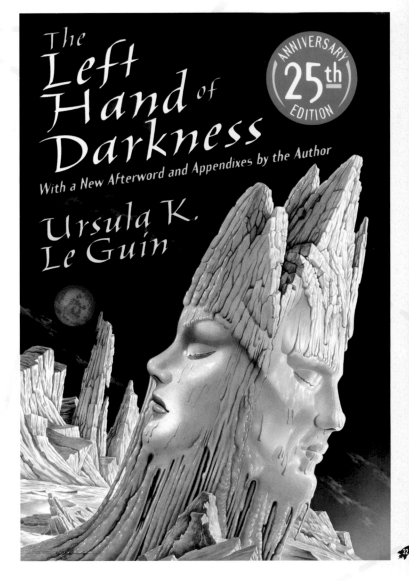

THE LEFT HAND OF DARKNESS
URSULA K. LE GUIN
1969
ALEX EBEL

A 1994 reprint of Le Guin's award-winning novel about the world called Winter whose inhabitants lack a fixed gender—becoming either male or female as circumstances demand.

TO YOUR SCATTERED BODIES GO
PHILIP JOSÉ FARMER
1971
IRA COHEN

Author Farmer first gained fame with *The Lovers*, published in *Startling Stories* and acclaimed for its open sexuality. One of his most famous novels, *To Your Scattered Bodies Go*, was part of the "Riverworld" series.

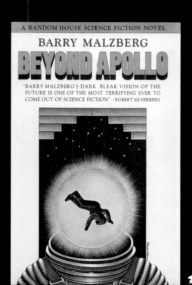

BEYOND APOLLO
BARRY MALZBERG
1972
ROGER HANE

Barry Malzberg has written mysteries and thrillers as well as science fiction. Editor of *Amazing* for a brief period, he was also the author of some twenty science-fiction novels.

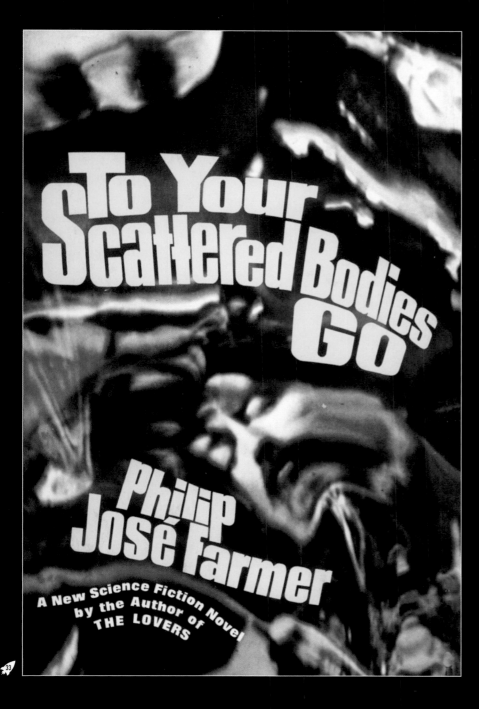

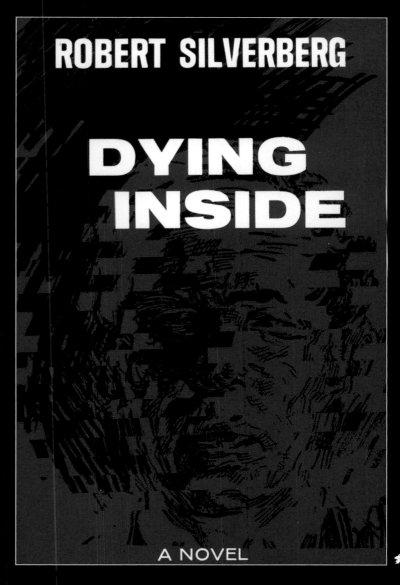

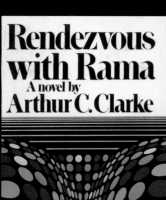

RENDEZVOUS WITH RAMA
ARTHUR C. CLARKE
1973
HAL SIEGEL

Perhaps the best-known modern science-fiction writer, Clarke is famous for his extrapolations based on scientific fact and his ability to make them accessible to the general reader as well as to the science-fiction buff.

DYING INSIDE
ROBERT SILVERBERG
1972
JERRY THORP

One of the most prolific of all science-fiction writers (utilizing a telephone book of pseudonyms), Silverberg's books have ranged from lighthearted space operas to well-crafted philosophical novels to fantasies, anthologies, and carefully researched nonfiction.

WHERE LATE THE SWEET BIRDS SANG
KATE WILHELM
1976
PHOTOGRAPH: JAMES KALETT OF
M.C. ESCHER'S *DAY AND NIGHT*

Sweet Birds is about an isolated community of clones in the Appalachians after a holocaust. Author Wilhelm specialized in people-oriented stories; she was also involved in the Clarion Science Fiction Writers Workshop.

several B movies based on short stories, *It Came From Outer Space* and *The Beast From 20,000 Fathoms*. A number of his stories were also adapted for *The Twilight Zone*.

Bradbury won fame not alone as a science-fiction writer but as…Ray Bradbury. He had transcended the field itself.

Robert A. Heinlein was a career science-fiction writer and known as one all of his professional life. A graduate of the U.S. Naval Academy at Annapolis, he retired because of ill health in 1934. He sold his first story, "Life-Line," to *Astounding* in 1939 and before he died in 1988 had published fifty-four books with more than forty million copies sold.

Before becoming a writer, Heinlein dabbled in politics (his knowledge of it continually showed up in his fiction) and ran but was defeated for the California State Assembly in 1939. Soon after that, his stories and novels made him the star of *Astounding* under his own and his pen name, Anson MacDonald.

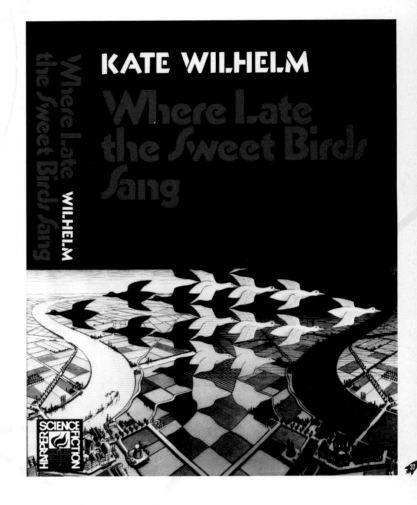

GATEWAY
FREDERIK POHL
1977
BORIS VALLEJO

Fred Pohl has been an editor, agent, and author. He won fame with *The Space Merchants* (with C.M. Kornbluth) and has collaborated extensively with Jack Williamson. *Gateway* won both the Hugo and the Nebula.

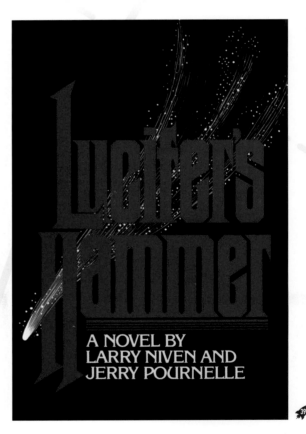

LUCIFER'S HAMMER
LARRY NIVEN AND JERRY POURNELLE
1977
ANTHONY RUSSO

Twenty years before *Armageddon* and *Deep Impact* were filmed, *Lucifer's Hammer* related what would happen if a comet struck the Earth. Authors Niven and Pournelle are justly famous for their "hard science" stories.

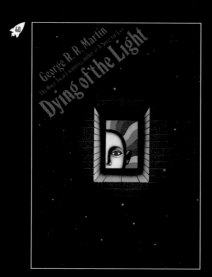

FRANKENSTEIN UNBOUND
BRIAN W. ALDISS
1973
PAUL BACON

Aldiss is a historian of science fiction as well as one of its leading award-winning authors. He and Michael Moorcock have been credited as two of the originators of the "new wave" in science fiction.

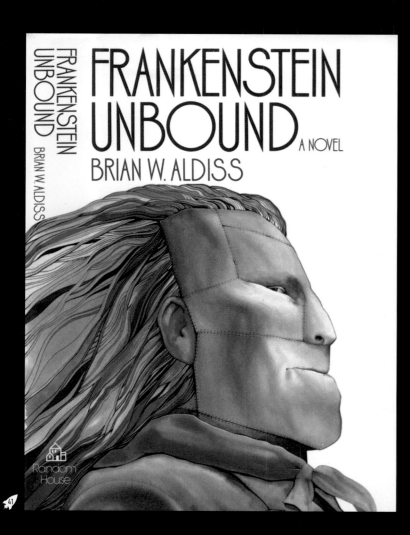

DREAMSNAKE
VONDA N. MCINTYRE
1978
STEPHEN ALEXANDER

A superb storyteller and a feminist with a large following, McIntyre writes stories that are largely character driven. *Dreamsnake* won the Hugo and the Nebula. McIntyre has also written movie tie-in novels for *Star Trek*.

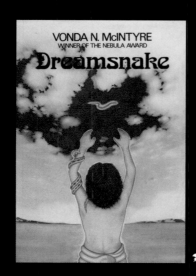

DYING OF THE LIGHT
GEORGE R.R. MARTIN
1977
SEYMOUR CHWAST/HARUO MIYAUCHI

A journalist and teacher, Martin has written both science fiction and horror stories. *Dying of the Light* is reportedly his only science-fiction novel, though he has won three Hugos and a Nebula for his shorter work.

Heinlein had a scientific background and an affection for the "hard sciences," though he also did surprisingly well with the sociology of his stories. After the war, he sold four science-fiction stories to the *Saturday Evening Post* and branched out with a series of juvenile novels.

His twelfth juvenile, *Starship Troopers*, was rejected by his editor at Scribner for being too militaristic. Putnam's bought it as an adult novel, and it won the Hugo. (It was also filmed in 1997. Previous films included *The Puppet Masters* and *Destination Moon*.)

His biggest success was *Stranger in a Strange Land*, which won the Hugo and was the first science-fiction novel to hit the *New York Times* best-seller list. Several years later, in paperback, it became a handbook for hippies. *Starship Troopers* and *Stranger in a Strange Land* were polar opposites as novels. Accused of being Fascistic in one, Heinlein was in turn accused of advocating free love in the other. The fact was that he had written portions of both at the same time, sometimes lifting notes he had made for one and using them in the other.

With succeeding novels Heinlein soon became the biggest kid on the block—he never denied writing science fiction but science fiction was whatever he said it was. In effect, he switched from writing stereotypical "science fiction" to writing mainstream novels without missing a keystroke. He made the best-seller lists again with *Job: A Comedy of Justice* (1984, written when he was 77), *The Cat Who Walks Through Walls*, and *To Sail Beyond the Sunset*, his last book published at age 80.

There was no writer who was more of a science-fiction writer than Heinlein—and who so successfully transcended the genre despite the label. But the real highpoint of his career, according to an interview

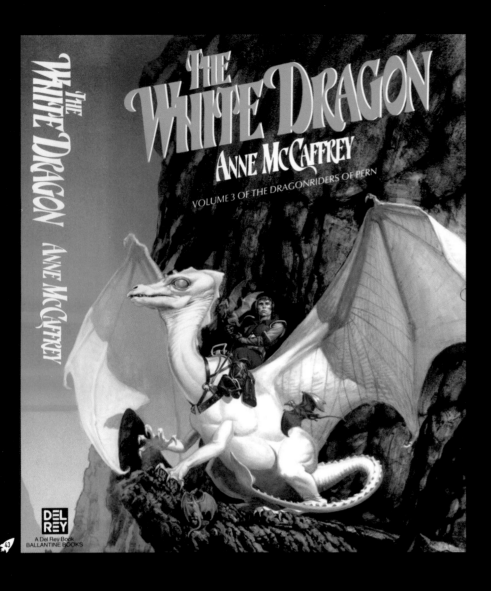

THE WHITE DRAGON
ANNE MCCAFFREY
1978
MICHAEL WHELAN

Wildly popular among younger readers, McCaffrey's stories about the dragons of Pern and their human riders are frequently considered fantasies though the series started as science fiction and first saw print in *Astounding*.

commissioned by *Playboy* (but published in its companion magazine, *Oui*), was watching the first Moon landing and feeling a wave of vindication sweep over him.

"It was the greatest day and the greatest experience in my life. Somebody standing behind me in the crowd shouted, 'They're really on their way to the *Moon*!' It was then I realized…that for the first time in history I was actually seeing a spaceship lift off on a journey to another celestial body…I (had) waited fifty years for this, literally fifty years. Half a century of being treated like a madman for believing what has been perfectly evident since the days of Sir Isaac Newton…"

Heinlein wrote science fiction not just to make a buck but because he was a true believer. His novels turned out to be more polemical as he grew older but he never stopped believing.

Like Isaac Asimov, whose career his own roughly paralleled, Arthur C. Clarke started as a young science-fiction enthusiast. He served in World War II as a radar instructor and graduated from Kings College, London, with honors in mathematics and physics.

Twice Chairman of the British Interplanetary Society, in 1945 he wrote an article for *Wireless World*, "Extra-Terrestrial Relays," about the feasibility of communication satellites. Twenty years later, they would be fact. (He frequently joked about how rich he might have become if he had patented the idea.) In the 1950s he moved to Sri Lanka and became fascinated with skindiving and photography, writing *The Coast of Coral* and other books about his adventures. His career was split between being a science-fiction writer and a science popularizer. He won numerous awards in both fields.

BIG PLANET
JACK VANCE
1978
STEVE HICKMAN

Jack Vance was educated as a mining engineer, physicist, and journalist. *Big Planet* was one of his best-known books. This edition by Underwood-Miller, a specialty house publisher, inadvertently left his byline off the cover.

SOME WILL NOT DIE
ALGIS BUDRYS
1978
KELLY FREAS

Some Will Not Die was originally published as *False Night*, Budrys' first novel. Budrys is known as a brilliant book reviewer and for many years was administrator of the Writers of the Future contest.

He had been well-established in the science-fiction field long before he co-scripted the screenplay (along with director Stanley Kubrick) of *2001: A Space Odyssey*, which has been called the first really modern science-fiction film. He novelized the script and wrote a sequel, *2010: Odyssey Two*, which was also filmed.

After the release of *2001*, Clarke became the most widely known science-fiction writer in the world. His novelization of the movie hit the best-seller lists, as did *Rendezvous With Rama* and *The Fountains of Paradise* (both books won the Hugo and the Nebula).

Known for the unique scientific concepts in his stories, Clarke also showed a broad streak of mysticism in his earlier books (*The City and the Stars*, *Childhood's End*).

Clarke was a commentator on the later moon missions for CBS-TV and remarked in an interview (incorporated in a "dialogue" with Zen expert Alan Watts for *Playboy*) that, like Heinlein, he had been moved to tears by the first Moon landing. He also agreed with Heinlein in speculating that perhaps mankind didn't belong on the Earth but in the sea or out in space, that we weren't "built" for the rigors of gravity.

What was astonishing about Clarke was his ability to spin off unusual concepts, to look at the world and its possibilities through a science-fiction writer's eyes. To speculate that receiving an interstellar communication would be the first real proof that intelligence had survival value; that the one thing a fish could never conceive of was fire; that the chief benefit of eyeglasses was that they multiplied the lifetime of the scholar; that the invention of the horse collar was important because for the first time it enabled a horse to pull more than its own weight without being strangled; that our skin is the functional equivalent

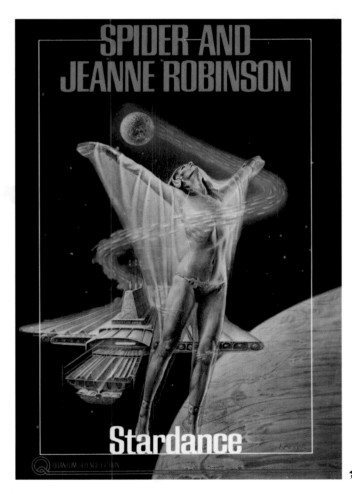

STARDANCE
SPIDER AND JEANNE ROBINSON
1979
LARRY KRESEK

Stardance won both the Hugo and Nebula awards when it first appeared as a novella in *Astounding*. The novel of the same name proved immensely popular with readers. Jeanne Robinson has been both a dancer and a choreographer.

BATTLEFIELD EARTH

L. RON HUBBARD
1982
PAUL STINSON

After an absence of more than thirty years, L. Ron Hubbard returned to the science-fiction field with *Battlefield Earth*, one of the longest science-fiction novels written. It immediately made the *New York Times* best-seller list.

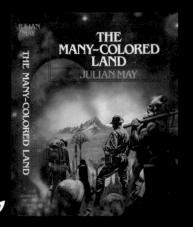

47

THE MANY-COLORED LAND

JULIAN MAY
1981
KEN BARR

Julian May wrote the well-received story "Dune Roller" for *Astounding* in 1951, then abandoned the field to write a series of nonfiction juveniles, returning to science fiction thirty years later with *The Many Colored Land* (nominated for both the Hugo and the Nebula).

47

48

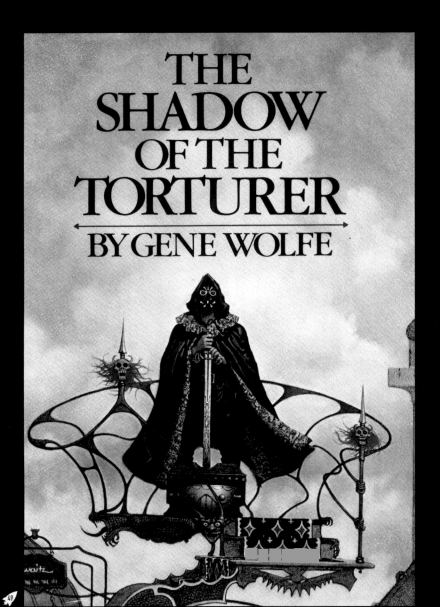

49

49

THE SHADOW OF THE TORTURER

GENE WOLFE
1980
DON MAITZ

Wolfe is best known for the four novels that make up *The Book of the New Sun* (*The Shadow of the Torturer* is the first). Wolfe is a superb stylist and *The Book of the New Sun* could be favorably compared to a science-fiction version of Lawrence Durrell's *The*

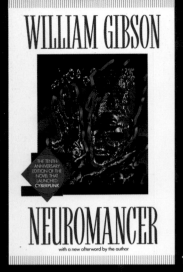

NEUROMANCER

WILLIAM GIBSON
1984
RICK BERRY

The tenth anniversary hardback edition of Gibson's *Neuromancer*, the novel that launched "cyber-punk," stories dealing with the new world of cyberspace. It won the Hugo, the Nebula, and the Philip K. Dick awards. Appropriately, the jacket by Rick Berry was the very first computer-generated cover.

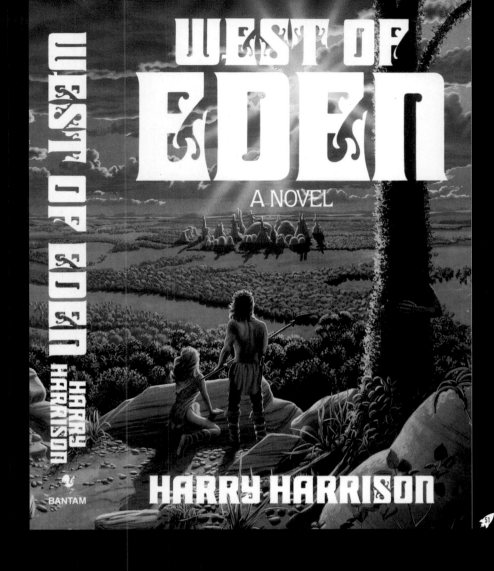

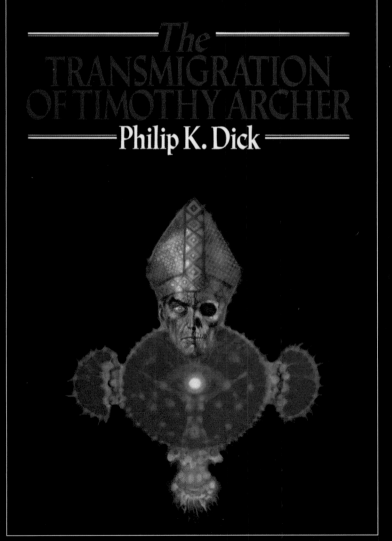

THE TRANSMIGRATION OF TIMOTHY ARCHER

PHILIP K. DICK
1982
RICHARD POWERS

One of the most important figures in science fiction, Philip K. Dick was a master stylist and idea man. Dick died before this book was published—nor did he live to see his stories filmed as the blockbusters *Blade Runner* (starring Harrison Ford) and *Total Recall* (with Arnold Schwarzenegger).

WEST OF EDEN

HARRY HARRISON
1984
DAVID SCHLEINKOFER

West of Eden is a novel of an alternative future in which a meteorite does *not* wipe out the dinosaurs, and they still rule the Earth.

DIE LAUTLOSE MACHT ("THE POWER")

FRANK M. ROBINSON
1982
DAVID MATTINGLY

A German book club edition of the editor's 1956 novel, *The Power*. Sometimes book jackets for foreign editions are far superior to those native born.

203

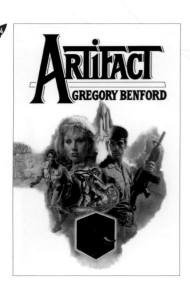

ARTIFACT
GREGORY BENFORD
1985
DAN GONZALEZ

Benford is a professor of physics and master of the "hard science" novel. (His *Timescape* won the Nebula and the John W. Campbell award.) The "artifact" proves to be of alien origin whose theft has disastrous consequences.

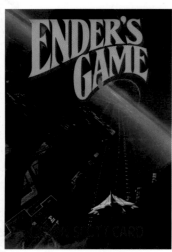

ENDER'S GAME
ORSON SCOTT CARD
1985
JOHN HARRIS

Winner of both the Hugo and the Nebula, *Ender's Game* was an auspicious introduction of Card to science fiction. His *Speaker for the Dead* also won a Hugo. A devout Mormon, Card's religion infuses his writing, though it hardly handicaps it—he's one of the most popular writers in the genre.

CONTACT
CARL SAGAN
1985
JON LOMBERG

A top science popularizer (PBS's series *Cosmos*— "billyuns and billyuns") and Pulitzer Prize winner (*Dragons of Eden*), Sagan tried fiction with *Contact*, a novel about the first contact between humans and extraterrestrials. It was a resounding success and filmed (starring Jodie Foster) in 1997.

LIFE DURING WARTIME
LUCIUS SHEPARD
1987
J. K. POTTER

Shepard has been a poet, a rock band leader while in his mid-twenties, and started writing science fiction in 1983 (he won the John W. Campbell Award for 1985). His *Life During Wartime* has been compared to a Vietnam war novel set in the Western Hemisphere.

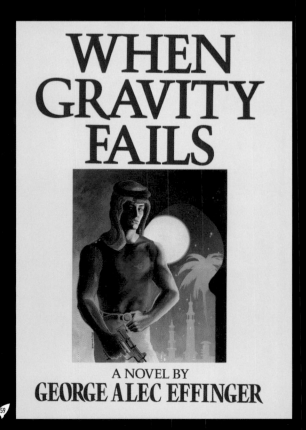

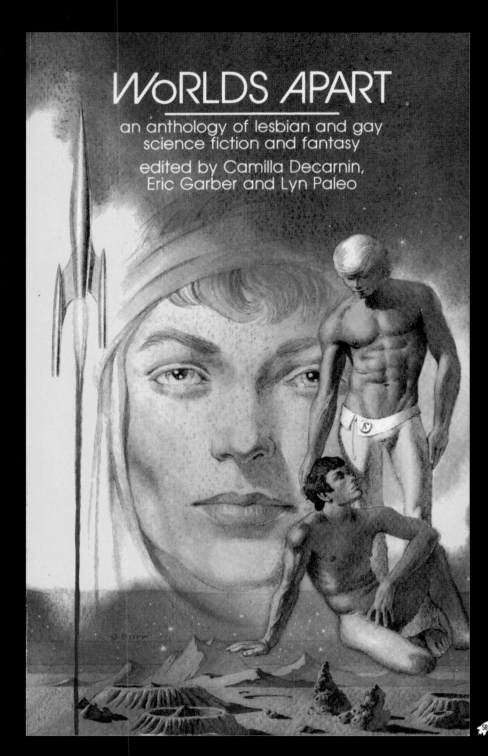

WORLDS APART
EDITED BY CAMILLA DECARNIN, ERIC GARBER AND LYN PALEO
1986
GEORGE BARR

One of the first anthologies of science fiction with gay and lesbian themes. Authors represented include Edgar Pangborn, James Tiptree, Jr., Marion Zimmer Bradley, Samuel R. Delany, Joanna Russ, John Varley, Elizabeth A. Lynn, Jewelle Gomez, and Walt Liebscher, among others.

WHEN GRAVITY FAILS
GEORGE ALEC EFFINGER
1987
MICHAEL HINGE

Effinger established an early reputation with his short stories, but his best works were his later novels dealing with a twenty-first century Middle East— *When Gravity Fails, A Fire in the Sun,* and *The Exile Kiss.*

THE UPLIFT WAR
DAVID BRIN
1987
WAYNE D. BARLOWE

Brin is a "hard science" writer best known for his "Uplift" series—*Sundiver, The Uplift War*—for which he won a Hugo, and *Startide Rising* (a Hugo and a Nebula). Brin knows his way around the galaxy but it was his more down-to-earth *The Postman* that was chosen to be filmed by Kevin Costner.

2061: ODYSSEY THREE
ARTHUR C. CLARKE
1988
MICHAEL WHELAN

Clarke shared an Oscar nomination with Stanley Kubrick for the screenplay of *2001: A Space Odyssey* but also wrote the book of the same title. Its sequel, *2010: Odyssey Two*, was also filmed. Like Isaac Asimov and Carl Sagan, Clarke has been a major science popularizer and written many nonfiction books, as well as hosting a TV show.

ADULTHOOD RITES
OCTAVIA BUTLER
1988
WAYNE BARLOWE

Octavia Butler has won both the Hugo and the Nebula. Her novels are primarily character driven, depicting the relationships between aliens and humans—and their offspring.

of a spacesuit; that the creation of a perfect synthetic food would solve one of the great moral dilemmas of our times (do animals feel pain? do plants?) and allow vast tracts of land to go back to nature; that an alien with a different persistence of vision could not "see" television as we do but only a dot of light moving across the screen; that with electronic aid someday a man or woman might be able to go to work without ever leaving home (the interview was taken in 1971, long before Web sites and the Internet)…

Clarke was living in the Chelsea Hotel in New York, on business in the States at the time of the interview. Surprisingly, his partner in the interview, Alan Watts, the apostle of the hippies, knew all the millionaires on Sutton Place. It was Clarke, on the other hand, who was friends with all the bookstore clerks on Eighth Avenue.

A fan of technology—it was one of Clarke's beliefs that biological life was merely a way station on the way to developing electronic life—he took Watts and the interviewer to the roof of the Chelsea to demonstrate a toy laser he had just bought. He flashed it on the sidewalk below where the beam appeared as a small circle of reddish light. Like a kid,

CONSIDER PHLEBAS
IAIN M. BANKS
1988
RICHARD HOPKINSON

A Scotsman, Banks is a relatively new writer to the genre whose *Consider Phlebas* was highly praised.

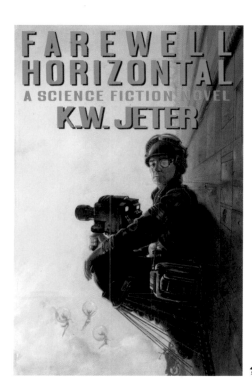

FAREWELL HORIZONTAL
K. W. JETER
1989
BRYN BARNARD

Perhaps better known as a horror novelist, Jeter wrote one of his few science-fiction novels with *Farewell Horizontal*. His ideas and concepts and ability with a light touch have earned praise from the critics.

HYPERION

DAN SIMMONS
1989
GARY RUDDELL

Hyperion won the 1990 Hugo and was followed a year later with *The Fall of Hyperion*. Some critics have classified the books as space operas—written with great skill and intelligence.

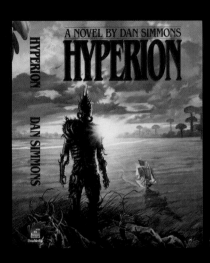

JURASSIC PARK

MICHAEL CRICHTON

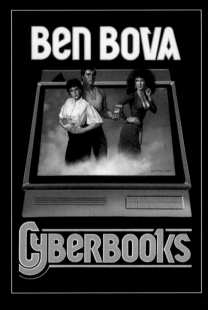

JURASSIC PARK

MICHAEL CRICHTON
1990
CHIP KIDD

The most commercially successful science-fiction writer of all time. Michael Crichton's novels include *The Andromeda Strain*, *Congo*, and *Sphere* (all filmed). Of all his novels, *Jurassic Park* was far and away the most successful, both as a book and as a film directed by Stephen Spielberg.

CYBERBOOKS

BEN BOVA
1989
BORIS VALLEJO

Ben Bova assumed the editorship of *Analog* in 1971, later became the editor of *Omni*, leaving that magazine to freelance. Bova is a "hard science" writer with a fondness for stories about the future of the space program.

THE SUMMER QUEEN
JOAN D. VINGE
1991
MICHAEL WHELAN

The Summer Queen was a sequel to Vinge's Hugo Award winning *The Snow Queen*, written ten years before. In between Vinge wrote movie tie-ins for *Star Wars: Return of the Jedi, The Dune Storybook, Willow*, and others.

he tried to distract pedestrians and was delighted when a drunk danced with the bobbing circle of light.

Clarke's stories were seldom noted for their characterization but were acclaimed for the novel concepts that the author brought to life on the printed page.

In Clarke's own words, he was a man nostalgic for the future.

Clarke was certainly not the last of the old-timers, but he could probably serve as a symbol of the changing times in the science-fiction field. The days when a magazine editor would ask an author to write a short story or a novelette based on a cover painting were over. Sixteen and seventeen-year-old wunderkinder still might contribute the occasional short story. But they were far fewer than before, and the chance that they would turn out a notable novel was vanishingly slim—the level of sophistication in both writing and story-line had increased tremendously since the 1930s.

The writers were getting older, and it showed in what they wrote. "Classics" were still being reprinted, primarily by the specialty presses, but yesterday's novels were not the stuff of which the future was made. The Old Guard had been children of the Great Depression. Few of them had degrees in the sciences—few of them had college degrees, period. Doc Smith was proud of his Ph.D. and so were his readers—never mind that he was a cereal chemist, an expert on doughnut mixes. And certainly management at Street & Smith had been impressed by Campbell's degree in physics.

Granted that there isn't necessarily a link between a degree and creativity, but at millennium's end any meeting of the Science Fiction Writers of America could boast more degrees than candy canes on the average Christmas tree.

Gregory Benford had a Ph.D. in physics, David Brin a B.S. in astronomy and an M.S. in applied physics, Larry Niven a B.A. in mathematics, Jerry Pournelle an undergraduate degree in engineering and Ph.D.s in psychology and political science, Pamela Sargent an M.A. in classical philosophy, Ursula K. Le Guin an M.S. in Romance literature of the Middle Ages and the Renaissance (she was also the daughter of Alfred and Theodora Kroeber, Alfred being a noted anthropologist and Theodora an accomplished writer).

Whatever these authors might write, it would not be "Hollywood on the Moon" or "Pariah Girls from Outer Space." They were writing for an adult audience, and what they wrote was no longer "product" —they wanted to present their own glimpse of what the future might bring, explore new thoughts and concepts, and fashion a subtext around something they thought important to say.

Science fiction was changing and so was the audience. The young kids and teenagers who had been so

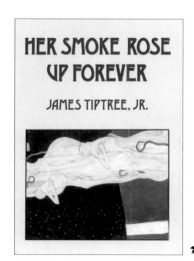

HER SMOKE ROSE UP FOREVER
JAMES TIPTREE, JR.
1990
GUSTAV KLIMT

"James Tiptree, Jr." was the pseudonym of Alice B. Sheldon. She had a talent for portraying relationships between males and females—and humans and aliens. *Her Smoke Rose Up Forever* is a collection of her best stories.

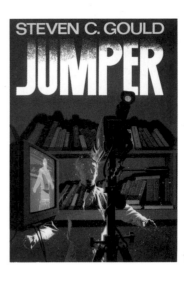

JUMPER
STEVEN GOULD
1992
ROMAS

Jumper is a coming-of-age story about a young man who can teleport himself—"jump"—from one location to another. But the ability can be dangerous, and the hero needs to find others who can jump. *Jumper* is a character-driven book and the author was much praised for his skill.

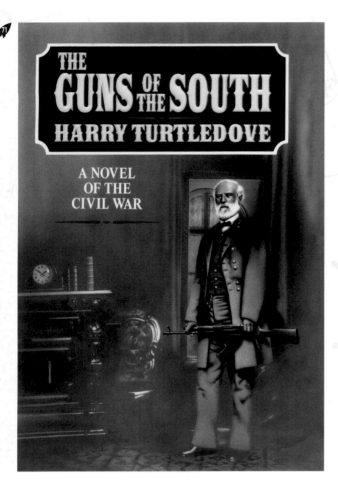

THE GUNS OF THE SOUTH
HARRY TURTLEDOVE
1992
TOM STIMPSON

Author Turtledove has a Ph.D. in history and, logically enough, is fond of the alternate history story. *The Guns of the South* is a novel of what might have happened in the Civil War if Robert E. Lee had access to AK47's.

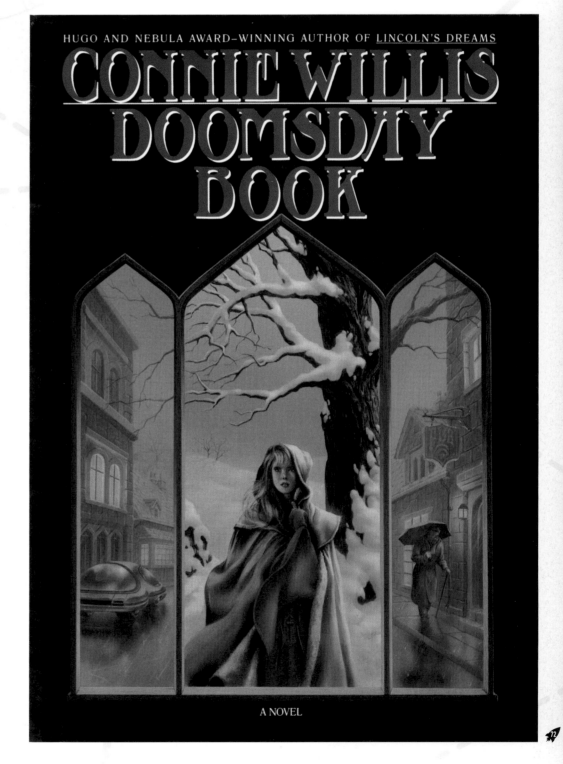

DOOMSDAY BOOK
CONNIE WILLIS
1992
TIM JACOBUS

A much honored author (five Hugos through 1997), Willis won the Nebula for her novel *Doomsday Book*. A tale of time travel back to the Middle Ages, it further solidified her reputation as a major talent in the field.

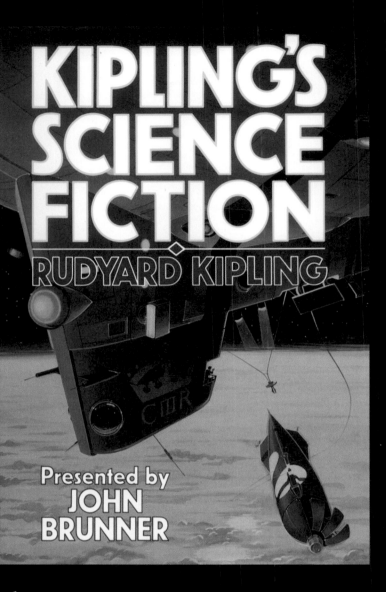

KIPLING'S SCIENCE FICTION
RUDYARD KIPLING

Presented by JOHN BRUNNER

CHINA MOUNTAIN ZHANG
MAUREEN F. MCHUGH
1992
UNKNOWN

A first novel that garnered rave reviews from *The New York Times*, *The Washington Post Book World*, and *Newsday* among a host of others. The book won the Locus Award for Best First Novel and was a Hugo and Nebula nominee.

KIPLING'S SCIENCE FICTION
RUDYARD KIPLING
(PRESENTED BY JOHN BRUNNER)
1992
DAVID R. DEITRICK

Kipling, who won the Nobel Prize for Literature in 1907, wrote a considerable number of fantasies and some science fiction in addition to *Kim* and *The Jungle Book*. His stories about the Aerial Board of Control, *With the Night Mail* and *As Easy as A.B.C.* stand up well even today.

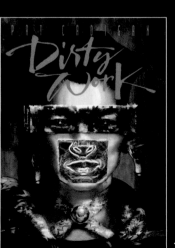

DIRTY WORK
PAT CADIGAN
1993
RICK BERRY

Pat Cadigan is another relatively new author whose short stories have been nominated for Hugos and Nebulas. *Dirty Work* is one of her best collections. The stunning jacket is by Rick Berry, a pioneer of computer art. This well-crafted book is from the Mark V. Ziesing specialty press.

GUN, WITH OCCASIONAL MUSIC
JONATHAN LETHEM
1994
MICHAEL KOELSCH

Lethem is one of the few science-fiction writers to break into mainstream with his first novel. Lethem's novels show an off-beat sense of humor and a flair for the unusual. The creases in the cover, incidentally, are a deliberate part of the art.

SUZY McKEE CHARNAS
THE FURIES

The long-awaited sequel to *Motherlines* and *Walk to the End of the World*

THE FURIES
SUZY MCKEE CHARNAS
1994
RICK BERRY

Charnas won the 1980 Nebula for Best Novella for "Unicorn Tapestry." Her short story "Boobs" won the 1990 Hugo; it was an intriguing title for an author noted for her skillfully developed feminist themes.

much of the market were now entranced by computers and video games, by film and TV. For those who read science fiction, the level of sophistication—as mentioned—had risen immensely. One author who had written what he considered an adult, mature novel was shocked at a signing when an eleven-year-old boy asked for an autograph on his book.

Most of the authors wrote at the top of their form, and some of them transcended the field to appeal to a mainstream audience (witness Clarke and Bradbury and Heinlein and a few others). But for those who didn't and who had quit their day job to become full-time writers, the blessing and the curse of being a genre writer quickly became apparent.

Anthony Boucher, the first editor of *Fantasy & Science Fiction* and one familiar with both the mystery and science fiction fields, had spelled it out years before. Being known as a genre writer offered a degree of security—you were guaranteed a certain minimum sale. The down side was that while there was a floor, there was also a ceiling. If you sold near the ceiling, you could do quite well. If you sold near the floor, you would starve to death in short order. Having your name on a book and living in the Village was fun, but sooner or later the realities of life set in.

FOREIGNER
C. J. CHERRYH
1994
MICHAEL WHELAN

One of the most prolific and successful science-fiction and fantasy writers, Cherryh is a master of the space opera and expert in linking most of her novels in one grand, well-developed plan. She won the Hugo for best novel in 1982 (*Downbelow Station*) and again in 1989 (*Cyteen*).

Escaping the "ghetto" wasn't easy. Bradbury did it early on by making his style of science fiction "acceptable" to a mainstream audience. Clarke would forever be associated with *2001* and, because of it, his novels were also "acceptable." Heinlein had managed to hew out a place for himself as…Heinlein. Frank Herbert hit the best-seller lists but primarily with *Dune* and its sequels. Kurt Vonnegut, after a brief apprenticeship in magazine science fiction, successfully ducked the genre bullet and became known as a contributor to mainstream literature. Walter Tevis started writing for *Galaxy* in 1957 and wrote several science-fiction novels, the best known of which was *The Man Who Fell to Earth*, filmed in 1976 and starring David Bowie. Tevis stepped outside the field long enough to write *The Hustler* (starring Paul Newman and Jackie Gleason in the movie version) and its sequel, *The Color Of Money* (Newman and Tom Cruise).

But the flirtation of Vonnegut and Tevis with the science-fiction field had been a casual one. If you had built a solid reputation as a science-fiction writer over a period of years, it was a hard one to

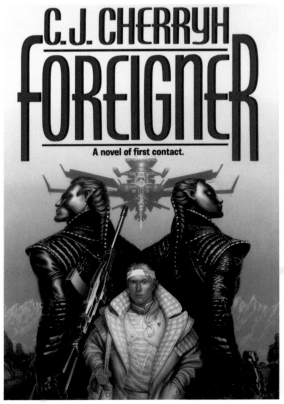

C.J. CHERRYH
FOREIGNER
A novel of first contact.

shake. Harlan Ellison fought most of his life to avoid being typecast and largely succeeded by broadening the nature of his output and the magazines and books in which he appeared (his varied film and television work helped as well).

The marketplace was complicated by mainstream authors who drifted into it with the occasional science-fiction novel that was never sold as such. Gore Vidal's *Messiah*, *Visit to a Small Planet*, and *Kalki* were peddled as satires. Ira Levin's *The Stepford Wives* and *The Boys from Brazil*—the latter about the cloning of cells from Hitler's body to produce a generation of young Fuhrers—were marketed as thrillers. (The book was written years before Dolly the sheep hit the headlines.)

The most commercially successful science-fiction writer at the end of the millennium was an author whose readers seldom associated his books with science fiction. *The Andromeda Strain*, *The Terminal Man*, *Congo*, *Sphere*, and *Jurassic Park*…all of them were best sellers (and all of them were filmed).

Michael Crichton, their author, was a film director as well, directing his own *Westworld* and Robin Cook's *Coma* (along with several other films outside the genre).

Crichton was accepted as a mainstream thriller writer and envied by many science-fiction authors for his success. But it wasn't easy to emulate him. Thrillers had their own demands as a genre, just as science-fiction novels did. Crichton was fortunate enough to be good at both.

But describing the problem facing many science-fiction writers at the end of the millennium wasn't of much help.

The major questions remained. What would science fiction be like and where would it be going in the year 2001?

Editor David Hartwell had once described the 20th century as the Science Fiction Century. But some critics claimed that the end of the century was the end of science fiction as well.

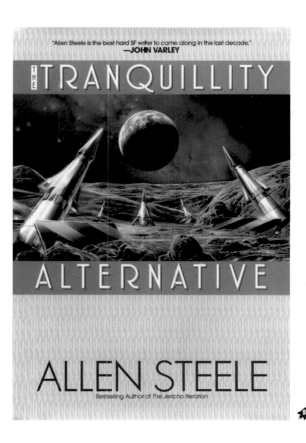

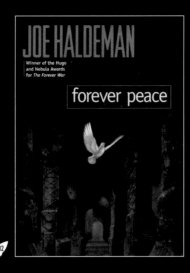

FOREVER PEACE
JOE HALDEMAN
1997
BRUCE JENSEN

Haldeman was severely wounded in Vietnam where he served as a combat engineer. The experience shadowed much of what he has written, especially *The Forever War*, which won both a Nebula and a Hugo. *Forever Peace* returns to the same theater of war.

OVER THE RIVER AND THROUGH THE WOODS
CLIFFORD D. SIMAK
1998
MICHAEL DASHOW

First published in 1931, Simak retired until 1938 when he began writing for the Campbell *Astounding*. His later stories were gentle and humane, about a period when man has all but disappeared and the dogs have taken over the earth. Best known for his collection of linked stories, *City*, he won the Nebula Grand Master Award in 1976. (Book: Tachyon Publications.)

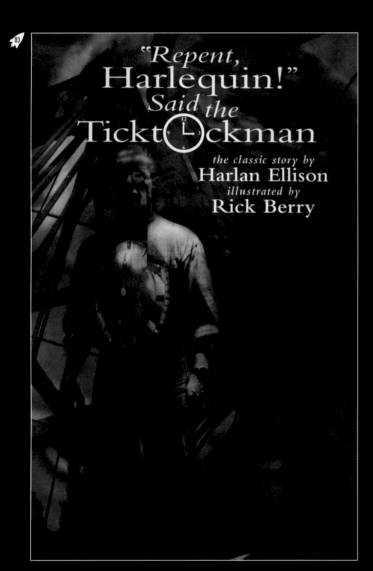

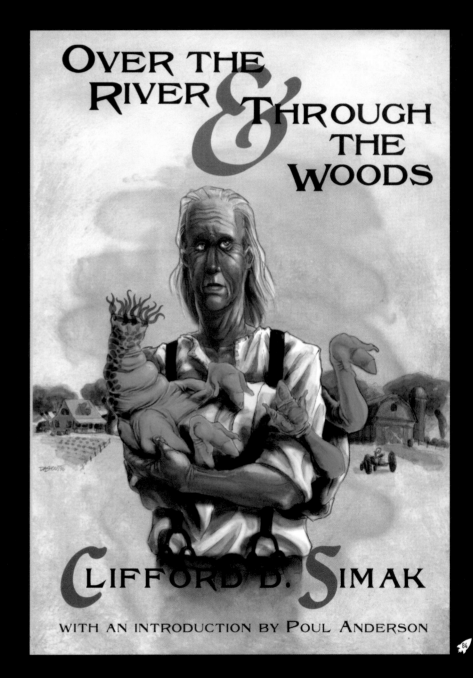

"REPENT, HARLEQUIN!" SAID THE TICKTOCKMAN
HARLAN ELLISON
1997
RICK BERRY

Originally published in magazine-form in 1965 (and winner of the 1965 Nebula and 1966 Hugo), the story was republished in 1997 as a deluxe hardbound book with jacket and interior illustrations by Rick Berry. Publisher: Underwood Books, a leading specialty press.

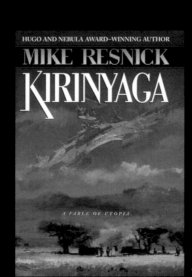

KIRINYAGA
MIKE RESNICK
1998
JOHN HARRIS

A prolific author, occasional screenwriter, and an anthologist with a flair for coaxing stories out of reluctant authors, Resnick has been a regular on the Hugo and Nebula lists. He's also an authority on Africa, where *Kirinyaga* and other stories are set, either geographically or culturally.

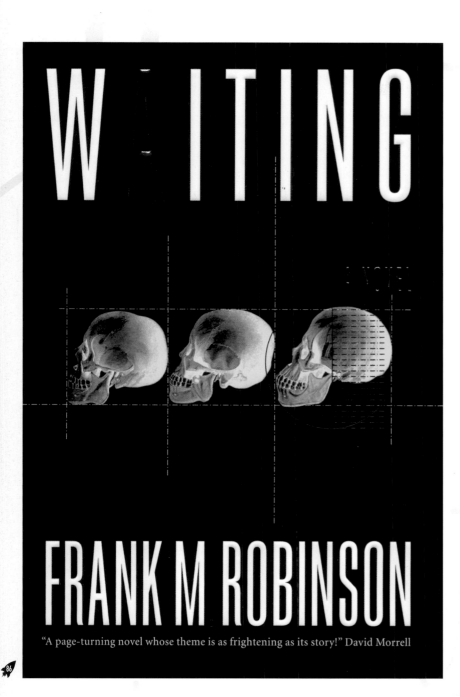

W∆ITING

FRANK M ROBINSON

"A page-turning novel whose theme is as frightening as its story!" David Morrell

 86

WAITING
FRANK M. ROBINSON
1999
DRIVE COMMUNICATIONS

Frank M. Robinson started with science fiction, switched to "techno thrillers," and mysteries (in collaboration) then returned to science fiction with *The Dark Beyond the Stars*. A science-fiction thriller, *Waiting* is set in modern day San Francisco.

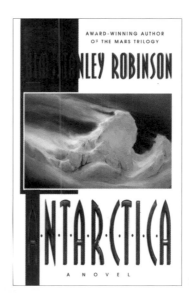

 87

ANTARCTICA
KIM STANLEY ROBINSON
1998
P. A. NISBET

Robinson won the Nebula for Best Novel for *Red Mars* and a Hugo for Best Novel for its sequels, *Green Mars* and *Blue Mars*. One of the few science-fiction authors to "cross over" into mainstream, *Antarctica* was a best seller in England and made the awards lists in the United States.

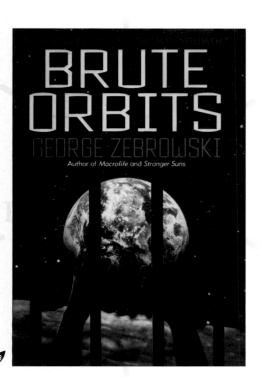

 86

 88

BRUTE ORBITS
GEORGE ZEBROWSKI
1998
DESIGN: CARL D. GALIAN

A prolific short-story writer and the editor of a number of anthologies, Zebrowski is perhaps best known for his novel *Macrolife*, praised by Arthur C. Clarke as "a worthy successor to Olaf Stapledon's *Star Maker*."

89

THE GOLDEN GLOBE
JOHN VARLEY
1998
DANILO DUCAT

One of the superstars of modern science fiction, Varley is a multiple Hugo and Nebula award winner with such books as *Titan*, *Wizard*, *Demon*, and *Steel Beach*. *The Golden Globe* details the adventures of an actor of the future — one with a price on his head.

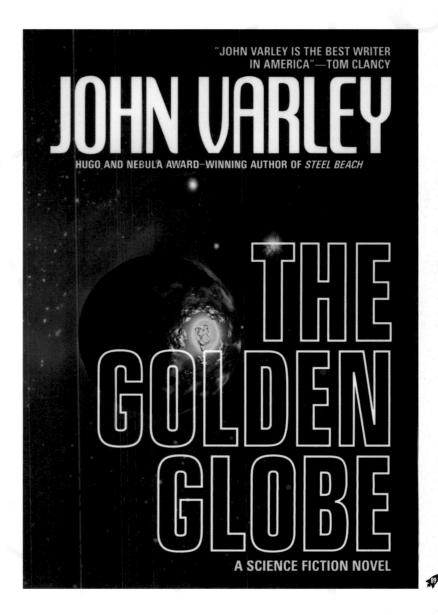

"JOHN VARLEY IS THE BEST WRITER IN AMERICA"—TOM CLANCY

JOHN VARLEY

HUGO AND NEBULA AWARD–WINNING AUTHOR OF *STEEL BEACH*

THE GOLDEN GLOBE

A SCIENCE FICTION NOVEL

89

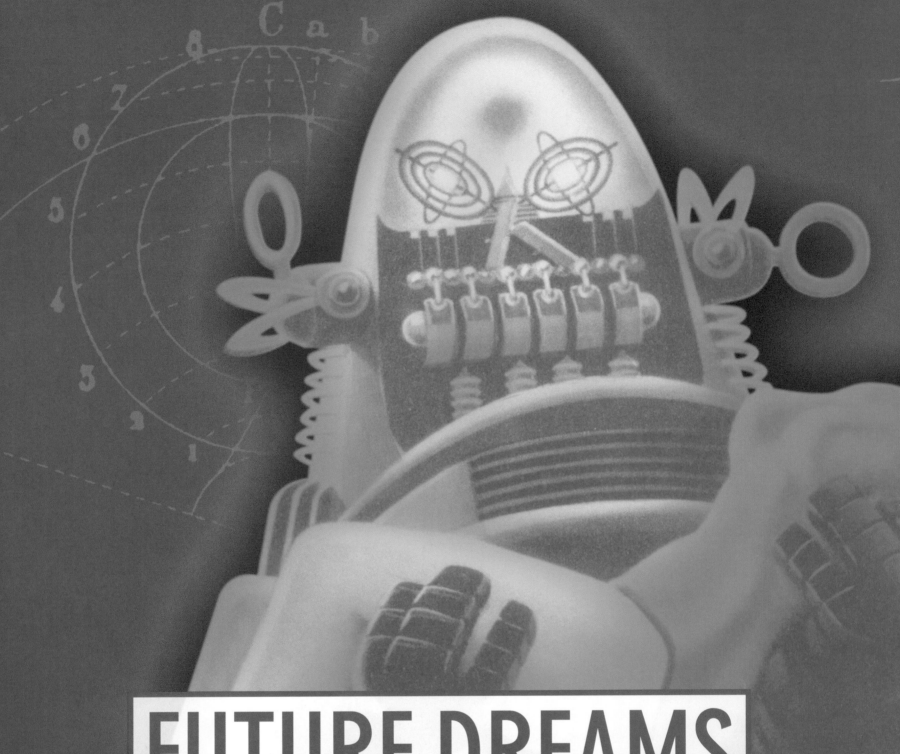

FUTURE DREAMS

CHAPTER 11

In the late 1920s and the early 1930s, science-fiction fans did not live by print alone. There was also the movies. The science-fiction enthusiast who religiously read *Science and Invention* for its fiction and bought the first issue of *Amazing Stories* probably had waited in line, popcorn in hand, to see the silent film *The Lost World*, adapted from the novel by A. Conan Doyle. It had a familiar story line by later standards—Professor Challenger, played by Wallace Beery, discovers a lost world complete with dinosaurs. The dinosaurs were brought to life by a master of stop-action motion, Willis O'Brien. (O'Brien had experimented with stop-action manipulation of models in the 1919 *Ghost of Slumber Mountain*, a short which also featured dinosaurs.) It was not, of course, the first science-fiction film. Edison invented the Kinetophonograph capable of recording

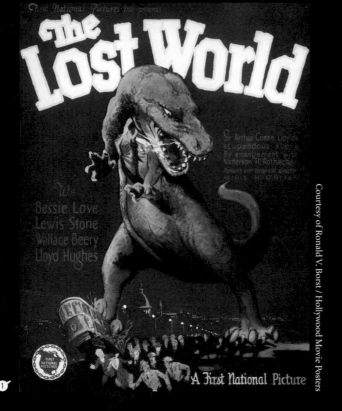

Courtesy of Ronald V. Borst / Hollywood Movie Posters

THE LOST WORLD
FIRST NATIONAL, 1925
(WINDOW CARD)

Sir Arthur Conan Doyle's story about explorers who find dinosaurs in a remote jungle is notable for Willis O'Brien's stop-action models of prehistoric animals, a technology that peaked with *King Kong* eight years later. (Directed by Henry Hoyt)

images on film (George Eastman had just invented celluloid film, complete with sprocket holes), Louis Lumière invented a way of projecting the film images, and Georges Méliès accidentally invented special effects. His camera had jammed while filming, and when he showed the film, the image he had photographed appeared and then suddenly disappeared, leaving only the background. Voila! Movie magic!

Méliès converted his theater (he had opened one for his own magic show) to showing films, founded his own company, built his own studio, and started producing movies. In 1902 he made *A Trip to the Moon*, a free adaptation of Verne's *From the Earth to the Moon*. Science-fiction movies had been launched.

A few years after *The Lost World*, Fritz Lang offered a change of pace with a glimpse of what the city of the future might look like in *Metropolis*, a 1927 German film. The movie offered dazzling vistas of a futuristic city plus a convincing female robot. In addition, it offered a glimpse of a society in which the wealthy, technological élite live at the expense of masses of proletarian workers who labor underground to keep the marvelous vistas above ground functioning. A "C" for politics but an "A" for its early special effects. (Anybody who wondered why early artist Frank R. Paul drew his men of the future wearing funny pantaloons had only to watch the film.)

In 1930, the comedian El (for Elmer) Brendel starred in a less-than-uproarious version of the future in *Just Imagine*, which offered a World's Fair view of a city of the 1980s. It looked nothing like the real thing.

The "talkies" arrived in the late 1920s but the 1931 *Frankenstein* featured a main character who didn't talk at all (though he did grunt a lot). Boris Karloff, who had acted in bit parts before, was chosen to play the monster, though Bela Lugosi, who had achieved

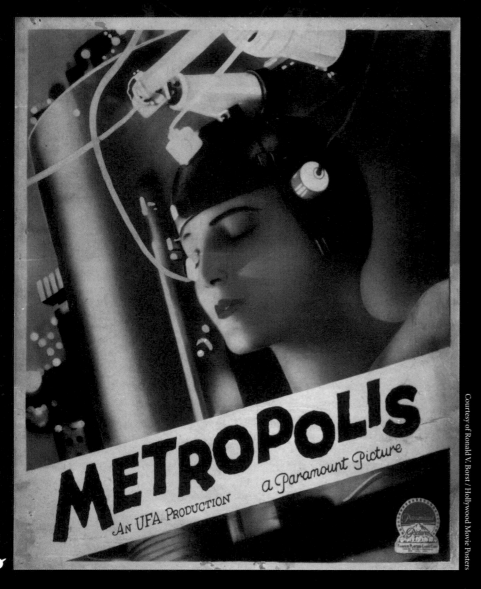

Courtesy of Ronald V. Borst / Hollywood Movie Posters

METROPOLIS
UFA (GERMANY), 1927
(OVERSIZE LOBBY CARD)

Fritz Lang's vision of a future city paved the way for the ultra-urban concepts of *Blade Runner* and *The Fifth Element*. Its depiction of a wealthy ruling class foreshadowed the totalitarianism of Orwell's *1984*. (Directed by Fritz Lang)

near stardom with *Dracula*, had been the early
choice. (Both Karloff and Lugosi later starred in the
Son of Frankenstein, with Lugosi playing Ygor, the
shepherd. In the early 1940s, Lugosi finally played
the monster in *Frankenstein Meets the Wolfman*.)
Eclipsing the original was its sequel, *The Bride of
Frankenstein*, in which Karloff recaps his role of the
monster—and this time speaks, though Karloff
thought it was a mistake—and Elsa Lanchester (the
wife of Charles Laughton) plays both the Bride and
Mary Shelley. The film also starred Dwight Frye, the
fly-eating acolyte of Count Dracula, but the film was
stolen by Ernest Thesinger as Dr. Pretorious, who
specializes in the miniaturization of human beings.

Between the original *Frankenstein* and its sequel,
director James Whale directed still another classic,
The Invisible Man, adapted from the novel by H. G.
Wells. You didn't hear Karloff talk in *Frankenstein*
and you didn't even see Claude Rains, who plays
the invisible man, until the last few frames of the
movie. Nevertheless, it made Rains a star, much as
the original *Frankenstein* had made one of Karloff.
(Obviously a director's lucky charm, Dwight Frye
was cast in four of the major genre movies of the era:
both of the "Frankensteins" plus *Dracula* and *The
Invisible Man*.)

The class act for pure science fiction was *Things to
Come*, another adaptation of a Wells book. It offered
a terrifying preview of what the next war might be
like, then suffered by comparison with the genuine
article a few years later. It ends with the launching of
a rocket to the moon (from a giant cannon) and
Raymond Massey proclaiming that mankind had a
choice as to what sort of future it wanted. "All the
universe or nothing—which shall it be?" The sets
and the special effects were tops for the period.

THE INVISIBLE MAN

UNIVERSAL, 1933
(LOBBY CARD)

Director James Whale's second great classic (the first was *Frankenstein*)
was *The Invisible Man*. It made a star of actor Claude Rains—whose
face you never see until the last shot. Like *Frankenstein*, it spawned a
number of sequels. Director Whale was the subject of the biopic
Gods and Monsters in 1998.

FLASH GORDON

UNIVERSAL, 1936
(ONE-SHEET POSTER)

First a serial, then a ninety-seven-minute feature. Ming the Merciless, ruler of the planet Mongo, tries to conquer the Earth, and Flash, Dale Arden, and Dr. Zarkov rocket to the rescue. Buster Crabbe starred (he also starred in later *Buck Rogers* serials). Adapted from the newspaper comic strip by Alex Raymond. (Directed by Frederick Stephani)

THINGS TO COME

LONDON FILMS, 1936
(VHS TAPE BOX)

This film version of H. G. Wells' saga of the far future revolutionized the use of architecture in movies—the sheer, sweeping structures dominate everything. It also idealized the purpose of space flight as man's ultimate destiny. (Directed by William Cameron Menzies)

Willis O'Brien had another go-around with stop-motion dinosaurs in the greatest monster movie of all, *King Kong*. Producer-directors were Merian C. Cooper and Ernest B. Schoedsack, who had filmed the silent documentaries *Grass* (in what is now Iran) and *Chang* (Thailand). Willis O'Brien had been working on stop-action dinosaurs for a project to be titled *Creation*, suspended when Cooper and Schoedsack got the go-ahead for *Kong*.

The story was by Edgar Wallace and Cooper; screenplay by James A. Creelman and Ruth Rose (Schoedsack's wife). The jungle set did double duty for both *Kong* and Schoedsack's *The Most Dangerous Game* (released the year before), starring Fay Wray, Robert Armstrong, and Noble Johnson, all of whom starred in *King Kong* as well. At the time, RKO was on the verge of collapse, so it was understandable that both sets and actors would double in brass. (For trivia fans, it was Cooper and Schoedsack playing the pilots who shoot down Kong from the Empire State Building.)

Kong himself consisted of six miniature models approximately eighteen-inches high, fully articulated and covered with rabbit fur; a full-sized head ideal for chomping people with three men inside to manipulate Kong's expressions; an enormous foot perfect for squishing natives; and an eight-foot hand with which to cradle Fay Wray. One peculiarity, unnoticed by most moviegoers, was the occasional rippling of the hair on Kong—the "fingerprints" of the technicians who moved the models.

Mae West got the credit for saving Paramount, Frankenstein for rescuing Universal, and King Kong for keeping the creditors away from RKO's door. Mae West was a force of nature, corset stays, and makeup—but two out of three wasn't bad for genre movies.

DESTINATION MOON
EAGLE-LION, 1950
(*VHS TAPE BOX*)

This pioneering movie was made by people who really believed in space flight: producer George Pal, astronomical artist Chesley Bonestell, and author Robert Heinlein (who co-wrote the script). With *Destination Moon*, they launched one of the greatest decades of science-fiction filmmaking. (Directed by Irving Pichel)

Some remarkable films showed up in the late 1930s —*Lost Horizon*, *The Man Who Could Work Miracles*, and the Saturday serials which included Gene Autry in *The Phantom Empire*, as well as twelve-parters about Flash Gordon and Buck Rogers.

The 1940s saw innumerable sequels (*The House of Frankenstein*, *The House of Dracula*, *Frankenstein Meets the Wolf Man*, *The Invisible Man Returns*); quickie horror films (*Devil Bat*, *Night Monster*); classic horror films (*Cat People*, *The Curse of the Cat People*, *I Walked With a Zombie*, *Bedlam* and *The Body Snatcher*—all produced by Val Lewton; and let's not forget *Phantom of the Opera*). Plus a selection of almost classic science-fiction films (*Doctor Cyclops*, *Mighty Joe Young*, *One Million B.C.*); a series of Boris Karloff thrillers with and without Bela Lugosi; a series of Bela Lugosi films with and without Boris Karloff; and a collection of serials—some of them starring comic-book heroes, one of whom would show up in major productions decades later (*The Batman*, *New Adventures of Batman and Robin*, *Adventures of Captain Marvel*, *King of the Rocket Men*).

The 1950s were a prelude to the 1970s and George Pal the predecessor of Kubrick and Lucas and Spielberg. The decade saw an enormous number of science-fiction films that matched the outpouring of science fiction in the digest magazines.

Disney filmed the definitive version of *20,000 Leagues Under the Sea* and Christian Nyby—but probably Howard Hawks, who let Nyby take credit —directed *The Thing From Another World* (adapted —loosely—from John W. Campbell's "Who Goes There?"). Robert Wise directed *The Day the Earth Stood Still* from the Harry Bates story, "Farewell to the Master." Ray Bradbury wrote the original treatment for the 3-D *It Came From Outer Space* and saw

Wade Williams Collection

Wade Williams Collection

⑧

TOM CORBETT: SPACE CADET
CBS, 1950
(*VHS TAPE BOX*)

Before there was *Star Trek*, before there was *Lost in Space* ("Danger, Will Robinson!"), before there was *Babylon 5*, there was *Tom Corbett: Space Cadet*. Based on the novel of the same name by Robert Heinlein, the series was broadcast live in 15-minute episodes. This tape contains five of them. (Directed by George Gould)

Courtesy collection of Vincent Di Fate

his *Saturday Evening Post* story, "The Beast From 20,000 Fathoms," turned into the movie of the same name. There was that classic of paranoia, *Invasion of the Body Snatchers*, plus *Forbidden Planet* (which starred Leslie Nielsen as a young, serious hero, though Robby the Robot stole the show; in later films, Nielsen would discover a profitable talent for comedy). Steve McQueen was featured in *The Blob* (his first starring role) and Vincent Price in *The Fly*.

Invaders From Mars* was one of a series of films fueled by American fears of a possible conflict between the United States and what would become known as "the Evil Empire," plus the drumfire of news stories about UFOs. The film was directed by William Cameron Menzies, best known for his cinematography and visual effects for *Gone With the Wind* and the silent version of *The Thief of Baghdad* (1924). *Invaders from Mars* is about a young boy who sees the landing of an alien craft, but nobody believes him when he reports the invaders are taking over human beings. It is understandable that the aliens sketched by people who later claimed to have been abducted by them looked much like the aliens from *Invaders* and similar movies.

Critics declared Ed Wood's 1956 release *Plan 9 From Outer Space* as probably the worst science-fiction movie ever made—and George Pal's *War of the Worlds* was praised as one of the best.

Pal was born in Hungary and came to the States in 1940 where he produced Puppetoons—stop action cartoons—for Paramount and won a special Academy Award for them in 1943. (He would go on to win five Oscars for special effects in his science-fiction and fantasy films.)

Pal's first science-fiction film was *Destination Moon*, co-scripted by Robert Heinlein, followed by *The War of the Worlds* (based on the novel by Wells), *The Conquest of Space*, and *The Time Machine*. Probably the best of all his films was *Tom Thumb*—a musical adapted from the fairy tale by the Brothers Grimm. A few years later Pal followed it with *The Wonderful World of the Brothers Grimm* (scripted by Charles Beaumont) and *7 Faces of Dr. Lao*, starring Tony Randall, who played six roles.

Pal's last two movies were *Doc Savage – The Man of Bronze* and this author's *The Power*. Critics said Pal made hash of *The Power*, though it wasn't entirely his fault. The first script was quite good, but the second was reportedly tailored to the wishes of the star, George Hamilton, who wanted a less ambiguous, "happy" ending.

Years later, when Pal met the author to discuss another deal, the first thing he said was, "How will you ever forgive me?"

George Pal was a talented man and a class act.

The 1960s were hardly without their share of excellent films—including Hitchcock's *Psycho*, adapted from the book by fantasy and science-fiction writer Robert Bloch. The rights were purchased by Hitchcock through a "stalking horse"—an unknown who bought it for a low fee, then turned around and immediately sold it to Hitchcock. (Obviously Bloch's agent would have asked for a lot more money if he had known that Hitchcock was the real buyer.) Bloch acknowledged that the rights for the largest grossing black-and-white movie ever made—up to that time

WHEN WORLDS COLLIDE
PARAMOUNT, 1951
(HALF-SHEET POSTER)

This George Pal film, adapted from the novel by Edwin Balmer and Philip Wylie, won an Oscar for special effects. Astronomical artist Chesley Bonestell was technical advisor, and it shows. (Directed by Rudolph Mate)

THE DAY THE EARTH STOOD STILL
20TH CENTURY FOX, 1951
(HALF-SHEET POSTER)

A cult classic, adapted from the Harry Bates story "Farewell to the Master." Michael Rennie played the alien, Klaatu, while Gort, his robot sidekick (actually his master), was played by Lock Martin, a seven-foot seven-inch doorman. Rennie later starred in *The Power*, and director Robert Wise directed *Star Trek— The Motion Picture* in 1979.

![3-DIMENSION. EXCITEMENT THAT CAN ALMOST TOUCH YOU! IT CAME FROM OUTER SPACE poster]

Starring RICHARD CARLSON · BARBARA RUSH
with CHARLES DRAKE · RUSSELL JOHNSON · KATHLEEN HUGHES · JOE SAWYER

Courtesy collection of Vincent Di Fate

⑫

IT CAME FROM OUTER SPACE
UNIVERSAL-INTERNATIONAL, 1953
(WINDOW CARD)

Based on a treatment by Ray Bradbury about shape-shifting aliens who crash in a southwestern desert, this is the first stereophonic, 3-D, and widescreen science-fiction movie. Steven Spielberg cited it as an influence on *Close Encounters of the Third Kind*. (Directed by Jack Arnold)

—were purchased for peanuts but also admitted the movie had made his reputation in Hollywood.

One Million B.C. (starring Raquel Welch) was released in 1964, *Fahrenheit 451*, directed by François Truffaut and adapted from Ray Bradbury's book, in 1968. Ron Borst in his book *Graven Images*, describes the film as being "…a futuristic allegory of firemen who burn books, librarians who die for books, and people who become 'books.'" In keeping with the nature of the story, the only printed words shown in the film are those that proclaim "The End."

The decade also saw *The Day of the Triffids*, *The First Men in the Moon*, *Dr. Strangelove*, and the first of the films starring Sean Connery as James Bond (*Dr. No*). 20th Century Fox released *Fantastic Voyage* (based on a story by Otto Klement and science-fiction writer and editor, Jerome Bixby) and *Planet of the Apes*, starring Charlton Heston, which was popular enough to spawn four sequels.

But the most important science-fiction movie of the decade was *2001: A Space Odyssey*, produced and directed by Stanley Kubrick and co-scripted by Arthur C. Clarke from his short story, "The Sentinel." MGM was in a stock option battle at the time the film was being shot in England and stateside, the company had almost shut down, its huge

![AT THIS VERY MOMENT SPACE SHIPS FROM THE BEYOND MAY BE ON THEIR WAY TO DESTROY OUR PLANET! H.G. WELLS' The War of the Worlds poster]

Starring GENE BARRY · ANN ROBINSON · TECHNICOLOR
PRODUCED BY GEORGE PAL · DIRECTED BY BYRON HASKIN · SCREENPLAY BY BARRÉ LYNDON
BASED ON THE NOVEL BY H. G. WELLS

Courtesy of Ronald V. Borst / Hollywood Movie Posters

⑬

WAR OF THE WORLDS
PARAMOUNT, 1953
(ONE-SHEET POSTER—1965 REISSUE)

Producer George Pal set *War of the Worlds* in mid-century Los Angeles instead of Victorian England. The film, which won the Oscar for Best Special Effects, opens with a tour of the solar system painted by Chesley Bonestell. (Directed by Byron Haskins)

FROM OUT OF SPACE… came hordes of green monsters!!
EDWARD L. ALPERSON presents
INVADERS FROM MARS
PHOTOGRAPHED IN COLOR

STARRING
HELENA CARTER · ARTHUR FRANZ · JIMMY HUNT

WILLIAM CAMERON MENZIES · RICHARD BLAKE · EDWARD L. ALPERSON, JR. · RAOUL KRAUSHAAR

Courtesy collection of Vincent Di Fate

THE BEAST FROM 20,000 FATHOMS
WARNER BROS.-FIRST NATIONAL, 1953
(ONE-SHEET POSTER)

Ray Harryhausen inherited Willis O'Brien's crown as king of the monster makers (O'Brien did *King Kong*) with his impressive "Rhedosaurus," a dinosaur awakened from its glacial bed by an A-bomb blast. The idea for the film was inspired by Ray Bradbury's story "The Foghorn." (Directed by Eugene Lourie)

GOJIRA / GODZILLA
TOHO JAPAN, 1954
(JAPANESE POSTER)

"Gojira" was a response to—and incarnation of—the Japanese dread of another atomic Armageddon. *Godzilla* is *Gojira* with English language inserts of actor Raymond Burr (before *Perry Mason*) as an American newspaper-man. (Directed by Inoshiro Honda)

Courtesy of Ronald V. Borst / Hollywood Movie Posters

INVADERS FROM MARS
20TH CENTURY FOX, 1953
(LOBBY CARD)

William Cameron Menzies not only directed but also designed the terrific look of *Invaders from Mars* to reflect a little boy's point of view. The film has super-saturated colors and sets with disorienting perspectives and a distorted sense of scale. The movie is a typical 1950s paranoid tale of American families being "taken over" by Martians.

Courtesy of Ronald V. Borst / Hollywood Movie Posters

THEM!

WARNER BROS.-FIRST NATIONAL, 1954
(ONE-SHEET POSTER)

The first—and the best—of the radioactive big bug movies. The U.S. military chases the lethal queen ant and her deadly consorts from their desert nest to the labyrinthine tunnels of the Los Angeles River. (Directed by Gordon Douglas)

17

20,000 LEAGUES UNDER THE SEA

BUENA VISTA, 1954
(ONE-SHEET POSTER)

The classic Jules Verne film—the "look" of the submarine captures the flavor of the mid-1800s, and James Mason is perfect as Captain Nemo. (Directed by Richard Fleischer)

19

INVASION OF THE BODY SNATCHERS

ALLIED ARTISTS, 1956
(ONE-SHEET POSTER)

Director Don Siegel's frightening movie about the duplication of human beings by aliens. Released during the McCarthy hearings and worries about Soviet espionage, the film played on people's fears of being turned into soulless citizens of a totalitarian state.

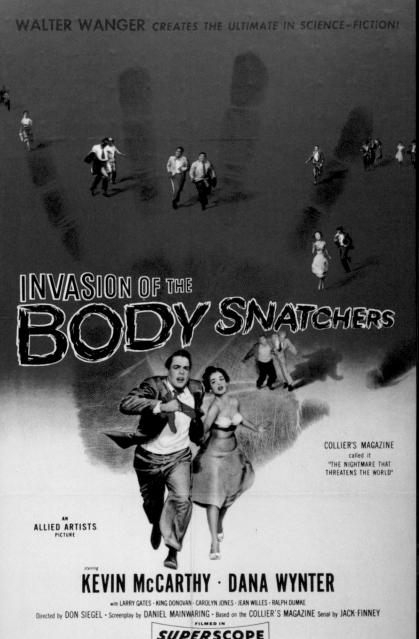

Courtesy of Ronald V. Borst / Hollywood Movie Posters

Courtesy of Ronald V. Borst / Hollywood Movie Posters

Courtesy of Ronald V. Borst / Hollywood Movie Posters

FORBIDDEN PLANET
MGM, 1956
(LOBBY CARD)

According to some critics, a science-fiction version of Shakespeare's "The Tempest." Starring Walter Pidgeon, Anne Francis, Leslie Nielsen (when he was playing heroic hunks), Robby the Robot, and the invisible "creature from the ID." (Directed by Fred McLeod Wilcox)

THE INCREDIBLE SHRINKING MAN
UNIVERSAL-INTERNATIONAL, 1957
(ONE-SHEET POSTER)

Adapted from a Richard Matheson novel by Matheson himself and made long before Disney started shrinking the kids. Our hero shrinks and eventually a pencil becomes a log, a pin a sword, and an ordinary house spider the equal of any science-fiction monster. (Directed by Jack Arnold)

THE FLY
20TH CENTURY FOX, 1958
(LOBBY CARD)

During a teleportation experiment, a fly buzzes into the chamber, and man and fly are freakishly blended. Not for the squeamish. (Directed by David Cronenberg)

EARTH VS. THE FLYING SAUCERS
COLUMBIA, 1956
(ONE-SHEET POSTER)

Special effects pioneer Ray Harryhausen's flying saucers destroyed Washington forty years before *Independence Day* and *Mars Attacks!*. The movie also got a jump on the Age of High Fidelity: the saucers are disabled by "sonic cannons" invented just for the occasion. (Directed by Fred F. Sears)

THE TIME MACHINE
MGM, 1960
(LOBBY CARD)

Director George Pal's adaptation of H. G. Wells' science-fiction novel of social criticism avoids being preachy in its depiction of the beautiful Eloi and their violent Morlock overlords. We're also introduced to the wonders of time-lapse photography as flowers bloom and wither and, in a hilarious view of female fashions, hemlines fall and rise and fall again.

sound stages silent except for the television series starring Richard Chamberlain as "Dr. Kildare" and George Pal's shooting of *The Power*.

2001 was reportedly referred to as "Kubrick's Folly" by management people who had seen the rushes and hadn't the foggiest idea what the film was about. What it was about was like nothing that had ever been filmed before. It was released to mixed reviews (in the science-fiction community as well as the general one), and it took a few weeks before the studio realized it had a hit on its hands. (It didn't help with the stock option battle—financier Kirk Kerkorian ran away with the studio.)

The movie was a seminal film—no other science-fiction film had even come close to touching it for visual grandeur and scientific accuracy. It hardly made Kubrick's reputation but it vastly enhanced it. The same could be said about Arthur C. Clarke. Special effects were by Douglas Trumbull, who won an Oscar and went on to produce his own science-fiction movie, *Silent Running*. The movie featured Keir Dullea and Gary Lockwood, but the real star was Douglas Rain as the voice of HAL, the computer. (The name of HAL was composed of the first letter of the alphabet preceding the letters IBM—an in-group joke.)

Science-fiction films would never again be the same.

Stanley Kubrick had been around the film world for a while (*Paths of Glory, Spartacus, Lolita, Dr. Strangelove*), but the next landmark in science-fiction films was made by a thirty-two-year-old neophyte with only two films to his credit.

George Lucas had gone to the School of Cinema and Television of the University of Southern California and while there had made a short titled *THX 1138*, which won first prize at the 1965 National Student Film Festival. He subsequently won a scholarship to observe the production of Francis Ford Coppola's *Finian's Rainbow* and developed into a protégé of Coppola's.

Somewhere along the line he became one of the cameramen on *Gimme Shelter*, a Rolling Stones documentary. In 1971, with Coppola acting as executive producer, Lucas co-scripted and directed the full-length version of *THX 1138*. Two years later, at age twenty-eight, he shot *American Graffiti* on a budget of seven hundred thousand dollars and with a shooting schedule of twenty-eight days. The actors included Richard Dreyfuss, Ron Howard, Charles Martin Smith, Cindy Williams, Suzanne Somers, and Harrison Ford, all of whom found fame in later films or television shows. But at the time of the shooting, probably the best-known member of the cast was Wolfman Jack.

Four years after the release of *American Graffiti*, Lucas, now an old fogy of thirty-two, wrote and directed *Star Wars* for a budget reported to be around ten million. The film won seven Academy Awards and for many years was the top-grossing film of all time. It was soon followed by two sequels, *The*

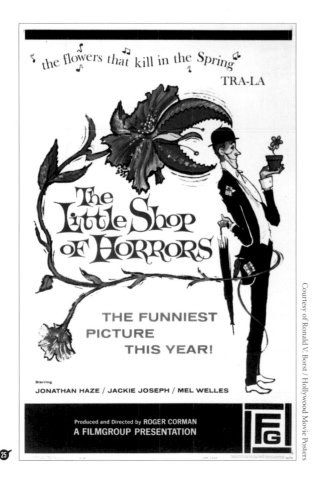

Courtesy of Ronald V. Borst / Hollywood Movie Posters

Courtesy of Ronald V. Borst / Hollywood Movie Posters

25

THE LITTLE SHOP OF HORRORS
FILMGROUP, 1960
(ONE-SHEET POSTER)

One of director Roger Corman's funniest films—shot in two days. A flower-shop clerk raises an alien, man-eating plant and is forced to kill people to feed it. Jack Nicholson plays a masochistic dental patient. It became a Broadway musical, remade as a film in 1986 with Rick Moranis as the clerk, Steve Martin the dentist, and Bill Murray the patient.

Empire Strikes Back and *Return of the Jedi*, both of them also huge winners at the box office—the worldwide gross for all three at the end of the century was $1.8 billion. (Three "prequels" were due to follow; the first—"*Star Wars: Episode I The Phantom Menace*" to be released in 1999.)

Star Wars has been credited as being an outgrowth of the old Saturday serials, of being a science-fiction remake of *The Wizard of Oz* with Luke Skywalker the unlikely embodiment of Dorothy and R2D2 and C-3PO the Tin Woodman and the Cowardly Lion, all of it inspired by Joseph Campbell's views on human myths.

To an extent, all of it was true. Lucas was certainly an admirer of Joseph Campbell, Oz might have been in the back of his head (much later he was an unpaid consultant on the film *Return to Oz*) and what boy hadn't been fond of the Saturday serials?

Lucasfilm Ltd. was one of a number of companies owned by Lucas, which also included LucasArts Entertainment Company Ltd. LLC (interactive entertainment software—computer games) and Lucas Digital Ltd. LLC (Industrial Light & Magic—his special effects company—and Skywalker Sound). Twenty years after the release of *Star Wars*, Lucas could have stocked a small warehouse with all the Oscars and awards his companies had won.

Lucas had directed four films—*THX 1138*, *American Graffiti*, *Star Wars*, and the first of the prequels—but was also executive producer of *Raiders*

26

THE NUTTY PROFESSOR
PARAMOUNT, 1963
(GERMAN POSTER)

Jerry Lewis directed and starred in this film about a college chemistry professor who concocts a potion that will change him into Buddy Love, man-about-town. Lewis's best film. Remade in 1996 with Eddie Murphy playing the professor.

Courtesy of Ronald V. Borst / Hollywood Movie Posters

27

FAHRENHEIT 451
UNIVERSAL-INTERNATIONAL, 1966
(FRENCH POSTER)

In a future where books have been outlawed, "firemen" destroy those that are left (paper burns at 451 degrees Fahrenheit). Adapted from the Bradbury novel, the author's paean to the printed word. This is the only movie that director François Truffaut filmed in English.

PLANET OF THE APES
20TH CENTURY FOX, 1968
(FRENCH POSTER)

The first of an extremely popular series. Charlton Heston, an astronaut caught in a time warp, ends up on an Earth ruled by apes. The last shot is memorable. Screenplay by Rod Serling. (Directed by Franklin J. Schaffner)

BARBARELLA
DINO DE LAURENTIS, 1968
(BRITISH QUAD POSTER)

Starring Jane Fonda, the movie became a popular midnight showing (à la *Rocky Horror Picture Show*). It took films like *Klute* and *On Golden Pond* to prove that Fonda is a fine actress. (Directed by Roger Vadim)

THE POWER
MGM, 1968
(ONE-SHEET POSTER)

Frank M. Robinson's suspenseful novel about the inevitable encounter between two scientists with psychokinetic powers was not fully realized in the cinematic version. But a retroactive reassessment has become necessary because of the movie's influence on David Cronenberg's very important *Scanners* (1981) that, in turn, inspired a series of similar films over the next twenty years. (Directed by Byron Haskins) *Caption by Bob Stephens.*

2001: A SPACE ODYSSEY
MGM, 1968
(BRITISH POSTER)

Producer-director Stanley Kubrick's classic science-fiction film, the one that set the standard. Adapted from an Arthur C. Clarke short story (Clarke co-wrote the screenplay with Kubrick); special effects by Douglas Trumbull won an Oscar.

of the Lost Ark, directed by Stephen Spielberg, and co-executive producer as well as story creator of I*ndiana Jones and the Temple of Doom*, directed by Spielberg again.

Lucas's credentials in the field of the imagination were impeccable—and so were Stephen Spielberg's. The same age as Lucas, Spielberg attended California State University at Long Beach and made a twenty-two-minute film titled *Amblin*. On the basis of it, Universal signed him to a seven-year contract.

Spielberg shot a number of television episodes, then directed the made-for-television film *Duel* (scripted by science-fiction writer Richard Matheson). A "duel" between a middle-aged salesman driving a car and the unseen driver of a huge truck, it won numerous prizes in European film festivals.

It was probably coincidence that saw the release of Spielberg's classic *Close Encounters of the Third Kind* in 1977, the same year that saw the release of *Star Wars*. In 1980 he and Lucas teamed up on *Raiders of the Lost Ark* and the rest was history.

MGM PRESENTS A STANLEY KUBRICK PRODUCTION

2001
a space odyssey
U

Super Panavision® and Metrocolor

PRINTED IN ENGLAND BY W. E. BERRY LTD., BRADFORD

31

Spielberg was to follow *Close Encounters* with *E.T. The Extra-Terrestrial* (1982), which at one time was second only to *Star Wars* in box office receipts. Later, Spielberg was to executive produce the popular *Back to the Future* trilogy, directed by Robert Zemeckis and starring Michael J. Fox and Christopher Lloyd, both of whom had been stars of TV sitcoms.

In 1993, Spielberg directed *Jurassic Park*, based on the novel by Michael Crichton, which totaled close to a billion dollars in world-wide receipts. (Spielberg began filming *Schindler's List*, a film about the Holocaust, while doing post-production work on *Jurassic Park*.)

Like Lucas, Spielberg soon started his own company, Amblin Entertainment, and ended the century as an associate in a new studio, DreamWorks.

(A side of Spielberg not generally known was the philanthropic. He established Survivors of the Shoah Visual History Foundation to videotape the testimonies of Holocaust survivors. He was also chairman of the Starbright Foundation formed to develop projects enabling seriously ill children to combat the emotional and physical challenges that accompany prolonged illness.)

But Lucas and Spielberg weren't the only players when it came to science-fiction films.

CLOSE ENCOUNTERS OF THE THIRD KIND
COLUMBIA, 1977 (LASER DISC SLEEVE)

Director Steven Spielberg's science-fiction masterpiece—a serious, intellectual approach to finally meeting the aliens in the UFOs. Douglas Trumbull, responsible for the special effects of 2001, also does the honors this time. French director François Truffaut plays a UFO investigator.

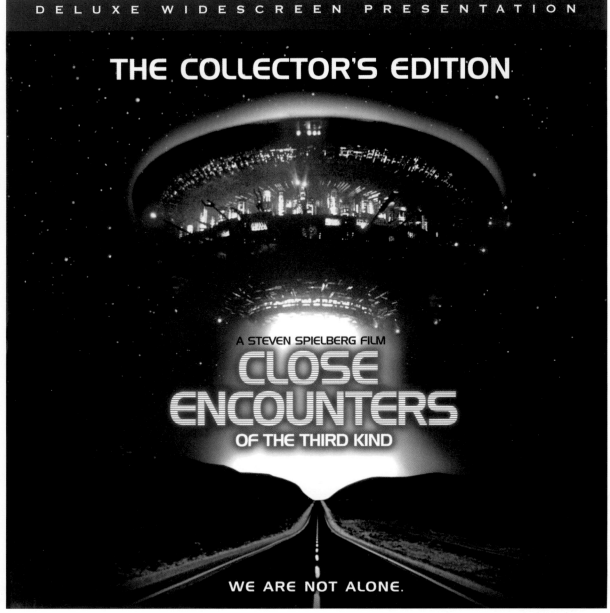

DELUXE WIDESCREEN PRESENTATION

THE COLLECTOR'S EDITION

A STEVEN SPIELBERG FILM

CLOSE ENCOUNTERS OF THE THIRD KIND

WE ARE NOT ALONE.

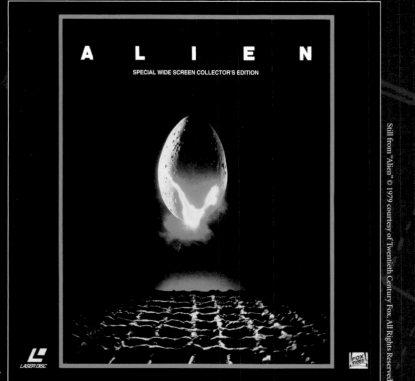

ALIEN
20TH CENTURY FOX, 1979
(LASER DISC SLEEVE)

The ultimate science-fiction horror movie. Director Ridley Scott had a sense of production design few other directors have matched. The film won the Oscar for Best Visual Effects. Muscular role for Sigourney Weaver made her a star and a hero of feminists everywhere. Several sequels.

It was director Ridley Scott's idea to "marry" the horror and science-fiction genres. *2001* and *Star Wars* had been immensely popular science-fiction releases. *The Exorcist, Carrie, The Omen,* and *Halloween* had been popular horror movies. With *Alien* (1979), Scott successfully combined the two—it had been done before, notably with *The Invasion of the Body Snatchers* and *The Thing* and even in *Frankenstein*, but never in a "hardware" science-fiction context of rocketships and space travel.

Scott had vastly admired *2001* but wanted his own film to involve a workaday spaceship and a blue-collar crew. For the design of his monster and the alien ship on the planet's surface, Scott chose Swiss designer H.R. Geiger who specialized in "bio-mechanicals," weird constructions of flesh and technology (a typical Geiger woman would probably have oil in her veins). For much of the design of the interior of the ship, he used Ron Cobb, a lover of science fiction and a political cartoonist for the old *Los Angeles Free Press*, an "underground" newspaper. (Between Geiger and Cobb, *Alien* won an Oscar for Best Visual Effects.)

Besides being one of the scariest films ever shot, *Alien* made the reputation of actress Sigourney Weaver, who played Warrant Office Ripley and became an icon for feminists everywhere. Weaver

intended to leave the series after the first sequel but came back to portray Ripley two more times. The first sequel, *Aliens*, directed by James Cameron, was very successful but was more of an action-adventure film than a horror movie.

Scott tried his hand at another science-fiction film again a few years later with *Blade Runner*, starring Harrison Ford as the "blade runner" who hunts "replicants," manufactured human beings. The setting was a Los Angeles of the future looking like a cross between present-day Los Angeles and Tokyo, smothered in smog and drenched with rain. Loosely adapted from Philip K. Dick's novel, *Do Androids Dream of Electric Sheep?*, by screenwriters Hampton Fancher and David Peoples, the film was visually stunning. Syd Mead did the set design while, once again, Douglas Trumbull was responsible for the special effects.

The test screening didn't go well and Harrison Ford was called back to add a *film noir* voice-over, while outtakes from *The Shining* were used to help provide a happy ending. Early reviews showed that while most critics admired the appearance of the film, they were confused by what they considered the dreary story line and unsympathetic characters.

Of such reviews are cult classics born.

Some years later, a "director's cut" was released with the voice-over eliminated and the original ending reinstated. The result was an entirely different film and a darker one. For the first time, it was obvious that the Harrison Ford character was a replicant designed to hunt down other replicants. The basic subtext also came to the fore—how important are memories in making us human?

One minor note: Of all the lines of dialog in the movie—and there were some great ones—some of the best were "ad-libbed" by actor Rutger Hauer

THE STORY THAT TOUCHED THE WORLD.

SPECIAL COLLECTOR'S EDITION

A STEVEN SPIELBERG FILM

E.T.
THE EXTRA-TERRESTRIAL

A STEVEN SPIELBERG FILM
E.T. THE EXTRA-TERRESTRIAL
DEE WALLACE · PETER COYOTE · DREW BARRYMORE
HENRY THOMAS AS ELLIOTT
MUSIC BY JOHN WILLIAMS   WRITTEN BY MELISSA MATHISON
PRODUCTION DESIGNER JAMES D. BISSELL
DIRECTOR OF PHOTOGRAPHY ALLEN DAVIAU   EDITED BY CAROL LITTLETON
PRODUCED BY STEVEN SPIELBERG & KATHLEEN KENNEDY
DIRECTED BY STEVEN SPIELBERG   A UNIVERSAL RELEASE
READ THE BERKLEY BOOK

digital
SOUND
STEREO

PG PARENTAL GUIDANCE SUGGESTED
SOME MATERIAL MAY NOT BE SUITABLE FOR CHILDREN

Original Soundtrack on MCA Records, Tapes and Compact Discs
©1982 Universal City Studios, Inc. All Rights Reserved.

MCA
HOME VIDEO

34

E.T. THE EXTRATERRESTRIAL
UNIVERSAL, 1982
(LASER DISC SLEEVE)

John Stanley in his book *Creature Features* summed it up
best: Young boy meets alien, boy loves alien, boy loses alien.
A touching, inventive film that refrains from becoming too
sentimental. (Directed by Steven Spielberg)

THE EMPIRE STRIKES BACK
LUCASFILM, 1980
(ONE-SHEET POSTER)

Luke Skywalker, Han Solo, and Princess Leia are back in the eagerly awaited sequel that some critics considered superior to the first. The special effects earned an Oscar. The film makes the assumption that you're seen the first in the series, but who hadn't? (Directed by Irvin Kershner)

during a read-around, where the cast is gathered around a table and read through their parts for the day. Rutger's contribution were the few lines the replicant Batty says just before dying, ending with "…like tears in rain."

Like *2001*, *Alien* and *Close Encounters*, *Blade Runner* was a triumph of science-fiction filmmaking, a seminal film that engendered more after-the-fact analysis than any film since *2001*.

Strangely enough, Ridley Scott never make another science-fiction film. He went on to make *Thelma and Louise* instead.

Another major science-fiction filmmaker surfaced with the release of *Terminator*. Directed by James Cameron, the story was about a humanoid robot from the future sent back in time on a mission of murder. His objective: to eliminate the future mother of a man who would become the savior of the human race in its forthcoming war against the robots.

The robot was implacable, unstoppable. Cameron's decision to cast Arnold Schwarzenegger in the role was brilliant. Schwarzenegger, whose dialog for the entire film wouldn't fill a page, had one of the greatest lines in movie making: "I'll be back." But of all the modern actors, probably only Schwarzenegger could have said it with as much menace in his voice.

Terminator gave a major boost to the careers of both Cameron and Schwarzenegger. Cameron went on to direct *Terminator 2: Judgment Day*, *The Abyss*, and the biggest blockbuster of all, *Titanic*. An accomplished screenwriter, Cameron was a hands-on director with the reputation of a perfectionist and the personality of a daredevil. In shooting *The Abyss*, a spectacular underwater adventure (it won the Oscar for Best Visual Effects), Cameron spent more time in a

③⑥

STAR TREK II:
THE WRATH OF KHAN
PARAMOUNT, 1982
(LASER DISC SLEEVE)

The most successful transfer of a TV show to the big screen. The show built up a huge audience in reruns and, after the success of *Star Wars*, moved to the local cineplex in all its widescreen glory. Captain Kirk, Spock, and Bones had become a part of popular culture. (Directed by Nicholas Meyer)

PRINTED IN U.S.A.

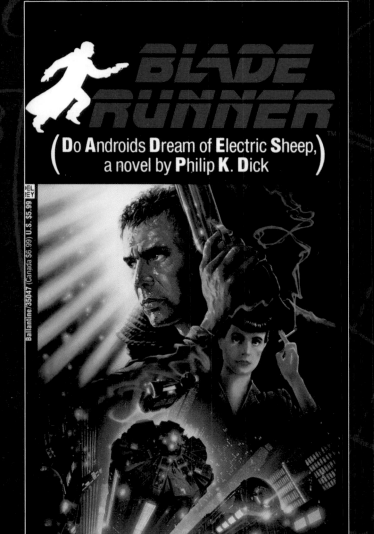

BLADE RUNNER
PAPERBACK TIE-IN, 1982
COVER ART SUPPLIED BY THE LADD COMPANY

An unusual movie tie-in book. The text is from the original novel (noted on cover); it's not a novelization of the script. Director Ridley Scott hadn't read much science fiction but vastly admired *2001* and *Star Wars*. The "happy ending" and voice-over, added after the test screening, were both eliminated in the director's cut. (Published by Ballantine Books)

wet suit under water than any of his stuntmen. He even had pages of the script laminated so he could write on them with a grease pencil while in the filming tank.

Schwarzenegger, who first appeared in *Pumping Iron*, a documentary on bodybuilding, starred in *Conan the Barbarian* and *Conan the Destroye*r prior to *Terminator*. After it, he became an action-adventure star and appeared in *Terminator 2: Judgment Day* as well as *Total Recall*, another film adapted from a story by Philip K. Dick, and *Predator*. Schwarzenegger showed a surprising talent for comedy in addition to action and soon was one of the highest paid stars in Hollywood.

(Not every science-fiction film was a smash success. One of the most eagerly awaited of all, *Dune*, directed by David Lynch, was close to a disaster, both critically and at the box office. It did no better in a later expanded release for television—from which Lynch removed his name—even with the added scenes.)

Most science-fiction films were now major Hollywood blockbusters, costing tens of millions of dollars to make and grossing in the hundreds of millions. The elementary special effects of stop-action photography had long since been replaced by the wonders of the computer which enabled an actor to seemingly walk through solid steel bars.

Visually, nothing was impossible anymore. Dinosaurs were frighteningly real, spaceships looked completely plausible (though some still made "whooshing" sounds when rocketing through the airless void of outer space—perhaps, in space, nobody could hear you scream, but you could still hear the *thrum* of rocket engines).

But all the action wasn't on the big screen, a lot of it was on the small.

RETURN OF THE JEDI
LUCASFILM, 1983
(ONE-SHEET POSTER)

The last of the original three *Star Wars* films. Darth Vader turns against the evil emperor, Han Solo ends up with Princes Leia, and the Empire is defeated. May the Force be with you! (Directed by Richard Marquand)

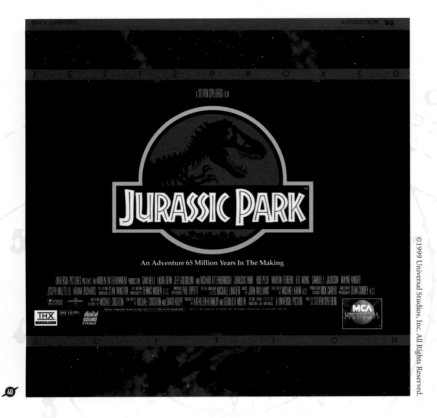

JURASSIC PARK ®
UNIVERSAL, 1993
(LASER DISC SLEEVE)

Another thriller from director Steven Spielberg starring the most terrifying dinosaurs since the original *King Kong*. An incredible hit at the box office.

First off the launching pad was *Captain Video* (1949-1953), telecast live by the DuMont network on a minuscule budget. A half-hour show starring the Captain and his Video Rangers, it was shown five nights a week. Many of the early episodes were scripted by Damon Knight, Cyril Kornbluth, Robert Sheckley, James Blish, and Jack Vance.

It was followed by *Space Patrol* featuring Commander Buzz Corry; *Tom Corbett: Space Cadet*, loosely adapted from Robert Heinlein's *Space Cadet*; *Science Fiction Theater*; *Space: 1999*, starring Martin Landau who went on to play Bela Lugosi in the film, *Ed Wood*. There was *Lost in Space*; *The Starlost*—which should have been a huge success but wasn't, created by Harlan Ellison (who repudiated it) and Ben Bova, with special effects by Douglas Trumbull; and let's not forget *Voyage to the Bottom of the Sea*, a television series spin-off from the Irwin Allen movie of the same name.

Twilight Zone had occasional science-fiction episodes, as did *Outer Limits* and *Stephen Spielberg's Amazing Stories*. Nothing succeeds like success in Hollywood and two years after the release of *Star Wars* saw the launching of the television series, *Battlestar Galactica*, closely patterned after *Star Wars* with John Dykstra, one of the special effects wizards of the film, masterminding—at least initially—

the special effects for the television series. Like most imitations, it never came close to matching the original. Later there would be the sitcoms, the "Coneheads" featured on *Saturday Night Live*, *My Favorite Martian*, and—as of 1999—*Third Rock from the Sun*.

But most importantly of all, there was…*Star Trek*. The brainchild of an ex-airline pilot, Gene Roddenberry, the original *Star Trek* ran for seventy-nine episodes on NBC during the 1960s. The ratings were hardly overwhelming, and the show was cancelled after its third season. A few stations picked up on the reruns…and then more…and still more. Years after cancellation, *Star Trek* was a hit.

Star Trek preceded *Star Wars* and there was little that the television show in its later incarnations borrowed from the Lucas film. The transporter, "Beam me up, Scotty!", the Klingons, and the Borg (the best science-fiction villains since Darth Vader and the Terminator) were all unique to the series.

After the success of *Star Wars*, a theatrical film featuring the original cast of Captain Kirk, Bones, Spock, and Scotty was inevitable. The first—*Star Trek–The Motion Picture*—was a disappointment. More feature films followed that enjoyed greater success. Then came another television series, *Star Trek: The Next Generation*, and when that had run its course, two more series—*Star Trek Voyager* and *Star Trek: Deep Space Nine*. Finally, there was small-screen competition in the form of *Babylon 5*, which earned a cult following of its own complete with spin-off novels, etc. *The X Files* had little to do with outer space but a great deal to do with government conspiracies, unidentified flying objects, aliens, and the like. It also spun off a feature film and the usual books and other cult paraphernalia.

STAR WARS: EPISODE I — THE PHANTOM MENACE
LUCASFILM, 1999
(ONE-SHEET POSTER)

The first of the three "prequels" to the original *Star Wars* starred Liam Neeson as Qui-Gon Jinn, a Jedi Knight, and Ewan McGregor as the young Obi-Wan Kenobi.

STAR WARS: EPISODE I — THE PHANTOM MENACE
LUCASFILM, 1999
(ONE-SHEET POSTER)

The young Anakin Skywalker, casting the shadow of the villain he will become—Darth Vader.

At the beginning of the 20th century, some of us still travelled by covered wagon. We were dazzled by the wonders of electricity, and, while a majority of us had indoor plumbing, few of us had telephones. Horses were a common sight on the street, and the ice man made regular deliveries. We got most of our news over the back fence or from newspapers in which the news was usually at least a day and sometimes a week old. We were proud to be living in modern times. By the end of the century we had walked on the Moon, sent probes that had landed on Mars, saw close-ups of the moons of Jupiter, had dropped atomic bombs, and manufactured electricity from atomic power plants. Half the homes in the United States had personal computers that the majority of owners couldn't operate very well and practically none of them could fix. The difference

THE DEATH

OF SCIENCE FICTION?

between modern engineering and black magic had become very thin indeed. Baffled by how our own computers work and the problems that might result (Y2K, for example), we also were just beginning to find out how we ourselves worked, how the immune system functioned, the heart pumped, the brain thought.

We were living in a future of our own making but not all of us were delighted. Our Brave New World had arrived slightly chipped around the edges. It was a world that had been almost completely explored, its promised wonders tarnished and rusty. At the start of the century, there was still the thrill of the exotic, when every issue of *National Geographic* showed us another corner of the globe that few people had ever seen. By the end of the century, sadly, we knew there were no more lost tribes, no lost continents, no priestesses, no noble barbarians. Opar and its fabled queen with all her jewels had vanished behind the curtain of time.

Science fiction had changed along with the country itself.

It was no longer possible for a Richard Seaton to build a spaceship in his garage (in the 1920s, where else would he have built it?). We had been to the Moon and discovered it wasn't covered with thigh-deep dust nor was it populated with Edgar Rice Burroughs' strange and savage Kalkars. Venus was a desert with a temperature of 900 degrees fahrenheit, and, while there was water on Mars, there were no canals into which we could stare and see the faces of the Martians staring back.

Not yet—and maybe never.

When we were kids, science fiction was something that set us apart from all the other kids on the block. We believed in rocket ships and debated the possibilities of time machines, wondered if telepathy was possible, followed the Rhine experiments avidly, and speculated that there might be life on Mars or that someday the evil aliens might land complete with hammer and sickle and make slaves of us all.

We thought it was literature (if not with a capital L), and we wanted everybody else to read it, too, and speculate about the same marvels that we speculated about. We thought we were smarter than average because we read science fiction. Or maybe it was just the reverse, that the reading of science fiction had made us smarter than average.

Most of us were kids who didn't fit in and had to seek refuge inside our own heads. We were in a culture war with our parents, with our teachers, with our peers. We believed and they didn't.

But that was then, and this is now.

We won the war.

Few at the end of the century disputed that there might be life on Mars, that time travel might be a hoot, that someday we might even send a probe to the stars or our radio telescopes might pick up a pattern from all the background noise, something that says we're not alone after all.

It's the last one that makes us uneasy.

The icons of science fiction are now common property; they don't belong to science-fiction fans anymore. Time travel, rocketships, life on other planets, immortality, aliens—they're a part of our common culture. It's no longer Us and Them—it's become all Us.

Editor David Hartwell called the 20th century the "Science Fiction Century," and, as it gradually dies, some critics claim science fiction is dying as well. Granted it may still be with us in one form or another but we won't call it that. And whatever it is, it will no longer be Our Thing.

The sense of wonder has died, the old-timers complain, and authors scurry about searching for the new idea, the new plot, or the new gimmick to resurrect it from its grave. Or maybe the sense of wonder was a part of being thirteen, like acne, and with increasing age we outgrew it.

But a sense of wonder is not part of the aging process or the secret of a few cherished authors. There's no mystery to it. A writer or a filmmaker conjures up a sense of wonder by enticing the reader into looking at the story's marvels through the eyes of its characters.

In movies, it was having Dr. Frankenstein cry, "It's alive!" Or Carl Denham (Robert Armstrong) in *King Kong*, his voice filled with awe, staring at a footprint of Kong and saying, "Look at the size of that— it must be as big as a house!" Or the family in *Jurassic Park* staring in wonder at the Brachiosaurus chomping on the tree leaves. Or the frightened boy watching the water in a glass jiggle and bounce as the Tyrannosaurus comes galumphing down the road. The characters were never so cynical or sophisticated that they were incapable of being amazed. And as members of the audience, looking at the events on the screen through their eyes, neither were we.

In books, it was much the same. Consider the young characters in Heinlein's juveniles who are surprised and delighted at the explanations of elementary science in the service of adventure. Or Jommy Cross, the young Slan, who just manages to escape the bloodthirsty mob intent on killing him for being different (how that must have resonated with some of the readers!). Or the kids in Bradbury's *Martian Chronicles* who *do* stare into the canals and see their first Martians—themselves. Or the seventeen-year-old boy on a generation ship who discovers his own death was a dream and that he has actually lived a hundred different lifetimes... As he discovers the marvels of the ship, so do the readers who see it all through his eyes. Or imagine Philip José Farmer's conceit that everybody who ever lived has been reincarnated along the banks of an infinite river. (A Hindu myth if ever there was one.)

Cynicism is the death of wonder and many of the old time filmmakers and authors knew it. They believed in the movies they made, the stories they wrote. But we've become a jaded society, and the delusion is that we constantly need something bigger and better or more unique to entertain us.

What is really needed is the connection between character and reader (or film goer) so the reader can see the world through more innocent eyes and perhaps really see it for the first time.

We've travelled from the start of the Confident Century, when some people thought science was dead because everything was known or had been discovered, through the Aspirin Age to a World Without Walls and with total insecurity. No wonder science fiction permeates our culture—it's the only crystal ball we have, flawed as it is.

Science fiction is more than just entertainment—it's a crash course in using your imagination, in sharpening your ability to speculate. Its predictive value is not that great; its ability to encourage that streak of curiosity in kids and even adults is enormous. NASA knows that—almost all its engineers read science fiction when they were younger, and NASA itself is one of the best producers of it with their snippets on television showing what the finished space station will look like or how a probe might appear as it parachutes into the atmosphere of Jupiter.

It's true that science fiction's most treasured icons have been stolen, that the vaults of the imagination have been plundered and the treasure distributed among the infidels. For the authors the questions are, Will books still sell? Will writers be able to make a living? Will the audience desert reading science fiction for watching it on film or television, for playing science-fiction computer games?

But more than 1,900 science-fiction, horror, and fantasy books were published last year, more than ever before, which should answer all of the above.

There's something both special and significant about science fiction and its writers that's not true of any other genre. Authors write science-fiction stories not just because they want to but because they have to. We look at the sensational views of the universe as revealed by the Hubble telescope and are awed by their beauty and their mystery. We're also frightened. The most spectacular views are those of a violent, exploding universe that could care less about Man and all his works.

It's human nature to make up stories about things we don't understand. We're not that much different from the primitive Bushmen or the African tribesmen or the early European barbarians who stared at the night sky and felt the same thing we feel looking at the Hubble photographs. They made up their myths and legends about the constellations, about Brother Sun and Sister Moon so that the universe would be a little less cold, a little less hostile, a little more understandable, and a lot more friendly.

And by doing so, perhaps they felt a little less …lonely.

It's no mistake that the most popular forms of science fiction were stories by Isaac Asimov and Frank Herbert that postulated countless worlds and thousands of solar systems all populated by human beings. (Granted a few writers postulated aliens as well—usually of a murderous mind who wanted to rape our women, steal our treasure, and roast us over a slow fire. But then, the unknown has always had its share of terrors.)

Carl Sagan devoted a lifetime urging us to listen to the heavens, to try and pick out a pattern from all the background noise so we would finally know that we were not alone. To ask the next question is to wonder what the world will be like when that first faint pattern is finally deciphered. With what panic, what hopes?

The fact is we're strangers and afraid in a universe we never made. We'll make up stories as long as we exist about what's out there, what's inside us here, what tomorrow might bring. They'll be written by authors working alone at their computers or God knows what because it's the individual mind that dreams the biggest dreams, not the corporate one. Science-fiction writers will continue to conceive of the inconceivable—that's their calling. They're our early warning system for the future, its probable wonders and possible dangers. They'll create new icons which will be borrowed by the films, by television, by computer games, by whoever wants to use them. And more power to the borrowers.

Nobody's a disbeliever now. With every passing year, the world grows smaller, the frontier that much closer. We're finally face to face with the universe itself, dangerous and beckoning. And when we're not looking outward, we'll be looking inward at that other great mystery—ourselves, searching for the universe in a grain of sand, looking for the God that dwells within.

As a genre, science fiction has long since ceased to be the province of the few; it's become the province of the many. We're no longer simply reading it or watching it; we're living it.

The critics are right.

The Science Fiction Century is dying.

Welcome to the Science Fiction Millennium.

Frank M. Robinson

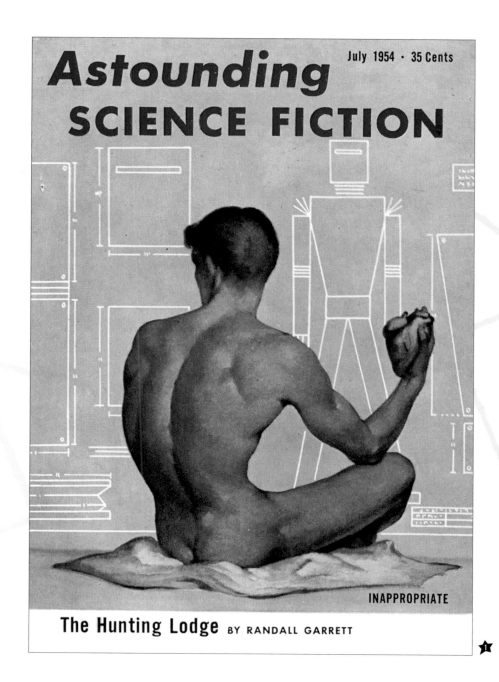

ASTOUNDING SCIENCE FICTION
JULY 1954
ALEJANDRO

A shocker of a cover for the 1950s. Wags in science-fiction fandom called it a portrait of "John's other wife" (referring to happily married editor John W. Campbell).

FOR SALE—
THE FUTURE
CREDITS & ACKNOWLEDGEMENTS

The Books—An Informal Bibliography Few books of this nature are the work of only one person. This one certainly wasn't. I'm indebted to Rob Edwards, Kris Etchison, Robert Gavora, Chris Hoth, Richard Meli, Steve Miller, Darrell Richardson, Dick Wald, and other collectors who opened up their files to me. My special thanks to Charles N. Brown of *Locus* who let me rummage through his library of books and paperbacks for rare and important items. Thanks are also extended to Dave Nee and Jan Murphy of Berkeley's *Other Change of Hobbit* bookstore for the same opportunity. I am especially grateful to Vincent Di Fate and Bob Stephens for help and suggestions when it came to films. And a special thanks to Ronald Borst of Hollywood Movie Posters who provided hard-to-get transparencies of early film posters, and to Wade Williams of Englewood Entertainment for providing new art for old movies.

Far from least, my thanks to Richard A. Lupoff, who acted as my unofficial editor and without whose help this book would not exist.

That said, what other books are recommended if you want to know more about science fiction than the snapshots I promised you at the start? One of the most enjoyable is *Infinite Worlds*, a collection of science-fiction art—arranged under the name of the artist—compiled by Vincent Di Fate, no mean artist in his own right. It's a mammoth volume containing a short biography of each artist along with representative samples of his work. Not to be missed.

If you're a film fan, you couldn't go wrong with *Graven Images*, a sampling of the collection of one-sheet posters, lobby cards, etc., of Ronald Borst, owner of Hollywood Movie Posters. (The book —technically out of print—can be had from Hollywood Movie Posters, 6727 5/8 Hollywood Boulevard; Hollywood, CA 90028.)

The most comprehensive book about writers is *The Encyclopedia of Science Fiction* edited by John Clute and Peter Nicholls. Absolutely indispensable for any collector or researcher. The volume is almost 1,400 pages long, a monumental work.

Equally valuable, though it concentrates more on magazines than on authors, is *Science Fiction, Fantasy*, and *Weird Fiction Magazines* edited by Marshall B. Tymn and Mike Ashley. One in a series of volumes about genre fiction, it's another huge volume of close to a thousand pages.

Other recommended reference books include *Trillion Year Spree*, a history of science fiction by Brian W. Aldiss and one densely packed with information. A somewhat older history is *Alternate Worlds*, edited by James Gunn and published almost twenty-five years ago. It's profusely illustrated with snapshots of authors so if you have a morbid curiosity about what your favorite author looked like way back when, this one is for you. Gunn is an academic as well as a science fiction author and the book is rewarding in many different ways.

Sam Moskowitz was the acknowledged historian of the field and published many valuable books about science fiction. All of them are recommended, especially *Explorers of the Infinite*, *Science Fiction by Gaslight*, and *Under the Moons of Mars*.

More specific in scope is the current edition of *The Hugo, Nebula and World Fantasy Awards* edited by Howard DeVore, listing all the stories that have won Hugos and Nebulas since the inception of the awards. Probably the most searching critical look at science fiction remains the latest edition of Damon Knight's *In Search of Wonder*.

Two autobiographies that give you an insider's look at growing up with science fiction are Jack Williamson's *Wonder's Child: My Life in Science Fiction* and Frederik Pohl's *The Way the Future Was*. Separated by a generation (though good friends and collaborators), the two authors offer a glimpse of what it's like to fall in love with your own imagination.

An overview of science fiction from the fan's point of view is *Forrest J Ackerman's World of Science Fiction*. An idiosyncratic but always entertaining look at the field by the former editor of *Famous Monsters of Filmland*.

The Marketplace

Many cities have "specialty" and independent bookstores that concentrate on the genres of science fiction, fantasy, and mystery books. (For example: Other Change of Hobbit, 2020 Shattuck, Berkeley, CA 94704 is a specialty store and Cody's—two locations in the same city—is an independent "mini-chain" that carries a large selection.) The larger chains—Barnes & Noble and Borders, etc.—usually have sections set aside for the latest releases in genre books, both hardback and paperback.

For older books and collector's items, recommended dealers include:

Claude Held, P.O. Box 515, Buffalo, NY 14225; Robert Madle, 4406 Bestor Dr., Rockville, MD 20853 (ask for catalog); R. F. Wald , 5 Becket, Lake Oswego, OR 97035; and L.W. Currey, Inc., Walter Street (Box 187), Elizabethtown, NY 12932.

The Magazines

Many of the dealers in specialty books also deal in magazine collectibles (Held, Madle, and Wald, listed above).

Other dealers include:

John Gunnison, Adventure House, 914 Laredo Rd., Silver Spring, MD 20901 (web page: www.adventurehouse.com); David Alexander, Box 273086, Tampa, FL 33618 (ask for catalog); Dark Star Books, 231 Xenia Ave., Yellow Springs, OH 45387; Graham Holroyd, 19 Borrowdale Dr., Rochester, NY 14626; Ray Walsh, Curious Book Shop, 307 E. Grand River, East Lansing, MI 49923.

Magazines currently being published include:

Aboriginal Science Fiction: Subscription Department, P.O. Box 2449, Woburn, MA 01888-0849.

Amazing Stories: Subscription Department, P.O. Box 707, Renton, WA 98057 (web page: www.wizards.com/Amazing)

Analog Science Fiction and Fact: Subscription Department, Penny Marketing, 6 Prowitt Street, Norwalk, CT 06855-1220 (web page: www.analogsf.com).

Asimov's Science Fiction: Subscription Department, Penny Marketing, 6 Prowitt Street, Norwalk, CT 06855-1220 (web page: www.asimovs.com).

Fantasy & Science Fiction: Subscription Department, 143 Cream Hill Rd., West Cornwall, CT 06796-9975.

Science Fiction Age: Subscription Department, P.O. Box 710, Mount Morris, IL 61054-9934 (editorial e-mail: scottedelman@erols.com).

Interzone: Subscription Department, 217 Preston Drove, Brighton BN1 6FL, United Kingdom.

Locus: Subscription Department, Locus Publications, P.O. Box 13305, Oakland, CA 94611 (web page: www.locusmag.com)

Some of the magazines—especially *Locus*—carry advertisements for dealers specializing in science-fiction books and magazines.

Conventions

As mentioned earlier in this book, science fiction, horror, fantasy, and "media" (films, games, etc.) conventions occur on the average of one per week. *Analog Science Fiction and Fact* usually has a listing in the back of the magazine every month. Every few months, *Locus* carries a more complete set of listings, frequently running to more than a hundred.

SMALLEST FAN MAGAZINE
1944

Fanewscard Weekly was the smallest fan magazine ever issued. Running as a weekly from 1943 to 1944, the postcard-sized "newsletter" related the travels of various fans as well as what books had just been published.

ACKNOWLEDGEMENTS

I'm indebted to Abigail Browning of PennyPress and Dell Magazines, Kim Mohan of Wizards of the Coast, Ed Ferman of *The Magazine of Fantasy & Science Fiction* and Joel Frieman of Argosy Communications, Inc., for permission to reprint numerous covers of their various magazines.

My appreciation to Colleen Benn of Universal Studios, Ashley Simmons and Rebecca Herrera of 20th Century Fox, Margarita Medina of Columbia TriStar Motion Picture Group, Kris Kelly of Amblin Entertainment, Jessica Closson of Viacom Consumer Products, and Jeanne Cole and Karen Rose of Lucasfilm Ltd. for their help in securing permissions from their respective companies.

All covers from the following magazines and their respective titles and distinctive logo designs are trademarks and are the property of Argosy Communications, Inc.: *Argosy All-Story Weekly, Astonishing Stories, Famous Fantastic Mysteries, Fantastic Novels, Super Science Stories*™ and Copyright © 1999 Argosy Communications, Inc. All Rights Reserved. Argosy Communications, Inc., is the successor-in-interest to Popular Publications, Inc., Fictioneers, Inc., The Frank A. Munsey Company, and The Red Star News Company. Reprinted by arrangement with Argosy Communications, Inc.

Covers for *Aboriginal Science Fiction* Copyright © 1986, 1987, 1988, 1999 by Aboriginal Science Fiction.

All covers from *Amazing Stories, Fantastic,* and *Fantastic Adventures* and their respective titles and logo designs are the property of Wizards of the Coast, Inc.™ and Copyright © 1999 by Wizards of the Coast, Inc. All rights reserved. Reprinted by permission.

All covers for the *Astounding/Analog* magazine series are copyrighted as follows:

Astounding Stories of Super-Science, January 1930. Copyright © 1930 by Clayton Magazines Inc., reprinted by permission of Dell Magazines, a division of Crosstown Publications. *Astounding Stories of Super-Science,* March 1930. Copyright © 1930 by Clayton Magazines Inc., reprinted by permission of Dell Magazines, a division of Crosstown Publications. *Astounding Stories,* January 1932. Copyright © 1931 by Clayton Magazines, Inc., reprinted by permission of Dell Magazines, a division of Crosstown Publications. *Astounding Stories,* October 1933. Copyright © 1933 by Street & Smith Publications, Inc., reprinted by permission of Dell Magazines, a division of Crosstown Publications. *Astounding Stories,* January 1934. Copyright © 1933 by Street & Smith Publications, Inc., reprinted by permission of Dell Magazines, a division of Crosstown Publications. *Astounding Stories,* October 1934. Copyright © 1934 by Street & Smith Publications, Inc., reprinted by permission of Dell Magazines, a division of Crosstown Publications. *Astounding Stories,* December 1934. Copyright © 1934 by Street & Smith Publications, Inc., reprinted by permission of Dell Magazines, a division of Crosstown Publications. *Astounding Stories,* March 1935. Copyright © 1935 by Street & Smith Publications, Inc., reprinted by permission of Dell Magazines, a division of Crosstown Publications. *Astounding Stories,* July 1936. Copyright © 1936 by Street & Smith Publications, Inc., reprinted by permission of Dell Magazines, a division of Crosstown Publications. *Astounding Science-Fiction,* April 1938. Copyright © 1938 by Street & Smith Publications, Inc., reprinted by permission of Dell Magazines, a division of Crosstown Publications. *Astounding Science-Fiction,* December 1938. Copyright © 1938 by Street & Smith Publications, Inc., reprinted by permission of Dell Magazines, a division of Crosstown Publications. *Astounding Science-Fiction,* February 1939. Copyright © 1939 by Street & Smith Publications, Inc., reprinted by permission of Dell Magazines, a division of Crosstown Publications. *Astounding Science-Fiction,* November 1939. Copyright © 1939 by Street & Smith Publications, Inc., reprinted by permission of Dell Magazines, a division of Crosstown Publications. *Astounding Science-Fiction,* October 1940. Copyright © 1940 by Street & Smith Publications, Inc., reprinted by permission of Dell Magazines, a division of Crosstown Publications. *Astounding Science-Fiction,* January 1941. Copyright © 1940 by Street & Smith Publications, Inc., reprinted by permission of Dell Magazines, a division of Crosstown Publications. *Astounding Science-Fiction,* April 1941. Copyright © 1941 by Street & Smith Publications, Inc., reprinted

FAN MAGAZINE COVER
1942
FRANK M. ROBINSON
Cover for prominent fan magazine, *Le Zombie*, spray-painted by hand by this author when he was a young science-fiction fan.

INDEX

Numbers in parentheses following page numbers refer to either an image or caption.